Rural-Urban Dynamics and the Millennium Development Goals

Global Monitoring Report 2013

Rural-Urban Dynamics and the Millennium Development Goals

A joint publication of the World Bank and the International Monetary Fund

The image on the cover is a segment of a painting by Sue Hoppe, an artist based in South Africa. Titled "Conflict Resolution," the painting explores the idea that people who seem irreversibly divided and with little in common can unite if they focus on what they have in common instead of what divides them. Hoppe's work examines war, conflict, and the plight of children and women in Africa, but is also inspired by nature and architecture. To learn more about Sue Hoppe and her work, visit www.southafricanartists.com/home/SueHoppe.

Cover design by Debra Naylor of Naylor Design

Photo credits: page xvi: Caroline Suzman; clockwise for pages 20–21, beginning at top: Tran Thi Hoa / World Bank, Julio Pantoja / World Bank, Arne Hoel / World Bank and Curt Carnemark / World Bank; page 25: Jonathan Ernst / World Bank; page 31: Simone D. McCourtie / World Bank; page 33: Dana Smillie / World Bank; page 34: Arne Hoel / World Bank; page 36: Arne Hoel / World Bank; page 40: Arne Hoel / World Bank; page 44: Curt Carnemark; page 84: Scott Wallace; and page 129: Gayatri Singh.

Contents

BOXES

FIGURES

Foreword

Global Monitoring Report (GMR) 2013 gauges progress toward the Millennium Development Goals (MDGs) through the lens of the changing urban-rural landscape. The goals encompass and promote a universal standard of being free from grinding poverty, being educated and healthy, and having ready access to clean water and sanitation. Urbanization has helped reduce poverty through the creation of new income opportunities, and has increased both access to and quality of services. However, the number of people living in urban slums is also rising, and cities often contribute to environmental degradation. At the same time, three quarters of the poor still live in rural areas, and better provision of basic services in those areas is essential to open up opportunities for the rural population. With this in mind, GMR 2013 calls for complementary rural-urban development policies and an integrated strategy of planning, connecting, and financing.

Against the backdrop of this changing urban-rural landscape and the macroeconomic growth that it has generated, success in reducing the proportion of people whose income is under $1.25 a day is a signal achievement. This proportion fell from 43.1 percent in 1990 to 20.6 percent in 2010. However, that still leaves 1.2 billion people in extreme poverty. This stark reality is only part of the story,

since the seven other goals are equally vital to improving the human condition.

The other targets and goals are crucial to human well-being, and they reinforce improvements in other areas. For example, providing access to safe drinking water and basic sanitation, part of MDG 7, is essential if people are to be healthy enough to complete school and join the job market. Improved sanitary conditions and better education help reduce infant and maternal mortality. In all of these areas, women play a key role, and ensuring equal opportunities for women is absolutely essential.

Yet, continued progress toward the MDGs will be increasingly difficult to achieve without far better stewardship of the environment. Pollution can get in the way of people's health and thus their productivity, whether on the farm or in cities. Poor people are the least able to protect their children from the effects of pollution on health and educational outcomes, which can in turn mean setbacks once they reach adulthood. Climate change is intensifying, putting the prosperity of future generations at risk and imperiling hard-won development achievements.

Global partnerships for development, which are enshrined in MDG 8, are necessary to tackle everything from supplying affordable essential drugs in poor countries to helping landlocked and small island developing states. To ensure that such partnerships can be deployed effectively, the international community needs to do a better job of facilitating joint public-private partnerships and harnessing technology to solve today's development challenges. For example, we need more dynamic innovation and more systematic sharing of lessons of experience. Also, resources matter. Enduring development solutions can only be realized if donors deliver on their pledges and,

through improved effectiveness, help countries absorb aid more productively.

With fewer than 1,000 days remaining until the current set of MDGs expire, it is imperative that all of us, wherever we are, make a greater effort to help more people escape poverty and improve their overall well-being. Accelerating progress toward the MDGs and maintaining that momentum beyond 2015 is not only the right thing to do, it is also in the best economic interests of nations.

Jim Yong Kim
President
The World Bank Group

Christine Lagarde
Managing Director
International Monetary Fund

Acknowledgments

This report has been prepared jointly by the staffs of the World Bank and the International Monetary Fund (IMF). In preparing the report, staffs have collaborated closely with partner institutions—the African Development Bank (AfDB), the Asian Development Bank (ADB), the European Bank for Reconstruction and Development (EBRD), the Inter-American Development Bank (IADB), the Organisation for Economic Co-operation and Development (OECD), Cities Alliance, and various nongovernmental institutions, such as SlumDwellers International (SDI) and Centre for Urban and Regional Excellence (CURE), India. The cooperation and support of these institutions are gratefully acknowledged.

Jos Verbeek was the lead author and manager of the report. Lynge Nielsen led the team from the IMF. The principal authors and contributors to the various parts of the report include Vandana Chandra, Shaohua Chen, Jorge Coarasa, William Cobbett, Uwe Deichmann, Amir Fouad, Jonas Frank, Yoichiro Ishihara, Somik Lall, Peter Lanjouw, Hans Lofgren, Mariem Malouche, Eugenia Suarez Moran, Siobhan Murray, Prem Sangraula, Rachel K. Sebudde, Forhad Shilpi, Gayatri Singh, Eric V. Swanson, and Quentin Wodon (World Bank) and Sibrabrata Das, Nisreen Farhan, Rodrigo Garcia-Verdu, Svitlana Maslova, Chris Papageorgiou, and Nicolo Spatafora (IMF). Amy Guatam was the principle editor of the text, and Kristina Tan Mercado and Hazel Macadangdang assisted with the overall preparation of the report. The work was carried out under the general guidance of Kaushik Basu and Hans Timmer at the World Bank. Supervision at the IMF was provided by Hugh Bredenkamp and Brad McDonald.

A number of other staff and consultants made valuable contributions, including the following from the World Bank: Shaida Badiee, Judy L. Baker, Grant Cameron, Asli Demirgüç-Kunt, Neil Fantom, Juan Feng, Deon Filmer, Cecile Fruman, Ejaz Ghani, Delfin Sia Go, Masako Hiraga, Vivian Hon, Sergio Kurlat, Jeffrey Lecksell, Xiao Li, Dennis Linders, Johan Mistiaen, Zia Qureshi, Israel Osorio-Rodarte, Martin Ravallion, and Saurabh Shome.

Contributors from other institutions include Suzanne Steensen and Andrzej Suchodloski (OECD), Josefina J. Balane, Debra Kertzman, Noriko Ogawa, Hong Wei (ADB), Amy M. Lewis, Luis Diaz, Marcos Robles, Federico Scodelaro Bilbao, Caroline Sipp, and Horacio Cristian Terraza (IADB), Murat Jadraliyev and Anita Taci (EBRD), Patricia N. Laverley, Nejmudin Bilal, and Lydiah Munyi (AfDB), Daniel Schensul and Jose Miguel Guzman (United Nations Population Fund).

Guidance received from the Executive Directors of the World Bank and the IMF and their staffs during discussions of the draft report is gratefully acknowledged. The report also benefited from many useful comments and suggestions received from the Bank and Fund management and staff in the course of its preparation and review.

The World Bank's Office of the Publisher managed the editorial services, design, production, and printing of the report, with Susan Graham anchoring the process. Others assisting with the report's publication included Stephen McGroarty and Denise Bergeron. Special thanks to Marty Gottron who edited the final draft.

The report's dissemination and outreach was coordinated by Indira Chand and Merrell Tuck-Primdahl, working with Vamsee Kanchi and Roula Yazigi.

Abbreviations and Acronyms

ADB	Asian Development Bank
ADF	African Development Fund
AfDB	African Development Bank
BRICS	Brazil, the Russian Federation, India, China, and South Africa
CDIA	Cities Development Initiative for Asia
CPA	Country programmable aid
CURE	Centre for Urban and Regional Excellence (India)
DAC	Development Assistance Committee
DDA	Doha Development Agenda
DEWAT	Decentralized Waste Water Treatment System (India)
DHS	Demographic and Household Surveys
FDI	Foreign direct investment
GDP	Gross domestic product
GMR	Global Monitoring Report
EBRD	European Bank for Reconstruction and Development
ESCI	Emerging and Sustainable Cities Initiative
EU	European Union
FINDETER	Financiadora de Desarrollo Territorial S.A. (Colombia)
FSI	Floor space index
G-8	Group of 8
G-20	Group of 20
GNI	Gross national income
HIPC	Heavily indebted poor countries
ICT	Information and communication technology
IDB	Inter-American Development Bank
IFC	International Finance Corporation
IFI	International financial institution
IIED	International Institute for Environment and Development

IMF	International Monetary Fund
MAF	MDG acceleration framework
MCI	Monetary Conditions Index
MDG	Millennium Development Goals
NGO	Nongovernmental organization
NSDFU	National Slum Dwellers Federation of Uganda
NWSC	National Water and Sewerage Corporation (Uganda)
OBA	Output-based aid
ODA	Official development assistance
OECD	Organisation for Economic Co-operation and Development
PARIS21	Partnership in Statistics for Development in the 21st Century
PISA	Program for International Student Assessment
PPP	Public-private partnership
SDI	Slum/Shack Dwellers International
SNG	Subnational government
SUN	Scaling Up Nutrition
TIMSS	Trends in International Mathematics and Science Study
U5MR	Under-five mortality rate
UKP	Urbanization Knowledge Platform
UN	United Nations
UNFPA	United Nations Population Fund
VT	*Vale transporte*
WDR 2009	*World Development Report 2009: Reshaping Economic Geography*
WDR 2012	*World Development Report 2012: Gender Equality and Development*
WDR 2013	*World Development Report 2013: Jobs*
WTO	World Trade Organization

Overview

The *Global Monitoring Report* (GMR), jointly produced by the World Bank and International Monetary Fund (IMF), is an annual report card on the world's progress toward the Millennium Development Goals (MDGs). Now in its 10th edition, the GMR also outlines prospects for the attainment of the MDGs and assesses the support of the international community. Achieving as many MDGs as possible before 2015 remains an urgent endeavor for the development community. This GMR highlights those MDGs that are lagging in progress and consequently need additional attention, while pointing out that accelerating toward attainment of one MDG will likely provide positive spillovers to the attainment of others. The Report shows that official development assistance (ODA) and progress with aid effectiveness have been less than stellar.

Each annual report has a thematic focus, an aspect of the development agenda on which the GMR provides a more in-depth assessment. The theme of GMR 2013 is rural-urban disparities in development and ways urbanization can better help achieve the MDGs. Not only is the theme highly relevant for assessing progress within the current MDG framework, but it also has the potential to inform discussions about the post-2015 development framework in which urbanization will be a major factor—96 percent of the additional 1.4 billion people in the developing world in 2030 will live in urban areas.

Urbanization matters. In the past two decades, developing countries have urbanized rapidly, with the number of people living in urban settlements rising from about 1.5 billion in 1990 to 3.6 billion (more than half of the world's population) in 2011. The report finds that urban poverty rates are significantly lower than rural poverty rates and that urban populations have far better access to the basic public services defined by the MDGs, such as access to safe water and sanitation facilities, even though within urban areas asymmetries in access are large. If the forces of urbanization are not managed speedily and efficiently, slum growth can overwhelm city growth, exacerbate urban poverty, and derail MDG achievements. As the GMR points out, however, people are located along a continuous rural-urban spectrum, and large cities are not necessarily places where the urban poor are concentrated. Smaller towns matter greatly for urban poverty reduction and service delivery. As urban centers continue their

GMR 2013

Rural-Urban Dynamics and the Millennium Development Goals

50% Urban

50% Rural

Urban/Rural Population Share

11.6%
Urban population that is poor

22.7%
Global population that is poor

29.4%
Rural population that is poor

2008

96% of the increase in population in developing countries between now and 2030 will be in urban areas

40% of urban population growth can be expected to come from migration and reclassification

76%
of the extreme poor live in rural areas

Rural

Four MDG targets have been met: MDG 1.a (halving extreme poverty), two parts of MDG 7 (access to safe water and improved lives of slum dwellers, and part of MDG 3.a (gender parity in primary education). Progress on the remaining MDGs is limited, except for MDG 3.a (gender parity in primary and secondary education), which is close to being on target.

Populations are typically seen as being spatially bipolar. In reality, people and poverty are located along a spectrum from rural to urban, with many types of settlements from small to large towns. The experience is that the smaller the town, the higher the poverty rate, with less access to MDG-related services.

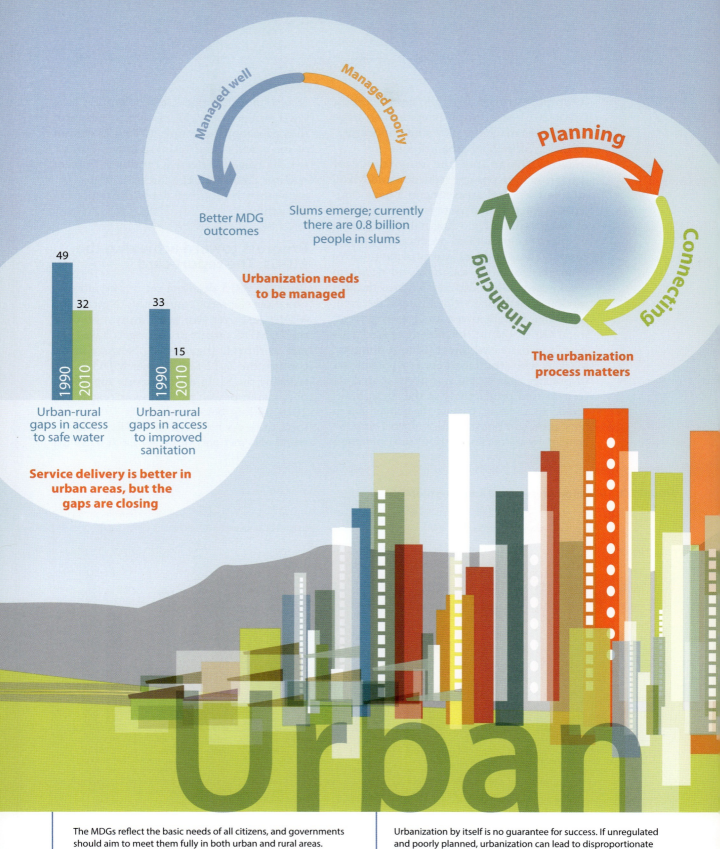

Managed well

Managed poorly

Better MDG outcomes

Slums emerge; currently there are 0.8 billion people in slums

Urbanization needs to be managed

Planning

Connecting

Financing

The urbanization process matters

49

32

1990 · 2010

33

15

1990 · 2010

Urban-rural gaps in access to safe water

Urban-rural gaps in access to improved sanitation

Service delivery is better in urban areas, but the gaps are closing

Urban

The MDGs reflect the basic needs of all citizens, and governments should aim to meet them fully in both urban and rural areas. But resources are scarce, and priorities must be set. Much of the sequencing will depend on local conditions regarding degree of urbanization and rural-urban differences in MDG outcomes.

Urbanization by itself is no guarantee for success. If unregulated and poorly planned, urbanization can lead to disproportionate increases in slums. GMR 2013 calls for an integrated strategy to better manage the planning-connecting-financing formula of urbanization.

inexorable growth over the next decades, GMR 2013 calls for an integrated strategy to better manage the planning-connecting-financing formula of urbanization.

Notwithstanding the importance of urbanization in poverty reduction and MDG attainment, rural areas remain a huge challenge—one that underscores the importance of being vigilant regarding policies that aim to improve agricultural productivity; if successful, these policies can provide positive synergies for farm incomes and nonfarm employment. GMR 2012 highlighted the promotion of increased yields through research, extension, and improved water management, improvements in the functioning of land markets, and increased integration of domestic markets with world markets as a possible set of policies that would positively contribute to increased productivity in the agricultural sector. In addition, closing the gender gap in education can boost rural women's empowerment by increasing agricultural incomes;

relative to male farmers, female farmers have lower productivity, which is directly related to their educational attainment. With 75 percent of the world's poor residing in rural areas, the challenge of effective rural development remains daunting but achievable with complementary rural-urban development policies and actions.

Progress toward achieving the MDGs: The report card

With the 2015 deadline set by the international development community to attain the MDGs just over two years away, only 4 of the 21 MDG targets or subtargets have been met worldwide (figure O.1). New estimates confirm the 2012 reports that MDG 1.a — reducing the $1.25-a-day poverty rate (2005 purchasing power parity)—was reached in 2010, falling below half of its 1990 value (box O.1). As reported in GMR 2012, the world also met part of MDG 7.c to halve the

FIGURE O.1 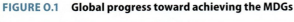 **Global progress toward achieving the MDGs**

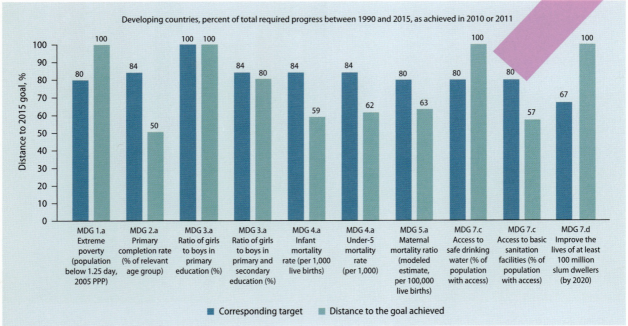

Source: World Bank staff estimates.
Note: Intermediate targets were calculated using a linear progression over 25 years, resulting in a needed progress of 4 percent a year. Note that the corresponding target for 2010 would equal 80 percent, and for 2011, 84 percent, to be on track to attain the MDG by 2015. Any value above those intermediate targets indicates that the world is ahead of the required pace to meet the MDG. A value of 100 percent means that the MDG has been met. PPP = purchasing power parity.

BOX O.1   MDG 1 for extreme poverty

New poverty projections for 2015 are the result of various updates of new and more recent household surveys and a new forecast of per capita consumption growth. Sufficient data do not exist to estimate progress on reducing extreme poverty in 36 developing countries. Consequently, the forecasts for these countries are based on changes in income poverty in the surveys of similar countries.

Updated economic projections for developing countries by the World Bank indicate that an estimated 970 million people will continue in 2015 to live below $1.25 a day, equivalent to 15.5 percent of the population in the developing world. That is lower than the previous estimate of 1 billion people (16.3 percent) done in 2012. New survey information on household budgets, used to estimate the 2010 figures, shows additional improvements in all regions except Sub-Saharan Africa compared with the 2012 extreme poverty estimates. Note that

because new and more complete surveys for Sub-Saharan Africa have become available this year, even the 2008 poverty number had to be revised upward from the 47.5 percent estimate last year to 49.2 percent this year. This new estimate adversely affected the projection of extreme poverty by 2015 for the region, which is now estimated at 42.3 percent, compared to 41.2 percent at the time of last year's GMR. The total projection of 970 million extremely poor people in 2015 is significantly lower than the 1.9 billion people living in extreme poverty in 1990 (43.1 percent).

Except for Sub-Saharan Africa, which had the worst starting position, all regions are expected to achieve the MDG 1.a target of halving extreme poverty by 2015. The poverty reduction in the East Asia and Pacific region has been spectacular as the rate of extreme poverty was reduced from 56.2 in 1990 to 12.5 in 2010.

TABLE BO.1.1   Poverty by region

Share of population below $1.25 a day (2005 PPP)

Region	1990	2005	2008	2010	2015 (forecast)
East Asia and Pacific	56.2	16.8	14.3	12.5	5.5
Europe and Central Asia	1.9	1.3	0.5	.07	0.4
Latin America and the Caribbean	12.2	8.7	6.5	5.5	4.9
Middle East and North Africa	5.8	3.5	2.7	2.4	2.6
South Asia	53.8	39.4	36.0	31.0	23.2
Sub-Saharan Africa	56.5	52.3	49.2	48.5	42.3
Total	43.1	25.0	22.7	20.6	15.5

Millions of people below $1.25 a day (2005 PPP)

Region	1990	2005	2008	2010	2015
East Asia and Pacific	926.4	332.1	284.4	250.9	114.5
Europe and Central Asia	8.9	6.3	2.2	3.1	1.9
Latin America and the Caribbean	53.4	47.6	36.9	32.3	30.0
Middle East and North Africa	13.0	10.5	8.6	8.0	9.3
South Asia	617.3	598.3	570.7	506.8	406.5
Sub-Saharan Africa	289.7	394.9	399.3	413.8	408.0
Total	1,908.6	1,389.6	1,302.8	1,214.9	970.2

Source: World Bank staff calculations from PovcalNet database. See http://iresearch.worldbank.org/PovcalNet/index.htm for additional information and data.
Note: PPP = purchasing power parity.

proportion of people without safe access to drinking water. MDG 7.d—to have achieved a significant improvement in the lives of at least 100 million slum dwellers by 2020—was also achieved.[1] Finally, the first part of MDG 3.a—to eliminate gender disparity in

primary education—was accomplished in 2010. Global progress on the full MDG 3.a (to eliminate gender disparity in primary and secondary education) is close to being on track.

Overall, global progress on the remaining MDGs has been less than stellar, however, particularly on those related to education (MDG 2.a) and health (MDG 4.a and 5.a), and a vast acceleration of progress is needed to achieve all of the goals by 2015. Accelerating progress toward attainment of these MDGs is not only intrinsically desirable but can produce positive spillovers between different development objectives. Reducing infant mortality and improving maternal health can pay additional dividends by increasing the returns to subsequent investments in human capital. A vast literature demonstrates that human capital formation is a cumulative process and that the first few years in a child's development are critical, as noted in GMR 2012. In addition, the accomplishment of the extreme poverty MDG bodes well for achievement of other MDGs, given the interrelationship between reduction of extreme (income) poverty and progress toward the various nonpoverty MDGs. For MDG 2.a (ensuring that, by 2015, children everywhere will be able to complete a full course of primary schooling), it is probably already too late, because completion rates depend on net enrollment rates, which have not reached 100 percent: in 2011, the net enrollment rate in primary education stood at only 88.8 percent globally.

Regional progress toward achieving the MDGs is more diverse. At one end of the spectrum, the East Asia and Pacific region is on target to meet most if not all of the MDGs, while at the other end, Sub-Saharan Africa is off target on most MDGs. Those regions still lagging started from positions that required the most absolute progress, however, and they have made significant progress in absolute terms, particularly on those MDGs that the world as a whole is struggling to meet. The relative nature by which many of the MDGs are defined masks to a large extent these accomplishments.

Evaluating progress toward attainment of the MDGs at the country level shows even further diversity (figure O.2). Sufficient progress toward MDG 3.a is most prevalent, with 72 countries on track, while only 18 countries are on track to meet MDG 4.a (reducing infant mortality). However, an additional 20 countries are projected to meet this MDG between 2015 and 2020. With a significant acceleration of effort, these countries could achieve MDG 4.a by 2015 or shortly thereafter. The same holds for the reduction in under-five mortality: 22 countries have made progress but require an additional push to achieve the target by or close to 2015.

Global growth and its implications for the MDGs

The global economy is expected to recover, but only very gradually. While the road to recovery in advanced economies will remain bumpy, downside risks to the global outlook have eased as policy intentions in developed economies have become clearer and commodity price volatility has abated. Although, important short- and medium-term downside risks remain—including adjustment fatigue in advanced economies and overinvestment and high asset prices in emerging market and developing countries—such risks are now more symmetric. A broadly appropriate current policy stance in emerging market and developing countries is supporting continued strong growth in these countries. Commodity prices trended down through most of 2012 and are expected to remain stable in 2013, providing room for a flexible implementation of monetary policy, particularly in emerging market and developing countries.

Were the downside risk of a protracted global slowdown extending through 2015 to materialize, it would have a significantly negative impact on growth in low-income countries and their ability to attain the MDGs. Despite sustained economic growth, progress in rebuilding policy buffers in low-income countries has been modest. Indeed, with policy buffers not yet restored to levels preceding the 2009 crisis and against the backdrop of reduced traditional sources of financing, most low-income countries would likely need to undertake adjustments in the face of such a shock. Differences across countries are large, however. Still-high international commodity prices are providing commodity exporters

FIGURE O.2 Extent of progress toward MDGs, by number of countries

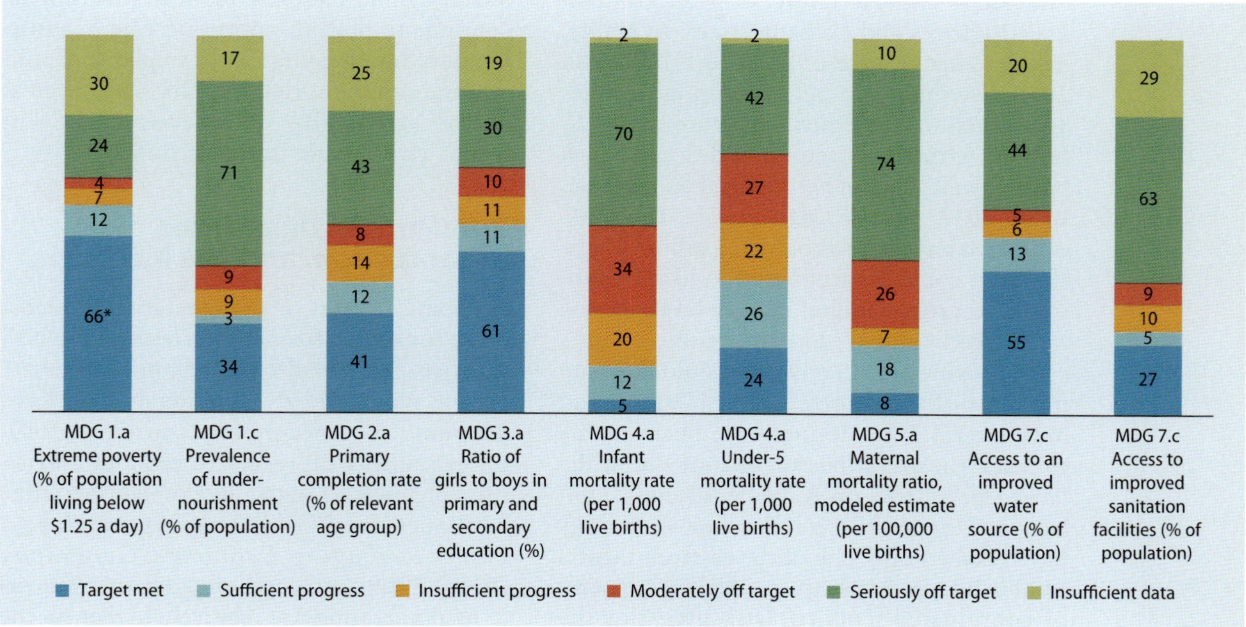
30
24
4
7
12
66*
17
71
9
9
3
34
25
43
8
14
12
41
19
30
10
11
11
61
2
70
34
20
12
5
2
42
27
22
26
24
10
74
26
7
18
8
20
44
5
6
13
55
29
63
9
10
5
27
MDG 1.a Extreme poverty (% of population living below $1.25 a day)
MDG 1.c Prevalence of under-nourishment (% of population)
MDG 2.a Primary completion rate (% of relevant age group)
MDG 3.a Ratio of girls to boys in primary and secondary education (%)
MDG 4.a Infant mortality rate (per 1,000 live births)
MDG 4.a Under-5 mortality rate (per 1,000 live births)
MDG 5.a Maternal mortality ratio, modeled estimate (per 100,000 live births)
MDG 7.c Access to an improved water source (% of population)
MDG 7.c Access to improved sanitation facilities (% of population)
Target met
Sufficient progress
Insufficient progress
Moderately off target
Seriously off target
Insufficient data

Source: Estimates based on World Development Indicators database.
Note: Progress is based on extrapolation of the latest five-year annual growth rates for each country, except for MDG 5, which uses the last seven years. Sufficient progress indicates that an extrapolation of the last observed data point with the growth rate over the last observable five-year period shows that the MDG can be attained. Insufficient progress is defined as being able to meet the MDG between 2016 and 2020. Moderately off target indicates that the MDG can be met between 2020 and 2030. Seriously off target indicates that the MDG will not even be met by 2030. Insufficient data points to a lack of enough data points to estimate progress or that the MDG's starting value is missing (except for MDG 2 and MDG 3).
* Includes 11 countries for which the extreme poverty rate is below 2 percent. Measuring changes in poverty rates at such low levels (< 2 percent) cannot be disentangled from measurement errors.

with relatively larger buffers than commodity-importing countries.

Aid flows and effectiveness

The international development finance architecture has changed markedly since the Millennium Declaration in 2000. In particular, the relative importance of ODA as a financing instrument for development has declined. The main drivers of that change are the increasing role of developing countries in the global economy, with a massive expansion of net private flows to those countries, and the emergence of middle-income countries as growth poles and important sources of non-ODA development finance.

Even though tough economic challenges have emerged in the developed world over the past few years, it is important that the Organisation for Economic Co-operation and Development (OECD) Development Assistance Committee (DAC) donors live up to earlier promises to maintain and expand aid flows and improve their aid effectiveness to strengthen the impact of that aid. Especially when the size of ODA flows relative to other financial flows is declining, the quality of aid flows and changes in the effectiveness of domestic policies that it can support become paramount. With improved policies in developing countries, the potential effectiveness of aid has increased. But if this potential is to be fully exploited, donors will have to follow up on aid effectiveness agreements and deliver on their pledges.

At the Gleneagles summit in 2005, DAC donors agreed to increase ODA by $50 billion between 2004 and 2010, with at least half of the increase designated for Africa—both Sub-Saharan Africa and North Africa. The promised increase of $50 billion made in 2004 prices and exchange rates would equal an increase in ODA to a level of $152.2 billion in 2010 prices and exchange rates. In reality, disbursements were only $128.5 billion in 2010, leaving a gap between initial pledges and actual disbursements of more than $25 billion. Africa received an additional $11.8 billion, well short of the pledged $25 billion. In its 2012 annual ODA report, the DAC estimated that only about $1.2 billion of the shortfall could be attributed to lower-than-expected gross national income levels caused by the recent global economic crisis.

Improving aid effectiveness could make up for some of the shortfalls, but bilateral and multilateral DAC donors have been unable to reach the ambitious targets set out in the Paris Declaration on Aid Effectiveness. Collectively, the multilateral development banks have reached only one of the thirteen targets established in Paris (to strengthen capacity by coordinated support). Disaggregating the data by the various multilateral development banks and other international organizations, such as institutions of the United Nations (UN) and the European Union (EU), yields a more nuanced picture. For example, the Inter-American Development Bank (IDB) has met four of the eight aid effectiveness indicators for which disaggregated data exist, the World Bank three, and the EU institutions two. All other multilateral development banks have met one indicator.[2]

The new Global Partnership for Effective Development, agreed upon in the Fourth High Level Forum on Aid Effectiveness in Busan, Republic of Korea, in 2011, represents a window of opportunity for a more balanced international dialogue among all development partners, including traditional DAC and non-DAC donors such as the BRICS (Brazil, the Russian Federation, India, China, and South Africa). The partnership provides space for these partners to agree on more realistic targets for aid effectiveness and to establish mutual accountability to implement agreed-upon actions. To date, more than 160 countries and 45 organizations from around the world have endorsed this partnership.

Notwithstanding these emerging trends in development finance and the aid effectiveness of DAC donors, development partners, including international financial institutions, continue to play an important role in assisting developing countries to implement policies and programs that help improve progress on the MDGs and other development outcomes, particularly in fragile states.

Rural-urban disparities, urbanization, and the MDGs

Economic aspects of agglomeration are most often looked at from a microeconomic perspective, but broad-based changes in where people work and live obviously also have profound macroeconomic consequences— for example, with regard to economic structural changes. Using an agglomeration index developed for *World Development Report 2009: Reshaping Economic Geography* (WDR 2009),[3] evidence suggests that returns to agglomeration are relatively higher on the lower rungs of development. Recent research at the IMF suggests that greater economic diversification is associated with improved macroeconomic performance. Another strand of research that has benchmarked Africa's transformation with that of Asia's provides some optimism with regard to Africa's economic prospects.

Poverty is lower in urban areas

Cities and towns are hubs of prosperity—more than 80 percent of global economic activity is produced in cities by just over half of the world's population. Economic agglomeration increases productivity, which in turn attracts more firms and creates better-paying jobs. Urbanization provides higher incomes for workers than they would earn on a farm, and it generates further opportunities to move up the income ladder. Between 1990 and 2008, rural poverty rates were, without exception, higher than urban poverty rates (table O.1). Indeed, more-urbanized countries have had greater success in attaining the MDGs than less-urbanized ones: countries with a degree of urbanization above 60 percent are expected to achieve 50 percent more MDGs than those with a degree of urbanization of 40 percent or less.

TABLE O.1 Poverty rates are falling in both urban and rural areas but are lower in urban areas
Share of the population below $1.25/day

	1990		1996		2002		2008	
	Rural	Urban	Rural	Urban	Rural	Urban	Rural	Urban
East Asia and Pacific	67.5	24.4	45.9	13.0	39.2	6.9	20.4	4.3
Europe and Central Asia	2.2	0.9	6.3	2.8	4.4	1.1	1.2	0.2
Latin America and the Caribbean	21.0	7.4	20.3	6.3	20.3	8.3	13.2	3.1
Middle East and North Africa	9.1	1.9	5.6	0.9	7.5	1.2	4.1	0.8
South Asia	50.5	40.1	46.1	35.2	45.1	35.2	38.0	29.7
Sub-Saharan Africa	55.0	41.5	56.8	40.6	52.3	41.4	47.1	33.6
Total	52.5	20.5	43.0	17.0	39.5	15.1	29.4	11.6

Source: World Bank staff calculations.

Urban poverty rates not only have been relatively low but have also declined in all regions between 1990 and 2008. East Asia's success in reducing urban and rural poverty has been spectacular, driven to a large extent by China's achievement. East Asia in 1980 had an urbanization level similar to that in South Asia and Sub-Saharan Africa but the highest poverty rate of all six regions. Its success in poverty reduction over the past three decades was linked to its rapid urbanization rate, which more than doubled from 21.5 percent in 1980 to 49 percent in 2010. In 1980, urbanization rates in South Asia and Sub-Saharan Africa were slightly above those in East Asia; by 2010 they had increased to only 37 percent. Urbanization by itself is no guarantee of success, however. If unregulated and poorly planned, rapid urbanization can lead to disproportionate increases in slums.

The challenge of poverty reduction, however, remains largely in rural areas and is concentrated in Asia and Sub-Saharan Africa. In 2008, 46 percent of Sub-Saharan Africa's rural population—but only 34 percent of its urban population—lived on less than $1.25 a day. In South Asia, the share of the poor in the population was 38 percent in rural areas and 30 percent in urban areas in 2008. Three-quarters of the poor in South Asia live in rural areas. Even in East Asia, the share of rural poor was approximately five times higher than in urban areas in 2008.

Services are better in urban areas

Apart from creating better-paying jobs, cities also make, through their density, public services more accessible. For example, on average, the cost of providing piped water is $0.70–$0.80 per cubic meter in urban areas compared with $2 in sparsely populated areas. South Asia and Sub-Saharan Africa have the largest rural-urban disparities in all service delivery indicators. The poor often pay the highest price for the water they consume while having the lowest consumption levels. For example, in Niger, the average price per cubic meter of water is CFAF 182 for piped water from a network, CFAF 534 from a public fountain, and CFAF 926 from a vendor. And poor access to basic infrastructure disproportionately affects rural women, because they perform most of the domestic chores and often walk long distances to reach clean water.

Even in the poorest of countries, people have higher expectations for service delivery in cities: that water will flow when a tap is turned on; that one will have access to a toilet; or that one will find a doctor when a child has malaria. In 2010, 96 percent of the urban population but 81 percent of the rural population in developing countries had access to safe drinking water. Disparities in access to basic sanitation were greater: 80 percent of urban residents but only 50 percent of rural residents had access to a toilet.

Schooling and health care can also be delivered with economies of scale in dense environments, close to where people actually live. Urban citizens in rich and poor countries have better access than rural citizens to basic services, including those associated with the attainment of the MDGs. Quite often, both access to and quality of services are better in urban areas.

While good outcomes in nutrition, health, and education are development goals in themselves, they also combine to form human skills and abilities that are strongly linked to productivity growth and poverty reduction. Rural children are disadvantaged because they have access to services of lower quality than do urban children. The inability to attract teachers to rural schools is only one of the reasons for the poor quality of schooling in rural areas.

The spectrum of urbanization is wide

Along the spectrum from rural to urban lie many types of settlements from small towns to small cities and peri-urban areas to large cities. In many middle-income countries, such as India and Vietnam, the urban population is concentrated in the largest cities, but the urban poor are dispersed along a continuum of medium, smaller, and very small towns, demonstrating that urban poverty is not just a large-city phenomenon. Research in India, for example, indicates that while poverty is primarily a rural phenomenon at the aggregate level, urban poverty is becoming a larger problem. The poverty rate for rural areas in India was 28 percent in 2004–05, compared with 26 percent in urban areas. Among urban areas, poverty rates were highest in small towns (population less than 50,000), at 30 percent, compared with 15 percent in large cities (population of 1 million or more). The urban spectrum is less pronounced in Sub-Saharan Africa, where many countries are small and sparsely populated and where urbanization is still in its early stages. Urban poverty there is thus more concentrated in capital cities.

Small rural towns often have high concentrations of poor people. Some poor want to migrate to cities to escape poverty but are reluctant to dispose of their rural assets. In Nepal, for example, where poverty is extreme, migrants prefer not to move too far from their rural residence but value proximity to paved roads and areas with higher housing premiums. Many want to maintain links with their farms, while others fear losing their land if they migrate too far.

Remaining close to one's land is an important factor in migration in the absence of efficient land markets.

Well-designed urbanization is needed to achieve the MDGs

As long as rural-urban disparities in income and service delivery persist, rural-to-urban migration will ensue. Nearly 50 percent of the population in developing countries was urban in 2011, compared with less than 30 percent in the 1980s. Urban dwellers are expected to double between 2000 and 2030, from 2 billion to 4 billion people, and the number of Chinese urban dwellers will increase from more than 622 million today to over 1 billion in 2030. This trend is not unique to developing countries—today's high-income countries underwent the same transformation in the 20th century. In fact, virtually no country has graduated to a high-income status without urbanizing, and urbanization rates above 70 percent are typically found in high-income countries.

For every ten people lifted out of poverty in the East Asia and Pacific region, two were facilitated by the urbanization process alone. Even in Sub-Saharan Africa, half of the decline in poverty originated in urban areas and through the urbanization process. Looking at the impact of urbanization on service delivery provides even stronger evidence of the importance of the process of urbanization itself: close to 30 percent of the improvement in the MDG on sanitation results from the process of urbanization, that is, the migration of people and the expansion of urban areas.

Policies to foster migration are important to enable the poor to move from lagging to leading areas, and governments can help reduce rural poverty by making migration more efficient. Equipping citizens with human capital assets while they are still in a rural area will increase the chance that their job search in the city is successful. Many developing countries have instituted land market policies in rural areas that discourage migration to urban areas. Restrictions in the

land market are not only detrimental to agricultural productivity growth but also hinder diversification into nonfarm activities that have higher returns. They should be relaxed.

However important facilitating the urbanization process is, it is not enough for successful development. Governments must also improve access to basic services in rural areas to achieve development goals, and they face important trade-offs in doing so. Priorities are not easily set, and financing local services is not straightforward. Moreover, governments must address the problem of slums in urban areas and mitigate the negative side effects of urbanization in the form of pollution caused by congestion or urban sprawl. To benefit fully from urbanization, smart planning of existing and new urban areas is needed.

Services in rural areas need improvement

Even as numerous towns emerge in rural areas and many poor people migrate to cities to seek better jobs and services, the prevalence of a large majority of the poor in rural areas remains of great concern. Rural areas need focused policies that help raise farm productivity and connect rural villages to input and output markets. Diversification of employment into nonagricultural activities can also reduce rural poverty. Growth of nonfarm activities is often driven by growth in agricultural productivity, at least at the initial stage of development. Roads and the provision of electricity are needed to improve connectivity to markets and increase agricultural productivity.

Because the MDGs reflect the basic needs of all citizens, governments should aim to attain them fully in both urban and rural areas. Given scarce resources, however, priorities must be set. Consequently, it is important that decision makers take country-specific circumstances into account when allocating resources.

For example, if the prime source of urbanization is domestic migration, then a strategy that focuses on MDG-related services that are portable (such as health and education) and that facilitate the integration of migrants seeking better opportunities in cities might have a higher payoff than one that indiscriminately tries to equalize MDG-related services across urban and rural areas. Early investments in education and health in rural areas will prove useful to those who seek jobs in cities but can also contribute to higher farm and nonfarm incomes for those who never migrate. Such a payoff seems particularly relevant for sparsely populated countries with both low urbanization and agglomeration rates, as in Sub-Saharan Africa.

If the prime source of urbanization is gradual thickening of population density, then the countrywide equalization of MDG-related services is more appropriate. This seems most relevant for countries with a low urbanization rate but an elevated level of agglomeration, as is the case in various countries in South Asia and those countries with a high urbanization rate and low expected migration.

If people get stuck in small towns, with little prospect of moving on to large cities, then policies should focus on improving connectivity with other urban centers. Poverty in small towns is often high, and the quantity and quality of services there differ little from those in rural areas and lag behind those in more mature urban settlements. Measures to better connect the activities in those small towns with economies of larger cities are then paramount.

In all cases, the challenges should not be underestimated. Many developing countries have been unable to provide a coordinated package of physical infrastructure and social services in rural areas. In part, that is because the financing of public goods in poor areas is a daunting task, a point about which more is said below.

New forms of service delivery are required in slums

Although poverty rates in cities are relatively low and declining, poverty in many countries is increasingly becoming an urban phenomenon as more and more people live in cities. Slums are the urban face of poverty and emerge when cities are unable to meet the demand for basic services and to supply the expected jobs. A likely 1 billion people live in urban slums in developing countries, and their numbers are projected to grow by nearly 500 million between now and 2020. Slums are growing the fastest in Sub-Saharan Africa, southeastern Asia, and western Asia. Currently, 62 percent of Africa's urban population lives in slums. Women and children bear a disproportionate burden of improper sanitation and poor health care in slums. The lack of urban planning by governments has implications for the urban poor, especially in Asia and Africa. Qualitative research, community surveys, and studies by nongovernmental organizations show that the actions taken by the urban poor in response to inadequate urban institutional support can produce severe indirect impacts.[4]

The absence of land tenure is a key factor. According to the UN's *MDG Report 2012*, slum evictions without due legal process are the most visible violation of housing rights confronting the urban poor. Household surveys carried out in a range of cities around the globe found that slum dwellers reported insecurity regarding possible eviction was high, ranging from 20 percent in São Paolo to nearly 45 percent in Lagos. Insecure tenure in slum settlements means that governments are unwilling or unable to provide basic services to these areas. In the absence of basic services, one coping strategy for the urban poor is dependence on informal providers, who offer low-quality services, often at higher costs than those paid by the nonpoor with access to formal services. This practice not only places higher economic costs on the urban poor but also leads to increased health costs, especially in the form of child morbidity from unclean water. Similarly, the lack of adequate sanitation facilities in low-income settlements can lower the school attendance of adolescent girls and eventually increase their dropout rates. This problem has been specifically detected in Kenya's urban slums, where qualitative and quantitative data show

that girls in grades four through eight who have reached puberty miss six learning weeks a year on average.

Combined with their informal employment, the inability of migrants living in slums to produce water or electricity bills or a formal rental lease to prove urban residence puts them in an even more precarious situation. In some countries, proof of urban residence is needed to access basic services, as is the case with health services in Kyrgyzstan, and can sometimes lead to reverse migration. For example, when the quality of health services is dismal or when a migrant is excluded for lack of required documentation, an illness can push a migrant back to a rural area. Additionally, the inability to provide required identification and proof of urban residence excludes the urban poor from accessing financial services, leaving them with little means of saving for future investment or insurance in the event of economic shocks. In a detailed qualitative study of 176 rickshaw pullers in Delhi, only 1 percent had bank accounts, although 95 percent consciously saved daily or periodically.

The most common coping strategies for saving in the absence of bank accounts include depositing money with a local shopkeeper or a relative or friend (with the risk of being cheated); carrying savings on one's person at all times; and burying small amounts in the ground or hiding money in perceived safe spots within one's residence. Savings handled in these ways are vulnerable to theft. In the event of economic shocks from periods of unemployment or illness, the absence of savings can lead to discontinuation of children's education, especially that of girls, and to interruption in remittances. Remittances are also affected by the high cost of sending money by informal means, given the lack of access to banking by both the urban and rural poor.

Impermanent, unsafe housing and the lack of basic services in slums force some migrants to maintain split households (separating spouses and leaving children with grandparents in rural areas), thus introducing instability into the urban transition. This continued dependence on rural areas has several negative implications, including the increased burden of child care on aging grandparents, the inability of migrants' children to access better-quality primary education and health services, and numerous other harmful psychological and health consequences. Several studies from Asia and Sub-Saharan Africa have documented the adverse effects arising from split households.

The key message is that governments should not discriminate between slum dwellers and the rural or urban poor. Slum dwellers should be provided access to basic services just like the poor in rural areas or cities, although the modalities may be different. Where land tenure issues are pervasive, and services cannot be or are not connected to informal dwellings, public connections may be more appropriate. Alongside increased instances of slum evictions and slum clearance in the past decade, a growing number of success stories of slum service provision and upgrades are beginning to be noticed. For example, in the Lao People's Democratic Republic, the government had never given land on a long-term lease to a low-income squatter community until recently, when two government projects did so, thus regularizing people's status on public land they already occupied. In Vinh, Vietnam, government has moved to provide slums with better services by adjusting existing planning standards to make them more realistic and to lower costs and make it easier for the urban poor to develop housing that matches their needs.

Uncoordinated urbanization can lead to pollution, sprawl, and congestion

Urbanization is largely a natural process, driven by the opportunities cities offer. Unregulated markets are unlikely to get densities right, however, and spontaneous development of cities can create negative side effects such as congestion or, alternatively, excessive sprawl. The consequences are pollution and inefficiencies. Without coordinated actions, cities will lack the proper investments to benefit from positive externalities generated by increased density. Higher-quality construction material and more sophisticated buildings are required to support greater densities, but if these higher costs must be fully internalized by firms and households, underinvestment is the result. In addition, complementary physical infrastructure is critical: roads, drainage, street lighting, electricity, water, and sewerage, together with policing, waste disposal, and health care. While a market-driven process could possibly gradually increase densities through shifting land values over time, the long-lived and lumpy nature of urban investment often inhibits such a process. A city's physical structures, once established, may remain in place for more than 150 years.

Under current trends, the expected increases in the urban population in the developing world will be accompanied by a tripling in the built-up area of cities, from 200,000 to 600,000 square kilometers. As an example, consider Shanghai, which has rapidly expanded over the past 20 years (map O.1). Such rapid population growth accompanied by an even faster spatial expansion of cities is likely to lead to low-density development dominated by individual-vehicle transportation—a largely irreversible pattern that runs the risk of dampening density-induced productivity and service delivery efficiencies. An additional consequence of rapid urban growth is worsening air quality. A recent study of the 189 largest cities using satellite data found that air quality worsened between 2002 and 2010, particularly in the largest cities of the Indian subcontinent, parts of Africa, the Middle East, and north China—places experiencing rapid urban growth.

Emissions from the burning of fossil fuels include fine particulate matter (PM10 and PM2.5), carbon monoxide, nitric oxides, and sulfur dioxide, which can cause allergies, respiratory problems, cardiovascular disease, and cognitive deficits. The impacts are significant. In Russia, a conservative estimate

MAP O.1 **Shanghai's spatial expansion as shown by average nighttime light intensity**

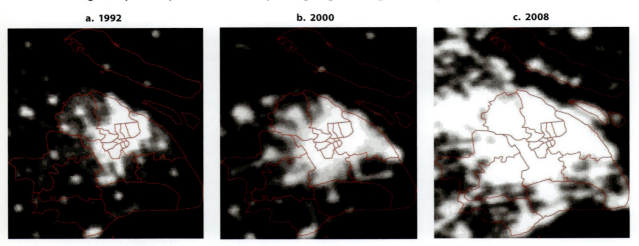

a. 1992   b. 2000   c. 2008

Source: China Data Center at University of Michigan.

suggests that annual health damage from fossil-fuel burning amount to $6 billion. The social cost of transport in Beijing is equivalent to 7.5–15.0 percent of its gross domestic product, with about half of that stemming from air pollution, including carbon emissions. The largest share of these costs comes from increased mortality.

Globally, acute respiratory infections associated with air pollution cause about 20 percent of all under-five deaths. In the former Yugoslav Republic of Macedonia, a country of about 2 million people, air pollution is the cause of an estimated 1,300 premature deaths annually. Beijing, Cairo, Delhi, Dhaka, and Karachi each see an estimated 3,500 to 7,000 premature deaths annually from cardiovascular disease caused by air pollution. Managing environmental quality while enhancing urban productivity is critical.

An integrated strategy

Three interrelated dimensions of urban development triangulate the coordinated approach needed to enable a country to take advantage of its urbanization process: planning, connecting, and financing.

- *Planning*—charting a course for cities by setting the terms of urbanization, especially policies for using urban land and expanding basic infrastructure and public services.
- *Connecting*—making a city's markets (labor, goods, and services) accessible to other neighborhoods in the city, to other cities, and to outside export markets.
- *Financing*—finding sources for large capital outlays needed to provide infrastructure and services as cities grow and urbanization picks up speed.

These are terms that policy makers use on a daily basis, but they often focus on financing first without fully considering the other two dimensions. Of the three, planning for land use and basic services is the most important. In fact, the key challenge for countries at all stages of urbanization is strengthening the institutions for land management. Yet because planning must allow for people and products to be mobile, it must be coordinated with and connected to all stages of a city's growth. Financing should be city leaders' last concern rather than their first.

In designing policies to manage the process of urbanization, it is paramount to enhance women's empowerment and to close the gender gap in earnings, largely by improving women's access to education. *World Development Report 2012: Gender*

Equality and Development (WDR 2012) details that the emergence of agglomeration economies can have disproportionate benefits for women with basic education through job opportunities in light manufacturing. Hence, in addition to the importance of getting polices right regarding planning, connecting, and financing, a priority is reducing gender gaps in human capital, specifically those that address women's education.

Urbanization should start with planning

Planning is fundamental to agglomeration economies in three ways. First, land use requires effective systems for land valuation. Second, land use must be allocated in a way that allows for infrastructure improvements as the city grows. Third, the most basic infrastructure services—water, energy, sanitation, and solid waste management—need to be provided for all residents, urban, peri-urban, and rural alike; natural market mechanisms are unlikely to provide those.

Lack of early planning often imposes very difficult corrective measures later on. Measures that could have worked well at an early stage are much less effective once city structures have been locked in. For example, to manage slum formation and reduce the hazards faced by slum dwellers, policy makers often try to move people to safe environments or provide better housing elsewhere. Initiatives include urban upgrades, such as community and household infrastructure projects; resettlement to new housing developments; housing subsidies; and land titling. But many of these policies do not work because people do not always willingly trade a good location for a better home with more modern utilities. People choose neighborhoods for their affordable services and amenities—but also for their proximity to jobs.

In many developing countries' cities, it can be difficult to live near one's job. One consequence of failed land markets and restrictive regulations is that the formal housing supply is low. But it may also be difficult and costly to commute to work, because transport infrastructure fails to connect urban neighborhoods. In many African cities, commuting by public transit costs more than half of a poor household's income. In Harare, the poor spend more than a fourth of their disposable income on transport. In Kampala, the figure is 50 percent.

To foster better living conditions, policy makers need to coordinate land market rules with urban infrastructure development. Hanoi has been able to grow without the formation of large slums because the government set prudent rules for land markets and infrastructure. It allowed the densification of former village areas. It pushed to modernize road networks just outside the city, yet it mostly avoided demolishing older houses. These roads have opened new land for formal developers while improving connections between existing village areas and the city. The village areas were allowed to grow and were integrated into the urban economy.

Policy makers in Bogotá similarly succeeded by coordinating land use with infrastructure development. The Programa de Mejoramiento Integral de Barrios aimed to improve mobility and living conditions in 26 of the poorest city areas, called Unidades de Planificacion Zonal. The Unidades comprised 107 neighborhoods of informal origin, with 1,440 informal settlements, 300,000 plots not formally titled, and about 500,000 structurally substandard dwellings. The program legalized homes and neighborhoods; it expanded infrastructure with roads, rainwater traps, and sanitary and aqueduct trunk networks; and it added urban facilities (stairs, parks, community rooms). Living conditions improved for about 650,000 people. Complementary improvements in communication and interregional transport can make it easier to integrate neighboring peri-urban and rural areas with urban economies.

Integrating planning, connecting, and financing is also key to the "greening" of growth and getting urbanization right. While there is a perceived trade-off between "building more cities" to accommodate rapid urban growth and "building cities right" to enhance social and environmental outcomes, compelling evidence shows that "building cities right" generates co-benefits in the near term and reduces the prohibitive costs of addressing sprawl, congestion, pollution, and climate change later. Integrating land use and transport plans effectively allows public transport (with its lower energy consumption and emissions) to be a major mode of transport in locations zoned for high density. The Brazilian city of Curitiba has managed to concentrate its population around public transportation lines and hubs, making it possible to maximize the share of trips with low-energy-consumption modes of transportation. Copenhagen redesigned its urban transport network to follow a transit-oriented and bike-friendly approach: it started with a "finger plan"— the identification of few priority development areas—and then invested in five-axis transit radials and corridors of new, satellite, rail-served towns.

Connectivity depends on more than infrastructure

To benefit from the opportunities that cities offer, commuting costs need to be low. Moreover, if connections with the surrounding areas are well developed, urban densities can also have a positive impact on rural areas. Research in India has shown a growing link between urban development and a reduction of rural poverty; higher demand for rural products and more options for rural nonfarm diversification followed India's economic liberalization in the early 1990s.

Connections, both between and within cities, benefit producers and consumers, both in urban and rural areas. Connections give producers access to input (including labor) and output markets. They give consumers options and, in many cases, better prices. And connections expose cities and rural areas to new economic opportunities. But policy makers who envision better transport connections for cities and neighborhoods face difficult choices. With limited resources, they cannot invest in everything. It is hard to know which new or improved connections will yield the highest returns over time. Setting priorities for connective investment means picking

winners and losers in the short run—but in the long run, thinking about priorities can make a vast difference for cities, surrounding rural areas, and even countries.

More than building and fixing, efforts to improve intercity connections are about the economics of the transport sector, which has a tendency toward natural monopolies. If the market structure for transport service provision does not promote competitive pricing, any cost reductions stemming from network investments will be absorbed as profit by monopolistic providers. The government regulates in large part to induce healthy competition, limiting monopolistic behavior but also limiting the number, or behavior, of competitors where required. Investments in infrastructure are more successful when bundled with regulatory reforms that promote competitive pricing while also ensuring compliance with safety standards.

In Uganda, as in many other African countries, a large gap between transport costs and prices attests to monopolistic behavior. Along the Uganda stretch of the Kampala–Mombasa corridor, home to most of Uganda's industrial production, transport prices average $2.22 a kilometer—double the average price in the United States—even though transport costs are about $0.35 a kilometer. According to trucker surveys, 86 percent of the corridor is in good condition. So the fact that providers are making more than 85 percent profit suggests a need for competition, which can be induced most effectively through policy measures and regulation.

Within many cities, the poorest residents are often deprived of affordable transport services. An extreme example is Mumbai, where, according to a study published in 2007, transport expenditures represented at least 16 percent of income for riders in the lowest income category, even though subsidies covered as much as 30 percent of transport costs. While subsidies have not always been successful, some targeted subsidies do reach the right groups and increase access to jobs. For example, South Africa uses highly subsidized weekly coupons, good for 10 journeys between black townships and industrial development areas, to connect low-income workers to jobs. Brazil requires formal sector employers to provide transit tickets to employees through a system called *vale transporte* (VT); firms then deduct the VT expenditures from taxable income. The VT system—albeit affecting only the formal sector—effectively spreads the cost of transport subsidies between employers and the government.

Finance is the difficult final part of the puzzle

Having identified priorities for planning and connecting, policy makers confront the problem of financing those investments. The main difficulty is the need for money up front. Large capital outlays are needed to provide infrastructure and services that are not fully in demand now but will become so as urbanization picks up speed. The large capital investments that are needed in the construction phase, whether for transport, water provision, solid waste management, or sewage removal and treatment, are likely to far exceed the budget of any city government. But financing can become more sustainable through taxes realized with increased economic growth, and with the ability of policy makers to leverage land markets and approach local currency debt markets.

More generally, financing of all local services is challenging. While services are best delivered locally, the local tax base is often narrow. That is true not only for cities, but for all subnational governments.[5] These governments are often better suited than agencies of the national government to address the challenges of service delivery. They can more efficiently detect citizens' needs given their informational advantage. That is particularly relevant for beneficiary identification in poverty programs. Subnational governments can direct resources toward these needs (*allocative efficiency*) and can provide some services more efficiently than national governments (*productive efficiency*). Decentralized management and execution of public investment can also be strengthened by joint

approaches to address infrastructural gaps. Chile, for instance, is coordinating public investment through regional investment windows, including cofinancing with municipalities. In addition, political decentralization lowers the "barriers to entry" for different groups of society, so they can more easily and directly participate in decision making. An example from Mexico underscores the importance of decentralization: because of political resistance, federal teachers were not decentralized to the states, resulting in a parallel hiring process at the state level that blurred the lines of accountability.

Local provision of services requires fiscal equalization across space to ensure that necessary resources flow toward the districts most in need of them. No country starts from a clean slate, however, and more often than not, reforms of intergovernmental transfers are done at the margin and incrementally. An example is Colombia's current royalty reform, which achieves more equitable distribution of royalty resources.

The financing challenges are largest in rural areas: they are home to the largest number of poor people, but, under growing disparities in fiscal capacity, they are increasingly resource constrained. Subnational governments in urban areas have higher fiscal capacity and are hence better able to influence outcomes through their own revenue decisions. Absent any convergence effects, fiscal capacity in urban areas will increase as agglomeration unfolds, putting rural areas at a further disadvantage. Given uneven advances and levels of autonomy in expenditures, rural governments are more constrained in their ability to provide a high-quality package of services to the poor or to target the incidence of spending on direct services where they are needed most.

Notes

1. The original target to improve the lives of at least 100 million slum dwellers by 2020 was based on an estimation of close to 100 million slum dwellers in the world. Upon measurement of slum populations using the internationally

agreed upon UN-Habitat definition of slums following the UN Expert Group Meeting of October 2002, it was learned that the global estimate of the slum population was in fact close to 1 billion (924 million). As a result, even though the slum target has been globally achieved, and in fact significantly surpassed 10 years ahead of schedule, there is little room for complacency given the existing magnitude of populations currently living in slums.

2. As detailed in the OECD's report "Aid Effectiveness 2005-10: Progress in Implementing the Paris Declaration" (2011).

3. Many reasons for the occurrence of urbanization were discussed in WDR 2009, which provided ample evidence of the benefits of agglomeration. WDR 2009 developed an agglomeration index with a uniform definition of what constitutes an urban or agglomerated area. An urban or agglomerated area is defined by population size of a settlement (more than 50,000 people), population density (more than 150 people per square kilometer), and travel time to the nearest large city (60 minutes).

4. The report draws upon an in-house desktop review of qualitative research, the findings of community-level surveys on slum dwellers in cities of developing countries, and fresh inputs sought from civil society organizations across a range of developing countries. This body of research has explored several themes affecting the urban poor, especially rural-urban migrants, and the strategies they apply to remain resilient to the challenges posed by urban poverty. Data and insights have been drawn from countries in Asia, Sub-Saharan Africa, and Latin America, including Bangladesh, China, India, Indonesia, Kyrgyzstan, Thailand, Ghana, Kenya, South Africa, Tanzania, Uganda, Zambia, Brazil, and Ecuador.

5. The term "subnational governments" encompasses, among other entities, regional or state governments, provinces, and municipalities.

Report Card

The Millennium Development Goals, 2013

4 targets out of **21** are already met.

Global Progress on MDGs

17 Countries on track to meet MDG 4: 2015

20 Countries projected to meet MDG 4: 2015–2020

Progress on MDG 4

All Countries

Countries met goals

MDG 3
Promote gender equality and empower women

72 out of 144 countries have met MDG 3

Goals and Targets from the Millennium Declaration

2

Achieve universal primary education

TARGET 2.A Ensure that by 2015, children everywhere, boys and girls alike, will be able to complete a full course of primary schooling

4

Reduce child mortality

TARGET 4.A Reduce by two-thirds, between 1990 and 2015, the under-five mortality rate

1

Eradicate extreme poverty and hunger

TARGET 1.A Halve, between 1990 and 2015, the proportion of people whose income is less than $1.25 a day
TARGET 1.B Achieve full and productive employment and decent work for all, including women and young people
TARGET 1.C Halve, between 1990 and 2015, the proportion of people who suffer from hunger

3

Promote gender equality and empower women

TARGET 3.A Eliminate gender disparity in primary and secondary education, preferably by 2005, and at all levels of education no later than 2015

6

Combat HIV/AIDS, malaria, and other diseases

TARGET 6.A Have halted by 2015 and begun to reverse the spread of HIV/AIDS
TARGET 6.B Achieve by 2010 universal access to treatment for HIV/AIDS for all those who need it
TARGET 6.C Have halted by 2015 and begun to reverse the incidence of malaria and other major diseases

5

Improve maternal health

TARGET 5.A Reduce by three-quarters, between 1990 and 2015, the maternal mortality ratio
TARGET 5.B Achieve by 2015 universal access to reproductive health

7

Ensure environmental sustainability

TARGET 7.A Integrate the principles of sustainable development into country policies and programs and reverse the loss of environmental resources
TARGET 7.B Reduce biodiversity loss, achieving by 2010 a significant reduction in the rate of loss
TARGET 7.C Halve by 2015 the proportion of people without sustainable access to safe drinking water and basic sanitation
TARGET 7.D Have achieved a significant improvement by 2020 in the lives of at least 100 million slum dwellers

8

Develop a global partnership for development

TARGET 8.A Develop further an open, rule-based, predictable, nondiscriminatory trading and financial system (including a commitment to good governance, development, and poverty reduction, nationally and internationally)
TARGET 8.B Address the special needs of the least-developed countries (including tariff- and quota-free access for exports of the least-developed countries; enhanced debt relief for heavily indebted poor countries and cancellation of official bilateral debt; and more generous official development assistance for countries committed to reducing poverty)
TARGET 8.C Address the special needs of landlocked countries and small island developing states (through the Programme of Action for the Sustainable Development of Small Island Developing States and the outcome of the 22nd special session of the General Assembly)
TARGET 8.D Deal comprehensively with the debt problems of developing countries through national and international measures to make debt sustainable in the long term
TARGET 8.E In cooperation with pharmaceutical companies, provide access to affordable, essential drugs in developing countries
TARGET 8.F In cooperation with the private sector, make available the benefits of new technologies, especially information and communications

Source: United Nations. 2008. *Report of the Secretary-General on the Indicators for Monitoring the Millennium Development Goals.* E/CN.3/2008/29. New York.
Note: The Millennium Development Goals and targets come from the Millennium Declaration, signed by 189 countries, including 147 heads of state and government, in September 2000 (http://www.un.org/millennium/declaration/ares552e.htm) and from further agreement by members states at the 2005 World Summit (Resolution adopted by the General Assembly—A/RES/60/1). The goals and targets are interrelated and should be seen as a whole. They represent a partnership between the developed countries and the developing countries "to create an environment—at the national and global levels alike—which is conducive to development and the elimination of poverty."

Progress toward the MDGs

Only two years away from the 2015 target set for reaching the Millennium Development Goals (MDGs), progress is diverse across goals and regions. Global estimates indicate that targets such as reduction of extreme poverty (MDG 1.a), gender equality in primary education (MDG 3.a), access to safe drinking water (MDG 7.c), and improved lives for at least 100 million slum dwellers (MDG 7.d) have been reached. The proportion of people whose income is less than $1.25 a day fell from 43.1 percent in 1990 to below 20.6 percent in 2010, leaving 1.2 billion people in extreme poverty. Gender equality in primary school enrollments was also achieved in 2010. Similarly, the goal of halving the proportion of people without sustainable access to safe drinking water has already been reached.

At the same time, progress on the remaining MDGs has been lagging, especially for education- and health-related MDGs. Global targets for infant, under-five, and maternal mortality (MDGs 4.a and 5.a), and to a lesser extent, access to basic sanitation (MDG 7.c) are significantly behind, and

progress needs to be greatly accelerated if all of the goals are to be achieved by 2015. The goal for primary school completion should have been within sight by 2011, but only half the progress needed has been made.

Regionally, progress toward the MDGs is more diverse, although most regions will likely miss health-related targets. In East Asia and the Pacific, the targets on extreme poverty, gender parity, and access to water and sanitation have been reached. The region is still lagging on the under-five, infant, and maternal mortality goals.

In Europe and Central Asia, the goals on poverty and water are likely to be met. This region has managed to achieve only 63 percent of the progress needed to meet the primary completion rate goal, 84 percent of the child mortality target, and 72 percent of the maternal mortality goal. The region is farthest behind on meeting the target for access to basic sanitation.

Latin America and the Caribbean have already reached the targets on extreme poverty,

FIGURE 1   Global progress toward achieving the MDGs
Developing countries, percent of total required progress between 1990 and 2015, as achieved in 2010 or 2011.

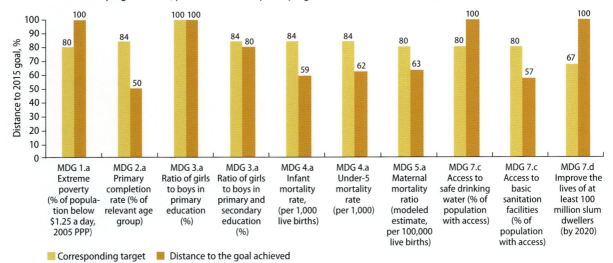

Source: World Bank staff estimates.

Note: Intermediate target calculated using a linear progression over 25 years, resulting in a needed progress of 4 percent per annum. Note that the corresponding target for 2010 would equal 80 percent, and for 2011 84 percent, to be on track to attain the MDG by 2015. Any value above those intermediate targets indicates that the world is ahead of the required pace to meet the MDG. A value of 100 percent means that the MDG has been met.

PPP = purchasing power parity.

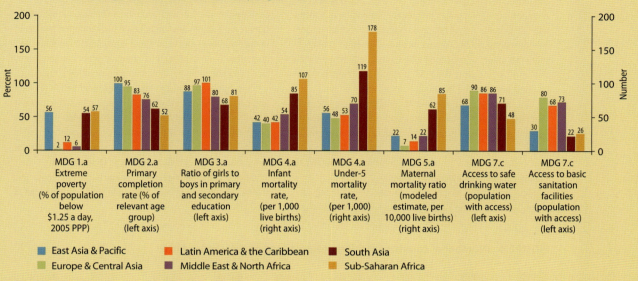

FIGURE 2   Starting position for each MDG by region, 1990

Legend:
- East Asia & Pacific
- Europe & Central Asia
- Latin America & the Caribbean
- Middle East & North Africa
- South Asia
- Sub-Saharan Africa

Source: WDI and GMR.

Note: Weighted by population. PPP = purchasing power parity.

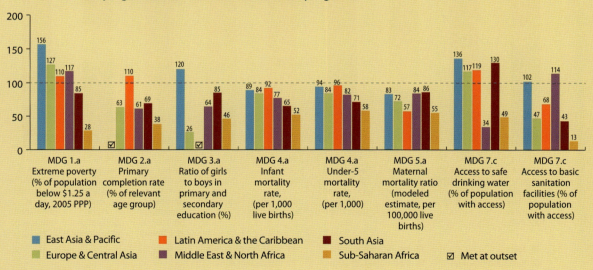

FIGURE 3   Global progress toward the MDGs achieved, by region

Legend:
- East Asia & Pacific
- Europe & Central Asia
- Latin America & the Caribbean
- Middle East & North Africa
- South Asia
- Sub-Saharan Africa
- ☑ Met at outset

Source: WDI and GMR.

Note: The corresponding target for 2010, 80 percent, and for 2011, 84 percent. Any value above those corresponding targets indicates that the region seems on track to meeting the MDG using a simple linear approximation. A value larger than 100 percent means that more progress has been made than is necessary at the year reported. A zero value indicates deterioration. PPP = purchasing power parity.

primary completion, and access to safe water. The region stagnated on the gender equality target but is very close to reaching it. Although the region has achieved more than 80 percent of the progress needed to reduce under-five mortality by two-thirds, progress on maternal mortality has been significantly slower than elsewhere, with the region moving only 57 percent of the distance needed to meet the goal.

The Middle East and North Africa region has also reached the targets on poverty and access to improved sanitation facilities. The region is making progress toward achieving universal primary education, gender equality, and child mortality. However more effort is needed to ensure access to safe drinking water.

South Asia has reached the target on access to safe water and has already achieved nearly 85 percent of the

goal to close the gender disparity gap in primary and secondary education. The region has also made progress on primary completion and child mortality rates. Progress on poverty reduction and access to basic sanitation has been slower, however. Faster progress is required to reduce child and maternal mortality and improve access to sanitation facilities if the region is to reach these goals by 2015.

Sub-Saharan Africa is lagging behind other regions and on most MDGs. However, this region had the furthest to go from the start. Currently, Sub-Saharan Africa has achieved more than 40 percent of the progress required to reach, by 2015, the targets for gender parity, child mortality, maternal mortality, and access to safe water.

Most countries need to pay particular attention to the health-related MDGs if they are to reach these goals by 2015.

FIGURE 4   Number of countries making progress toward the various MDGs

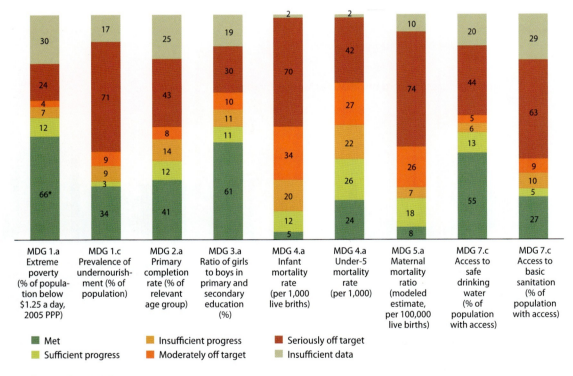

Source: WDI and GMR team estimates.

Note: Progress is based on extrapolation of latest five-year annual growth rates for each country, except for MDG 5, which uses the last seven years. "Sufficient progress" indicates that an extrapolation of the last observed data point with the growth rate over the last observable five-year period shows that the MDG can be attained. "Insufficient progress" is defined as being able to meet the MDG between 2016 and 2020. "Moderately off target" indicates that the MDG can be met between 2020 and 2030. "Seriously off target" indicates that the MDG will not even be met by 2030. "Insufficient data" points to the fact that not enough data points are available to estimate progress or that the MDG's starting value is missing (except for MDG 2 and MDG 3). PPP = purchasing power parity.

* In the poverty target, 11 out of the 66 countries that have met the target have less than 2% of people living below $1.25 a day.

Eradicate extreme poverty and hunger

The proportion of people living on less than $1.25 a day fell from 43.1 percent in 1990 to 20.6 percent in 2010, leaving 1.2 billion people in extreme poverty. Although the food, fuel, and financial crises over the past five years have worsened the plight of vulnerable populations and slowed poverty reduction in some countries, global poverty rates have continued to fall. Between 2005 and 2008, both the poverty rate and the number of people living in extreme poverty fell in all six developing-country regions, the first time that all regions had posted declines in poverty. Preliminary estimates for 2010 show that the extreme poverty rate fell further, reaching the global target of halving world poverty five years early, as close to 90 million more people were lifted out of extreme poverty.

Further progress is not only possible but likely before the MDGs' 2015 target date. Current economic forecasts suggest that gross domestic product (GDP) in developing economies will maintain a growth rate of 5.5–6.0 percent over the next three years. Economic growth will be fastest in East Asia and South Asia, regions that are home to more than half of the world's poorest people. Growth will be slower in Sub-Saharan Africa, the poorest region in the world, but faster than in preceding years, quickening the pace of poverty reduction. According to these forecasts, the proportion of people living in extreme poverty will fall from 20.6 percent in 2010 to 15.5 percent by 2015, leaving slightly more than 1 billion people in extreme poverty. Of these, 42 percent will live in South Asia and 42 percent in Sub-Saharan Africa.

The pace of poverty reduction depends not just on the growth of GDP but also on its distribution. A common assumption is that growth is "distribution neutral"; that is, growth in average income results in similar changes in the incomes of everyone, rich or poor. Although that has been the general experience over the past 20 years, there are notable variations: income distribution has improved in some countries, such as Brazil, while worsening in others, such as China. To accelerate progress toward the elimination of extreme poverty, development strategies should attempt to increase not only the mean rate of growth but also the share of income going to the poorest segment of the population. Sub-Saharan Africa, where average incomes are low and the average incomes of those below the poverty line are even lower, will face great difficulties in bringing its poorest people to an adequate standard of living.

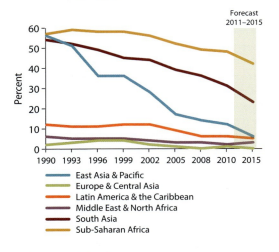

FIGURE 1a Poverty rates (living on $1.25 per day) by region

Forecast
2011–2015

Percent

1990 1993 1996 1999 2002 2005 2008 2010 2015

- East Asia & Pacific
- Europe & Central Asia
- Latin America & the Caribbean
- Middle East & North Africa
- South Asia
- Sub-Saharan Africa

Source: World Bank Povcalnet.

Note: Regional poverty rates are measured at US$1.25 a day (2005 purchasing power parity), with forecasts to 2015. Surveys cover less than half of the population of Sub-Saharan Africa in 1990; of South Asia in 1999; and Europe and Central Asia in both 2002 and 2008.

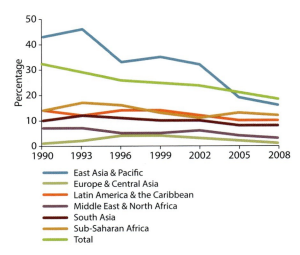

FIGURE 1b The decreasing gap in the urban and rural poverty headcount by region

Percentage

1990 1993 1996 1999 2002 2005 2008

- East Asia & Pacific
- Europe & Central Asia
- Latin America & the Caribbean
- Middle East & North Africa
- South Asia
- Sub-Saharan Africa
- Total

Sources: World Bank Staff calculations and Household Surveys.

The distribution of the poor is notable in the differences between poverty rates in rural and urban areas. As global poverty declined, so did the differential between urban and rural poverty. East Asia and the Pacific narrowed the gap by almost half by 2008. In other regions, such as Sub-Saharan Africa, Latin America and the Caribbean, and South Asia, there was less progress in closing this gap.

Hunger and malnutrition are measured by two different MDG indicators. Undernourishment reflects a shortage of food energy to sustain normal daily activities and is affected both by changes in the average amount of food available and by its distribution. Undernourishment declined steadily in most regions from 1991 to 2005, but further improvements have stalled since, leaving 13 percent of the world's population, almost 900 million people, without adequate daily food intake.

Malnutrition, measured in children by comparing their weight with other children of similar age, reflects a shortfall in food energy, poor feeding practices by mothers, and a lack of essential nutrients in their diets. Malnutrition in children often begins at birth, when poorly nourished mothers give birth to underweight babies. Malnourished children develop more slowly, enter school later, and perform less well. Based on available data, malnutrition rates in developing countries have dropped substantially, from 28 percent of children under age five in 1990 to 17 percent in 2011. Every developing region except Sub-Saharan Africa is on track to cut child malnutrition rates in half by 2015. However, data collection on malnutrition using surveys that directly measure children's weight and height is costly, and many countries lack sufficient information to calculate time trends.

FIGURE 1c **Average daily income of the poor by region, 2008**

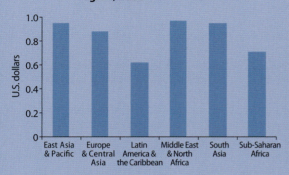

Source: World Bank, Povcalnet.

FIGURE 1d **Malnutrition prevalence (weight for age) by region, 1990–2011**

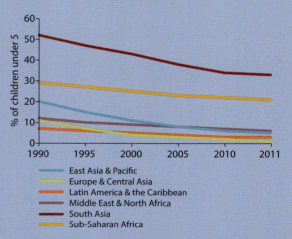

Source: World Development Indicators database, 2013.

FIGURE 1e **Undernourishment prevalence by region, 1991–2011**

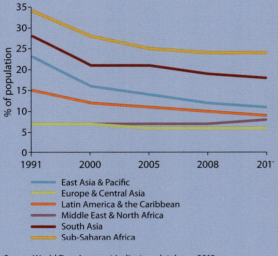

Source: World Development Indicators database, 2013.

MDG 2

Achieve universal primary education

The commitment to provide primary education to every child is the oldest of the MDGs, having been set in 1990 at the first *Education for All* conference, in Jomtien, Thailand. Achieving this goal has often seemed tantalizingly near, but it has been reached only in Latin America and the Caribbean, although Europe and Central Asia is close. (This goal had been reached at the outset by East Asia and the Pacific; then there was some backtracking, but the region is now close to reaching the goal again.) Progress among the poorest countries, slow in the 1990s, has accelerated since 2000, particularly in South Asia and Sub-Saharan Africa, but full enrollment remains elusive. Many children start school but drop out before completing the primary stage, discouraged by cost, distance, physical danger, and failure to progress. Even as countries approach the MDG target, the education demands of modern economies are expanding. In the 21st century, more than ever before, primary education is a critical stepping stone in building the human skills necessary for continued growth and prosperity.

In most developing regions, school enrollment rates picked up after the MDGs were promulgated in 2000, when the completion rate was 80 percent. By 2009, that rate had climbed to nearly 90 percent but has stalled since.

Completion rates in the Middle East and North Africa have stayed at 90 percent since 2008. Sub-Saharan Africa and South Asia, which started out farthest behind, have made substantial progress in absolute terms: South Asia has reached 88 percent but progress has been slow, while Sub-Saharan Africa lags far behind, at 70 percent. Even if schools in these regions were to begin now to enroll every eligible child in the first grade, those children would not be able to achieve a full course of primary education by 2015. But they would at least be on their way.

Many children enroll in primary school but attend intermittently or drop out entirely. This is particularly true for girls. Almost all school systems with low enrollment rates show underenrollment of girls in primary school. In rural areas, the work of children of both sexes may be needed during planting and harvest. Other obstacles, including school fees, lack of suitable facilities, and absence of teachers, discourage parents from sending their children to school. The problem is worst in South Asia and Sub-Saharan Africa, where more than 48 million children of primary school age are not in school.

Urban and rural primary completion rates are very similar in many countries around the world. The *quality* of primary education, however, differs more substantially, as

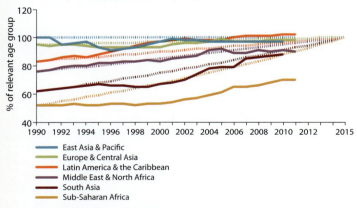

FIGURE 2a Progress toward achieving complete primary education by region

Source: UNESCO Institute of Statistics and World Development Indicators database.
Note: Dotted lines show path to goal.

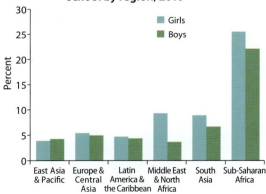

FIGURE 2b More girls than boys remain out of school by region, 2010

Source: UNESCO Institute of Statistics and World Development Indicators database.

Note: Progress assessment in East Asia and Pacific does not include China, which is believed to have completion rates close to 100 percent.

evidenced by the notable differences in the percentage of pupils reaching competency levels in reading in urban versus rural areas.

In Ghana, for example, enrollment in basic education nearly doubled by 2011, to 7 million pupils, and government expenditures on basic education more than tripled in real terms. More children are accessing basic education, graduating from junior high school, and enrolling in senior high school than at any time in Ghana's history.

Despite these achievements in access to basic education, inequity remains a persistent feature of Ghana's education service delivery and its most critical challenge. The primary net enrollment ratio has remained close to 80 percent over the past five years, meaning that nearly 1 million primary school-age children are not in school. These students are disproportionately from poor households and rural or marginalized areas or language groups (including the three northern regions) or are living in foster situations. Instead of compensating for deprivation, public expenditures appear to exacerbate the inequality by allocating fewer resources per child to the regions with the majority of deprived districts. Such a system perpetuates poverty and inequality.

This picture of inequity is mirrored in data on Ghanaian children's primary learning outcomes, primary completion rates, and access to senior high school. Notably, although the Ministry of Education has introduced several equity-improving initiatives, challenges with program design, targeting, and implementation have not been overcome, and the initiatives disproportionately benefit individuals from wealthier populations. Hence, Ghana's scores in the Trends in International Mathematics and Science Study (TIMSS) 2003 were lower than any other African country evaluated, including Botswana, the Arab Republic of Egypt, Morocco, South Africa, and Tunisia. Ghana's scores on the TIMSS 2007 were better but still among the lowest among African countries whose students took the tests.

FIGURE 2c Urban and rural primary completion rates are not very different worldwide

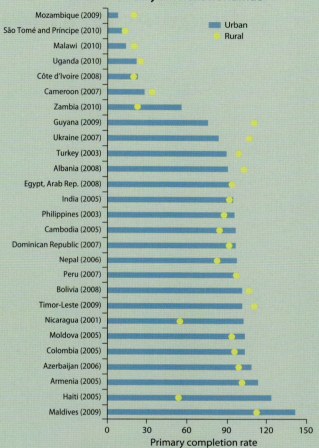

Sources: Demographic and Health Surveys; World Bank 2012; and staff calculations.

FIGURE 2d Reading competency levels (4-8) in urban and rural areas, 2007

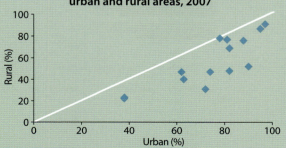

Source: Southern and Eastern Africa Consortium for Monitoring Educational Quality (SACMEQ).

Promote gender equality and empower women

Women make important contributions to economic and social development. Expanding opportunities for them in the public and private sectors is a core development strategy. Education is the starting point. By enrolling and staying in school, girls gain the skills they need to enter the labor market, care for families, and make decisions for themselves. Achieving gender equity in education is an important demonstration that young women are full, contributing members of society.

Girls have made substantial gains in primary and secondary school enrollment. In 1990, the primary school enrollment rate of girls in developing countries was only 86 percent that of boys. By 2011, the average was 97 percent.[1] Similar improvements have been made in secondary schooling, where girls' enrollments have risen from 78 percent to 96 percent of that of boys. Progress has been greatest in richer countries. In countries classified by the World Bank as upper-middle-income, girls' enrollments in primary and secondary schools now exceed those of

boys. But averages can obscure large differences between countries: overenrollment of girls in one country does not counterbalance underenrollment in another. At the end of the 2011 school year, 31 upper-middle-income countries and 23 lower-middle-income countries had reached or exceeded equal enrollment of girls in primary and secondary education, but only 9 low-income countries had done so. Two regions lag behind: South Asia and Sub-Saharan Africa. The differences are also notable for urban-rural areas. For several African countries, the gap between male and female enrollment remains large, especially for secondary enrollment. Only a few countries in Sub-Saharan Africa have higher enrollment rates for girls (Niger, Rwanda, and Senegal in urban areas). However, most of the countries included in figure 3b show that boys have higher enrollment rates compared with girls.

More women are participating in public life at the highest levels. The proportion of parliamentary seats held by women continues to increase. The Latin America and Caribbean region, where women now hold 23 percent of all parliamentary seats, remains in the lead. The most impressive gains have been made in South Asia, where the number of seats held by women more than tripled between 1999 and 2010. In Nepal, women held one-third of parliamentary seats in 2011. In Sub-Saharan Africa, Rwanda leads the way: since 2008, 56 percent of its parliamentary seats have been held by women. The Middle East and North Africa lag far behind.

Full economic empowerment of women remains a distant goal. While many women work long hours and make important contributions to their families' welfare, they often work in the informal sector, typically as unpaid family workers. Women's share in paid employment in the nonagricultural sector has risen marginally but remains less than 20 percent in South Asia and in the Middle East and North Africa. The largest proportion of working women is found in Europe and Central Asia, where in recent years, 47–48 percent of nonagricultural wage employees were women.

FIGURE 3a Gender parity in primary, secondary, and tertiary education by region, 2011

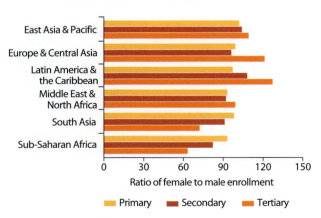

Source: UNESCO Institute of Statistics and World Development Indicators database.

1. The ratio between the enrollment rate of girls and boys (gender parity ratio) increased from 91 in 1999 to 97 in 2010 for the developing regions as a whole—falling within the plus-or-minus 3-point margin of 100 percent that is the accepted measure for parity.

FIGURE 3b   Gap in male-female enrollment ratios

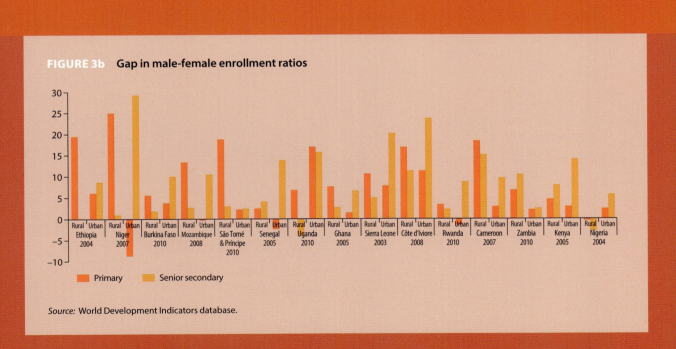

Source: World Development Indicators database.

Reduce child mortality

In most countries around the world, most children's deaths occur in the first year. In developing countries, the under-five mortality rate fell from 87 per 1,000 live births in 1990 to 51 in 2011. This progress is not sufficient to meet the health-related MDG target of a two-thirds reduction by 2015. Only 25 countries have achieved this target, and only an additional 26 have made enough progress to be able to meet the target by 2015.

For the infant mortality rate, the numbers are worse: only 5 countries met the target of reducing the infant mortality rate by two-thirds between 1990 and 2015, and only 13 countries are making enough progress to reach it by 2015. More than 120 countries still have not made sufficient progress to meet the goal on time. Overall, the MDG health indicators have seen the least progress of all the MDGs.

As a country urbanizes, children in urban areas tend to have access to better health services and thus lower rates of child mortality than children in rural areas. In addition, as countries become more urbanized, the proportion of children in rural areas declines, further narrowing the difference between the mortality rates of rural and urban children. Notably, the highest rates of child mortality are in Sub-Saharan Africa, whose countries are the least urbanized.

The disparities between urban and rural infant mortality rates display a similar pattern. Higher infant mortality rates in rural areas are in part attributable to the disadvantages faced by rural households, such as lack of access to a safe source of drinking water and electricity. As discussed in chapter 2 of the *Global Monitoring Report* (GMR), governments need to provide basic services in rural areas as well as in urban ones to correct such deficiencies, to the extent possible.

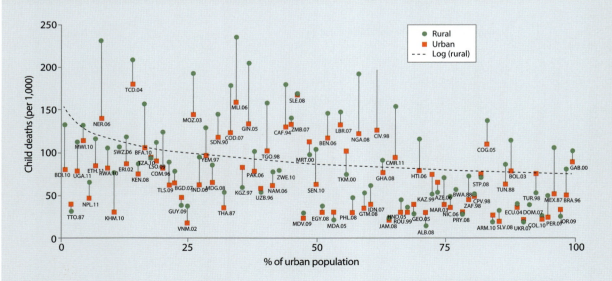

FIGURE 4a Urban versus rural child mortality gap

Source: Demographic and Health Surveys (DHS).

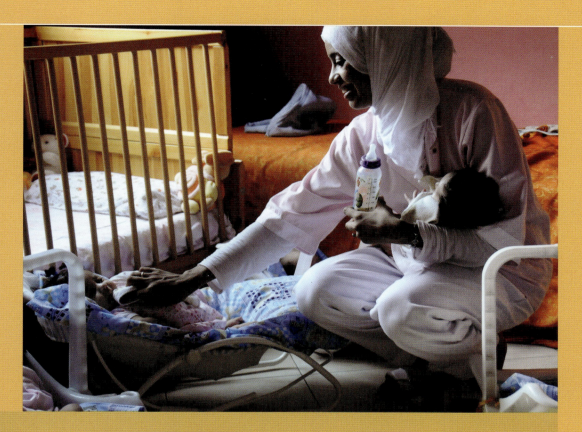

FIGURE 4b Urban versus rural infant mortality gap

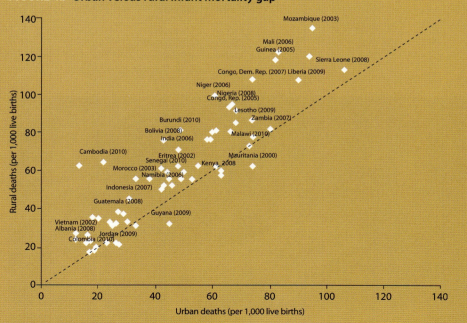

Source: Demographic and Health Surveys (DHS).

Reduce maternal mortality

MDG 5 centers on improving maternal health, with a target of reducing the maternal mortality ratio by three-quarters between 1990 and 2015. With only two years remaining before the target date, progress on maternal health is still lagging. Despite some notable exceptions such as Sri Lanka and Malaysia, the level of maternal mortality remains high in much of the developing world. Although on the aggregate the rate of progress has doubled across the globe from 2005 to 2010, it is unlikely that this MDG will be achieved by 2015.

South Asia is the only region on track to reach the target for reducing maternal mortality, assuming the region continues at the same rate of progress made from 2005 to 2010. The Middle East and North Africa might also be able to reach the MDG target if it doubles the effort it made from 2005 to 2010. The starting point in the level of maternal mortality obviously affects progress made in achieving the target but is not the only factor. Europe and Central Asia started with 70 maternal deaths per 100,000 live births in 1990, while Sub-Saharan Africa started with 850. However, if Sub-Saharan Africa doubles the progress made during 2005 to 2010, it will be able to reach its goal by 2016—just a year past the target, while Europe and Central Asia would need to more than double its effort to meet the goal in 2015.

The starting point for the maternal mortality ratio in middle-income countries in 1990 was nearly half that of low-income countries (370 deaths per 100,000 live births compared to 810). However, neither group of countries is close to achieving the goal on time . Although they will miss the 2015 target date, middle-income countries could reach the maternal mortality goal by 2016 if they doubled their effort. The low-income group will need even longer

Despite this bad news, there are some bright spots. Fragile states as a group started with a similar number of maternal deaths to Sub-Saharan Africa (780 deaths per 100,000 live births in 1990), but several of them have managed, or are on track, to achieve this particular MDG. Nepal reduced its maternal mortality rate from 770 deaths per 100,000 live births in 1990 to 170 in 2010, earning it the MDG Millennium Award in 2010. Nepal has also made extraordinary progress in reducing its proportion of poor people in recent years. Other fragile states such as Afghanistan, Angola, Eritrea, Timor-Leste, and the Republic of Yemen are still on track to meet the MDG, some with acceleration, and others following their current growth trend.

The issue of teenage pregnancy still requires significant attention, especially in rural areas, where the rate of teen pregnancy is higher than in urban areas.

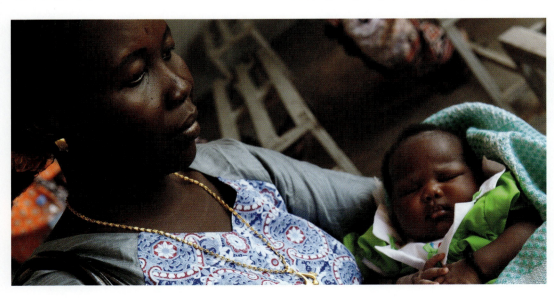

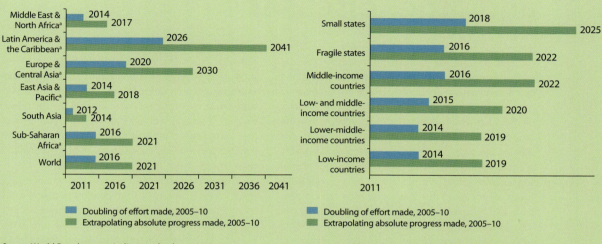

FIGURE 5a Expected year when maternal mortality goal will be met, by region

Middle East & North Africa[a]
2014
2017

Latin America & the Caribbean[a]
2026
2041

Europe & Central Asia[a]
2020
2030

East Asia & Pacific[a]
2014
2018

South Asia
2012
2014

Sub-Saharan Africa[a]
2016
2021

World
2016
2021

2011 2016 2021 2026 2031 2036 2041

■ Doubling of effort made, 2005–10
■ Extrapolating absolute progress made, 2005–10

Source: World Development Indicators database, 2013.
a. Developing countries only.

FIGURE 5b Expected year when maternal mortality goal will be met, by income level and by fragile and small states

Small states
2018
2025

Fragile states
2016
2022

Middle-income countries
2016
2022

Low- and middle-income countries
2015
2020

Lower-middle-income countries
2014
2019

Low-income countries
2014
2019

2011

■ Doubling of effort made, 2005–10
■ Extrapolating absolute progress made, 2005–10

Source: World Development Indicators database, 2013.

FIGURE 5c The percentage of teenagers who had children or are currently pregnant is higher in rural areas than in urban ones

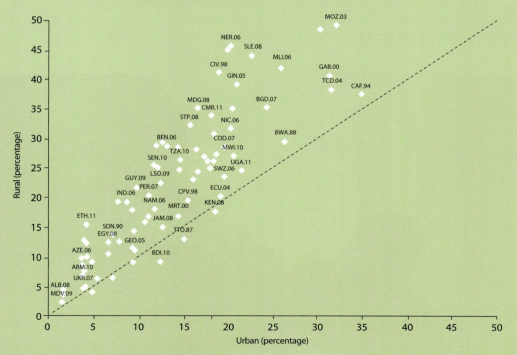

Source: Demographic and Health Surveys (DHS).

35

Combat HIV/AIDS, malaria, and other diseases

Epidemic diseases exact a huge toll in human suffering and lost opportunities for development. Poverty, armed conflict, and natural disasters contribute to the spread of disease and are made worse by it. In Africa, the spread of HIV/AIDS has reversed decades of improvement in life expectancy and left millions of children orphaned. It is draining the supply of teachers and eroding the quality of education. Malaria takes a large toll on young children and weakens adults at great cost to their productivity. Tuberculosis caused the deaths of some 1 million people in 2011, most of them aged 15–45, and sickened millions more. Tuberculosis is one of the principal causes of adult death from a single infectious agent in developing countries.

Some 34 million people were living with HIV/AIDS in 2011, and 2.5 million people acquired the disease during the year. Sub-Saharan Africa remains the center of the epidemic, but the proportion of adults living with AIDS has begun to fall as the survival rate of those with access to antiretroviral drugs has increased. By the end of 2010, 6.5 million people worldwide were receiving anti-retroviral drugs. That represented the largest one-year increase in coverage but fell far short of the target of universal access. In Africa, 58 percent of adults with HIV/AIDS are women; among youth aged 15–24, the prevalence rate among women is more than twice that of men. The second highest prevalence rate is in Latin America and the Caribbean, where 0.5 percent of adults are infected.

The prevalence of HIV infection in urban and rural areas varies significantly from country to country. For most Sub-Saharan Africa countries, the rates of HIV infection are higher in urban areas than in rural ones. Because evidence from health surveys confirms that a prominent decline in prevalence is associated with higher education, increased condom use, and a reduced number of sexual partners, most of the effort to prevent HIV/AIDS should continue to be concentrated in urban areas.

In 2011, 8.7 million people were newly diagnosed with tuberculosis, but its incidence, prevalence, and death rates are all falling. The global incidence rate

FIGURE 6a Population infected with HIV, ages 14-49

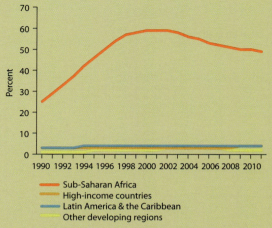

- Sub-Saharan Africa
- High-income countries
- Latin America & the Caribbean
- Other developing regions

Source: UNAIDS and World Development Indicators database.

FIGURE 6b Tuberculosis-infected population in low- and middle-income countries

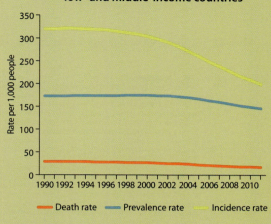

- Death rate
- Prevalence rate
- Incidence rate

Source: UNICEF and World Development Indicators database.

FIGURE 6c Millions of people still afflicted with HIV/AIDS

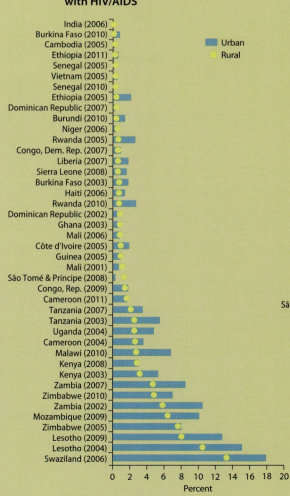

Source: Demographic and Health Surveys (DHS).

FIGURE 6d Urban versus rural children under age 5 who sleep under insecticide-treated bed nets

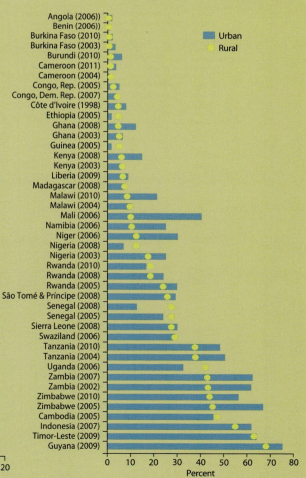

Source: Demographic and Health Surveys (DHS).

FIGURE 6e   Children under age 5 who use insecticide-treated bed nets

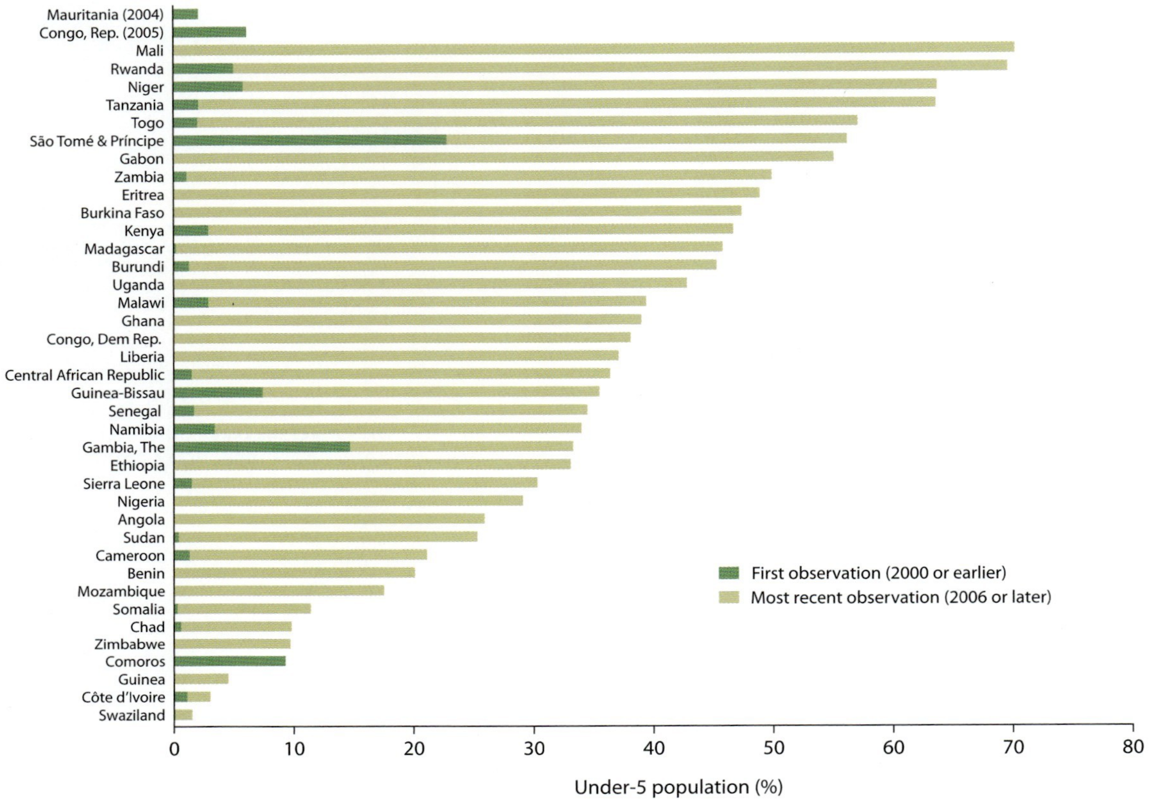

Sources: UNICEF and World Development Indicators database.

peaked in 2002; the prevalence rate—the proportion of people living with the disease—began to fall in 1997. If these trends are sustained, the world could achieve the target of halting and reversing the spread of tuberculosis by 2015. People living with HIV/AIDS, which reduces resistance to tuberculosis, are particularly vulnerable, as are refugees, displaced persons, and prisoners living in close quarters and unsanitary conditions. Well-managed medical intervention using appropriate drug therapy is the key to stopping the spread of tuberculosis.

There are 300 million–500 million cases of malaria each year, leading to more than 1 million deaths. Encouraging progress against the disease is being made. In 2011, Armenia was added to the list of countries certified free of the disease. Malaria, a disease of poverty, occurs in all regions, but Sub-Saharan Africa, where the most lethal form of the malaria parasite is

most abundant, is the epicenter. Prevention and control measures, such as the use of insecticide-treated mosquito bed nets, have proven effective and their use is spreading. In Sub-Saharan Africa, the use of treated nets is estimated to have grown from 2 percent in 2000 to 39 percent in 2010. Better testing and the use of combination therapies with artemisinin-based drugs are improving the treatment of at-risk populations. But malaria is a difficult disease to control. Emerging resistance to artemisinins and to the pyrethroid insecticides used to treat mosquito nets has been detected.

The differences in the rate of use of treated mosquito nets between rural and urban areas are minor. The cost of distributing nets is lower in urban areas thanks to agglomeration effects, likely contributing to the typically higher usage there.

Ensure environmental sustainability

As part of the MDGs, most countries have agreed on the principles of sustainable development, and there is international consensus to protect the environment. To this end, MDG 7 includes a target of halving the proportion of the population without access to improved sanitation and water sources by 2015. For many people in developing countries, however, access to safe water and sanitation remains a problem.

Fifty-six countries have still not made enough progress to reach the target of improved water sources on time; moreover, 20 countries do not have enough data to measure their progress on this target. Sub-Saharan Africa is lagging the most, although it has improved access to clean water in rural areas from 35 percent in 1990 to 49 percent in 2010; access in urban areas has not changed and remains at 83 percent. East Asia and Pacific made impressive improvements in rural areas, from a starting position of only 58 percent in 1990 to 84 percent in 2010; in urban areas access was nearing 100 percent. In general, the other regions have already managed to reach access rates of more than 80 percent in urban and rural areas.

Poor sanitation causes millions of people worldwide to contract illnesses. Around 1.7 million people die each year because of unsafe water and sanitation, and 90 percent of those are children under age five. Almost all sanitation-related deaths occur in the rural areas of developing countries, where sanitation problems are more severe (and access to adequate health care is less available). Some regions have made more progress than others, but even though most regions have improved access to sanitation by more than 20 percentage points, differences between urban and rural areas are considerable.

South Asia and Sub-Saharan Africa are the only regions where progress has not been significant, with an increase in access of only 17 percentage points in South Asia and 4 percentage points in Sub-Saharan Africa from 1990 to 2010. These regions also had the worst starting positions.

The increase in access to improved sanitation has not been impressive in urban areas either. The biggest advance came in the East Asia and Pacific region, where access increased about 22 percent during 1990–2010.

Although the gap between urban and rural access to sanitation is still wide, it has decreased in all regions. Between 1990 and 2010, for example, the gap narrowed from 42 percent to 25 percent in Latin America and the Caribbean, and from 44 percent to 31 percent in South Asia. Most striking, in Europe and Central Asia, the gap narrowed from 20 percent in 1990 to 7 percent in 2010, suggesting that even though progress is slow, it does reach underserved rural populations.

FIGURE 7a   Access to water by region, 1990 and 2010

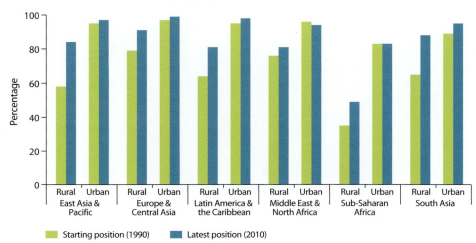

Source: World Development Indicators database, 2013.

FIGURE 7b   Access to sanitation by region, 1990 and 2010

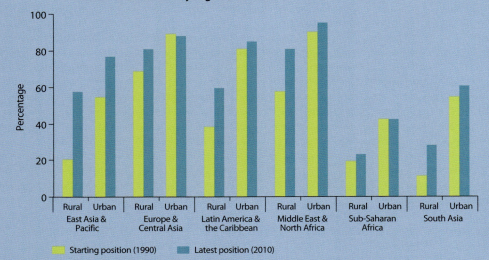

Starting position (1990)   Latest position (2010)

Source: World Development Indicators database, 2013.

FIGURE 7c   Urban-rural gap in access to sanitation by region

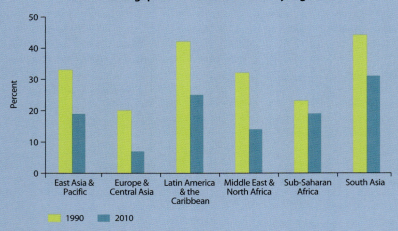

1990   2010

Source: World Development Indicators database, 2013.

Develop a global partnership for development

The use of information and communication technology (ICT) for economic development is part of the MDG 8 indicator, which focuses on the deepening of a global partnership for development. A specific description of this specific target was chosen and indicators identified. Target 8.F states that, in cooperation with the private sector, the benefits of new technologies, especially those related to information and communications, will be made available. The indicators measuring this progress are the number of fixed telephone lines, cellular subscribers, and Internet users.

These indicators show that mobile phone subscriptions have risen impressively across the world, while the growth in the number of fixed telephone lines has stagnated. Remarkable increases have also taken place in Internet usage, although here progress is more diverse, with stronger growth in high-income countries than in low- and middle-income countries. Even though access challenges remain, particularly in low-income countries, the spectacular rise in mobile phone penetration has led to the emergence of a variety of innovations that allow citizens, governments, and international organizations to be more engaged and better informed, and that enable aid providers to identify and communicate more directly with beneficiaries.

FIGURE 8a   Use of information and communication technology by region and income group

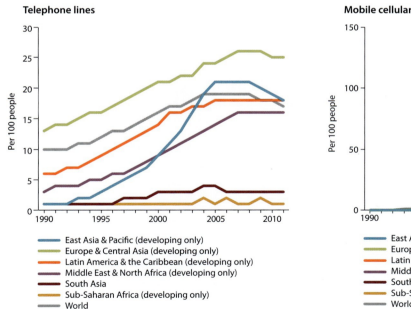

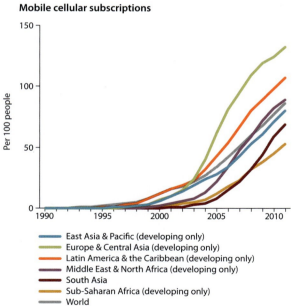

Source: World Development Indicators database, 2013.

Source: World Development Indicators database, 2013.

Improving the measurement of development goals

The Millennium Development Goals (MDGs) provide a yardstick against which to measure development outcomes. They have also stimulated demand for better statistics and new programs to increase the capacity of developing countries to produce and use statistics. The United Nations and its specialized agencies, including the World Bank and the International Monetary Fund, and the Organisation for Economic Co-operation and Development responded to these demands by creating new partnerships and mobilizing additional resources to provide support for statistics in developing countries. The result has been a marked improvement in the quality and availability of statistics on core development outcomes: poverty and income distribution, school enrollments, mortality and morbidity rates, and environmental conditions.

The MDGs posed three challenges: the selection of appropriate targets and indicators with which to monitor them; the construction of an international database to use for global monitoring; and the need for significant improvements in the quality, frequency, and availability of the relevant statistics, especially at the national level. The selection of goals and targets was determined by the Millennium Declaration adopted unanimously by the member states of the United Nations. Building the database and strengthening the statistic systems of developing countries has required the efforts of many partners over many years. When countries produce statistics to monitor their own development programs, differences in definition and methodology often limit comparability across countries. Whether monitored at the national, regional, or global level, international monitoring of the MDGs requires indicators that are comparable across countries and over time.

To produce harmonized statistics suitable for international comparisons, agencies often revise national data or recompile data using different reference periods or standards, such as the "dollar a day" poverty indicator. They may also impute values for missing data or use statistical models to combine multiple estimates. Interagency efforts such as these have been very important for filling the gaps in child and maternal mortality series. However, they inevitably result in data series that differ from nationally reported data and international assessments of country progress that differ from those produced by the countries.

When the MDGs were adopted, few developing countries had the capacity or resources to produce statistics of the requisite quality or frequency. Many countries had not conducted a recent census or a household survey capable of producing information on income, consumption, or health status. Values for many indicators disseminated by international agencies were based on unverified reports from national authorities. Statistical activities sponsored by bilateral donors and multilateral agencies often focused narrowly on securing data of interest to them but doing little to increase the capacity of the national statistical system to serve the needs of local decision makers or citizens.

The early efforts to monitor the MDGs revealed large gaps in both the international database and in many national databases. In 2003–04, the Partnership in Statistics for Development in the 21st Century (PARIS21) conducted six case studies of developing-country statistical systems. The studies found that the countries generally had very limited capacity to manage their own statistical programs.

Although the developing world has made some headway in improving its data collection and reporting, the systems are characterized by underfunding, reliance on donor support, particularly for household surveys, and very weak administrative data systems. The basic demographic information needed to underpin key indicators is out of date in some countries, and funding for major activities, such as population censuses, is particularly difficult to secure. Overall, there continues to be a shortfall in funding for core statistical systems required to provide information both for economic management and for monitoring the MDGs.

The proportion of countries with two or more data points (the bare minimum needed for assessing trends)

TABLE 1 Proportion of countries with two or more observations

Selected MDG indicators with two or more observations in period show	2005 database				2013 database			
	Number of countries 1990–2000	Number of countries 2001–12	Population covered (%) 1990–2000	Population covered (%) 2001–12	Number of countries 1990–2000	Number of countries 2001–12	Population covered (%) 1990–2000	Population covered (%) 2001–12
MDG 1.a Extreme poverty (% of population below $1.25 a day, 2005 PPP)	63	—	40.9	—	67	75	65.7	85.8
MDG 1.c Malnutrition prevalence, weight for age (% of children under age 5)	77	—	88.9	—	77	72	83.6	61.5
MDG 2.a Primary completion rate (% of relevant age group)	111	83	88.5	54.6	110	123	86.1	70.9
MDG 3.a Ratio of girls to boys in primary and secondary education (%)	105	62	86.3	17.7	116	126	89.5	95.5
MDG 4.a Infant mortality rate (per 1,000 live births)	135	2	99.0	0.3	141	141	99.9	99.9
MDG 4.a Under-5 mortality rate (per 1,000)	135	1	99.0	0.2	141	141	99.9	99.9
MDG 5.b Births attended by skilled health staff (% of total)	86	1	63.4	4.2	108	119	90.6	94.8
MDG 6.c Immunization, measles (% of children, ages 12–23 months)	134	135	99.5	99.6	137	139	99.7	99.7
MDG 7.c Improved sanitation facilities (% of population with access)	—	—	—	—	136	138	99.6	99.8
MDG 7.c Improved water source (% of population with access)	—	—	—	—	138	137	99.8	99.6

Source: World Development Indicators.
Note: — = not available; PPP = purchasing power parity.

for selected MDG indicators in 2005 and 2013 is shown in table 1. For some indicators, the improvement has been much more dramatic. But for other less prominent indicators, progress has been slower.

Despite the progress made in the past decade, national systems face immense difficulties on many fronts including funding, sectoral shortcomings, and poor data access, and the development of skills needed to use statistics effectively in planning and management. In 2011, the High Level Forum on Aid Effectiveness meeting in Busan, Republic of Korea, endorsed a new action plan for statistics. Several statistical domains have been identified as priorities for international action because of large deficits

in data quality and availability. The high-priority domains include agricultural statistics, poverty statistics and household surveys, gender statistics, labor force statistics, environmental accounting and the system of national accounts, and vital registration systems. The Busan Action Plan for Statistics provides an agreed framework for addressing capacity limitations in developing countries and work is already under way in some domains. Resources are limited, however, and even with greater resources, capacity building is a slow, deliberate process. The MDGs have contributed to the development of a statistical infrastructure that is increasingly capable of producing reliable statistics on a variety of topics.

Macroeconomic, Trade, and Aid Developments in Developing Countries

Growth and macroeconomic adjustment in developing countries

The global economy is expected to recover, but only very gradually. While the road to recovery in advanced economies will remain bumpy, downside risks to the outlook have eased as policy intentions in advanced economies have become clearer and commodity price volatility has abated. Although important downside risks remain—including adjustment fatigue in advanced economies and overinvestment and high asset prices in emerging market and developing countries—overall risks are now more symmetric. In emerging market and developing countries, economic activity is picking up. A broadly appropriate current policy stance in emerging market and developing countries is supporting continued strong growth in these countries, but some tightening of the policy stance appears appropriate over the medium term, beginning with monetary policy and prudential measures. Commodity prices trended down through most of 2012 and are expected to remain stable in 2013, providing room for a flexible implementation of monetary policy, particularly in emerging market and developing countries.

Despite sustained economic growth, progress in rebuilding policy buffers in low-income countries has been modest. There are large differences across countries, however. Still-high international commodity prices are providing commodity exporters with relatively larger buffers than commodity-importing countries. The downside risk of a protracted global growth slowdown extending through 2015 would have a significantly negative impact on growth in low-income countries. With policy buffers not yet restored to levels preceding the 2009 crisis and against the backdrop of reduced traditional sources of financing, most low-income countries would likely need to undertake adjustments in the face of such a shock.

This year's *Global Monitoring Report* (GMR) focuses on agglomeration as an important driver of development. As factors of production agglomerate, they become more productive because it becomes easier to exploit economies of scale and scope. These economic aspects of agglomeration are most often looked at from a microeconomic perspective, but broad-based changes in where people work and live also have profound macroeconomic consequences. Using a World Bank agglomeration index, evidence is presented below suggesting that there are relatively higher returns to agglomeration on the lower rungs of development. Recent research at the International Monetary Fund (IMF) suggests that greater economic diversification is associated with improved macroeconomic performance. Another strand of research, which has benchmarked structural transformation in Africa with that of Asia's, provides some optimism with regard to Africa's economic prospects.

Growth should rebound by 2014, but risks remain

Global economic growth continued to slow in 2012 to 3.2 percent, from 4.0 percent in 2011 (table 1.1). Growth slowed in advanced economies as well as in emerging market and developing countries, but the former group of countries grew significantly less than the latter group (1.2 percent and 5.1 percent respectively). The growth slowdown in 2012 was more pronounced than foreseen in GMR 2012. Importantly, however, the two country groupings most challenged in meeting the Millennium Development Goals (MDGs)— low-income countries and fragile states— both grew broadly as expected (5.5 and 5.8

percent, respectively).[1] The low and falling growth in the global economy was accompanied by low consumer price inflation in most countries.

There were large regional differences in growth performance across emerging market and developing countries in 2012. The recession in the euro area weighed heavily on central and eastern European countries. With Poland and Turkey tightening policies and several southeastern European countries falling back into recession, growth in this region fell to just 1.6 percent. As in previous years, growth in emerging market and developing countries was led by those in Asia (6.6 percent). Growth in the Middle East and North Africa countries recovered to 4.8 percent (from 4.0 percent in 2011), as these countries progressed in their political and social transitions, in particular in Libya, where gross domestic product (GDP) more than doubled after the economic collapse the year before. In Sub-Saharan Africa, robust growth continued in 2012, but the average growth rate of 4.8 percent masks large cross-country differences. Whereas conflicts negatively affected growth in Guinea-Bissau and Mali, growth in Côte d'Ivoire rebounded following election-related disturbances in 2011. Despite the

TABLE 1.1   Global output
Annual % change

	2010	2011	2012	2013	2014	2015
				Projections		
World	**5.2**	**4.0**	**3.2**	**3.3**	**4.0**	**4.4**
Advanced economies	3.0	1.6	1.2	1.2	2.2	2.6
Emerging market and developing countries	7.6	6.4	5.1	5.3	5.7	6.0
Central and Eastern Europe	4.6	5.2	1.6	2.2	2.8	3.3
Commonwealth of Independent States	4.9	4.8	3.4	3.4	4.0	4.0
Developing Asia	9.9	8.1	6.6	7.1	7.3	7.6
Middle East and North Africa	5.5	4.0	4.8	3.1	3.7	4.5
Sub-Saharan Africa	5.4	5.3	4.8	5.6	6.1	5.9
Western Hemisphere	6.1	4.6	3.0	3.4	3.9	3.9
Low-income countries[a]	6.4	5.7	5.5	6.0	6.2	6.6
Emerging market countries[b]	7.7	6.4	5.0	5.2	5.7	5.9
Fragile states[c]	5.0	3.6	5.8	6.4	6.8	7.3

Source: World Economic Outlook.
a. Low-income countries are those eligible for financial assistance under IMF's Poverty Reduction and Growth Trust, and Zimbabwe.
b. Emerging market countries are emerging market and developing countries that are not low-income countries.
c. A subset of emerging market and developing countries included in the World Bank's list of Fragile and Conflict-Affected States.

weaker overall economic outcome, per capita incomes rose in most countries (figure 1.1).

The IMF's World Economic Outlook projects 3.3 percent global growth in 2013. The expected growth is subdued as the underlying fragilities that caused the slowdown in 2012 take time to unwind. The ongoing fiscal consolidation and financial sector deleveraging will continue to weigh on the euro area, and its economy is projected to contract for a second year in a row. Other advanced economies are projected to expand, but growth will be held back by headwinds that include subdued external demand in, and financial spillover effects from, the euro area, and fiscal consolidation (for example, in the United States). Overall, advanced economies are projected to grow 1.2 percent as in 2012.

In the emerging market and developing countries, prospects are for a strengthening of growth to 5.3 percent in 2013. Growth is being supported by appropriate policies for the most part, but held back by weak demand in advanced economies. Lower commodity prices will also lead to terms-of-trade losses for commodity exporters, with knock-on effects on growth. Diminished policy space, policy uncertainty, and supply bottlenecks hamper growth in some countries (for example, India). As in 2012, the countries in central and eastern Europe and the Asian countries would be the slowest and fastest growing groups of countries (projected to grow by 2.2 and 7.1 percent respectively). The countries in central and eastern Europe—with their deep trade and financial links to western Europe—will continue to be negatively affected by spillovers from the euro area, while the strong growth in Asia is predicated on continued expansion in China and a strong recovery in India. Growth in the Middle East and North Africa will be modest, reflecting ongoing political transitions and a slowdown among the region's oil exporters. Notwithstanding a somewhat weaker outlook for commodity prices, Sub-Saharan African economies are expected to expand by 5.6 percent.

Strong domestic government revenue mobilization is key to emerging market and

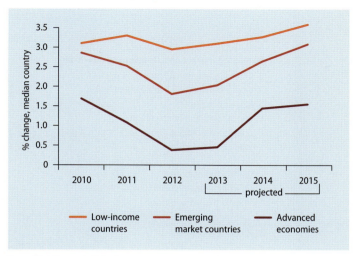

FIGURE 1.1   GDP per capita growth

Source: World Economic Outlook.

developing countries having the resources needed to address their development challenges, including enhancing infrastructure provision and achieving the Millennium Development Goals (MDGs). In that regard, the 2009 global crisis was a major setback as the crisis led to a drop in revenues of 3 percentage points of GDP. Since then, revenues have recovered somewhat, but not fully, and are expected to remain below pre-crisis levels through 2015 (table 1.2).

Global current account imbalances—which widened in the run-up to the crisis—narrowed as the crisis hit and have since remained broadly stable (figure 1.2). Robust net financial flows to emerging market and developing countries have also remained fairly constant from 2009 onward, with prospects of no major changes for 2013 (table 1.3). Emerging market countries receive on average about 8 percent of GDP in net financial flows, with most of these flows being private sector financial flows (including transfers). Relative to GDP, low-income countries receive net financial inflows that are about twice as high, averaging 14 percent of GDP in recent years. Relative to emerging market countries, low-income countries receive more private capital flows and private transfers, but the main factor behind the higher inflows to low-income

TABLE 1.2   Government revenue excluding grants

Weighted averages, % of GDP

	2008	2009	2010	2011	2012	Projections		
						2013	2014	2015
Emerging market and developing countries	29	26	27	28	28	28	27	27
Central and Eastern Europe	36	35	35	37	37	37	37	36
Commonwealth of Independent States	39	35	35	37	37	36	35	34
Developing Asia	20	20	20	21	22	21	21	22
Middle East and North Africa	43	33	34	38	38	37	37	35
Sub-Saharan Africa	28	23	24	28	27	26	26	25
Western Hemisphere	30	28	30	30	31	31	31	30
Low-income countries[a]	24	19	21	23	23	23	22	22
Of which: Fragile states[b]	22	17	19	20	20	21	20	20
Emerging market countries[c]	30	26	27	28	28	28	28	27

Source: World Economic Outlook.
Note: General government.
a. Low-income countries are those eligible for financial assistance under IMF's Poverty Reduction and Growth Trust, and Zimbabwe.
b. A subset of low-income countries included in the World Bank's list of Fragile and Conflict-Affected States.
c. Emerging market countries are emerging and developing countries that are not low-income countries.

FIGURE 1.2   Global current account imbalances

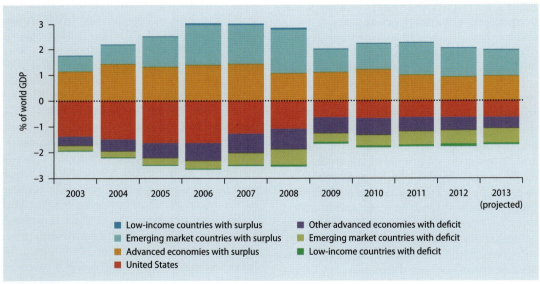

Source: World Economic Outlook.

countries is the significantly higher level of official inflows (capital and transfers). Fragile states receive significantly higher net inflows (relative to their GDP). In 2012, fragile states received net inflows that averaged 16 percent of GDP and the prospects are for a similar level of inflows in 2013.

World trade was stagnant in 2012, reflecting weak import demand in advanced economies and relatively stable international commodity prices. Trade in emerging market and developing countries expanded by 4 percent, down sharply from 25 percent the previous year (in nominal U.S. dollars). In contrast,

TABLE 1.3   Net financial flows

% of GDP[a]

	2008	2009	2010	2011	2012	2013 Projected
Emerging market countries	9.6	7.3	7.7	7.3	7.0	7.0
Private capital flows, net	6.0	1.4	2.7	3.1	2.9	2.6
Of which: private direct investment	5.1	3.8	3.2	3.3	3.0	3.0
Private portfolio flows	−1.2	−1.0	0.4	0.4	0.4	0.5
Private current transfers	3.5	3.5	3.5	3.3	3.4	3.3
Official capital flows and transfers (net)	0.1	2.5	1.6	0.9	0.8	1.1
Memorandum item:						
Change in reserve assets (−, accumulation)	−1.7	−2.8	−2.0	−1.2	−0.6	−1.0
Low-income countries	14.9	13.6	12.4	14.7	13.2	13.1
Private capital flows, net	4.7	2.7	3.4	4.0	2.3	2.4
Of which: private direct investment	6.6	5.2	5.9	6.7	5.7	5.4
Private portfolio flows	−1.0	−1.2	−1.0	−0.7	−0.9	−0.9
Private current transfers	5.0	4.6	4.5	4.7	4.8	4.5
Official capital flows and transfers (net)	5.2	6.3	4.5	6.1	6.0	6.2
Memorandum item:						
Change in reserve assets (−, accumulation)	−2.1	−1.9	−1.9	−1.9	−1.2	−1.2
Fragile states[b]	16.3	13.0	9.9	19.0	15.9	16.6
Private capital flows, net	6.3	2.3	3.0	5.3	2.4	4.5
Of which: private direct investment	4.4	3.3	3.7	5.4	4.5	4.3
Private portfolio flows	0.1	−0.3	−0.1	−0.4	−0.4	−0.5
Private current transfers	5.6	5.8	5.6	5.6	5.9	5.3
Official capital flows and transfers (net)	4.4	4.9	1.4	8.1	7.6	6.8
Memorandum item:						
Change in reserve assets (−, accumulation)	−1.6	−1.7	−1.8	−2.1	−0.3	−1.1

Source: World Economic Outlook.
a. Equally weighted.
b. A subset of emerging market and developing countries included in the World Bank's list of Fragile and Conflict-Affected States.

advanced economies' trade contracted by 2 percent. The typical low-income country is highly integrated into the world economy with import and export shares of GDP of about 50 and 30 percent, respectively (figure 1.3). The current account deficits (including foreign direct investments) in these countries remain higher than before the 2009 crisis and little change is expected for 2013. Official reserves, in months of imports—a standard measure of reserve adequacy for an emerging market or low-income country—changed little in 2012, reflecting modest increases in both imports and reserve accumulation (figure 1.4). About a quarter of all emerging market and developing countries maintain reserves of less than three months imports.

Macroeconomic policies

In 2012, the continuing challenge for policy makers in most advanced economies was how concurrently to support a feeble recovery and address concerns about medium-term fiscal sustainability. With inflation expectations well-anchored, monetary policy continued to remain supportive, while firm expenditure controls allowed room for a narrowing of fiscal deficits. Food and other commodity

FIGURE 1.3   Low-income countries: Imports, exports, and current account balance including FDI

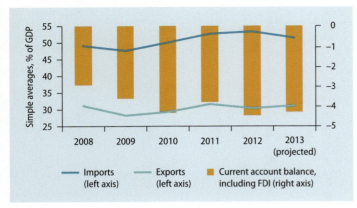

Source: World Economic Outlook.
Note: Median country. FDI = foreign direct investment.

FIGURE 1.4   Official reserves

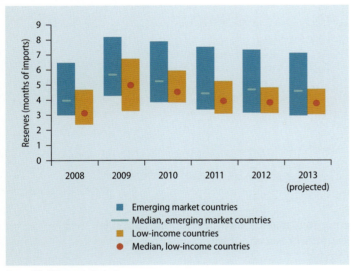

Source: World Economic Outlook.
Note: Bars represent the range between the 25th and 75th percentiles.

making in emerging market and developing countries.

Fiscal deficits in 2012 remained broadly stable in both emerging market and low-income countries (figure 1.7). Thus, the trend toward reinforcing fiscal buffers has stalled. In the 2009 crisis, large buffers made possible an unprecedented countercyclical fiscal response on the order of about 3 percentage points of GDP, but three years after the crisis, less than half of this buffer has been reconstituted.

Slightly more than half of all emerging market countries continued to tighten monetary policy in 2012 (figure 1.8). Among the countries that loosened monetary policy, the loosening took the form of reduced nominal short-term interest rates and depreciation of the currency in about equal measure. In low-income countries, a significant majority of countries loosened monetary policy in 2012, in sharp contrast to 2011. In these countries, the monetary loosening mostly took the form of currency depreciation although the number of countries using the interest rate instrument increased significantly from 2011 to 2012. Against this background, growth in monetary aggregates relative to GDP in emerging market countries broadly reverted to trends prevailing before the 2009 crisis (figure 1.9).

The macroeconomic policy mix varied sharply across emerging market countries and low-income countries in 2012; the mix also changed appreciably from 2011 to 2012 (figure 1.10). Among emerging market countries, twice as many countries (close to 40 percent) loosened both monetary and fiscal policy than tightened both policies. Among low-income countries, more countries tightened than loosened both type of policies. Emerging market countries shifted markedly toward relaxing fiscal policy in 2012, with an offsetting tightening of monetary policy. In low-income countries, the trend was in the opposite direction.

Quality of macroeconomic policies in low-income countries

Since 2003, the quality of macroeconomic policies in low-income countries has been

prices in global markets rose sharply from late 2010 to late 2011, followed by some pull-back through most of 2012 (figures 1.5 and 1.6). In emerging market and developing countries, commodity price movements impact consumer prices, terms of trade, and income to a larger extent than in advanced economies. For that reason, commodity price volatility complicates macroeconomic policy

FIGURE 1.5   Commodity price indexes

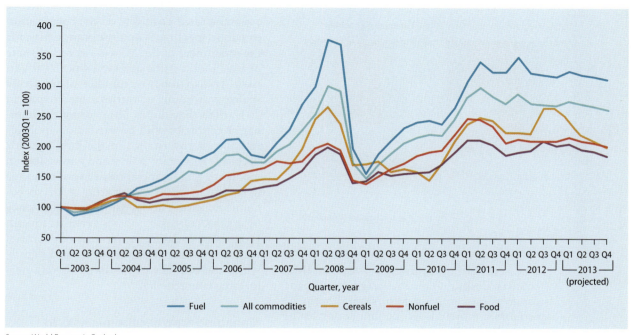

Source: World Economic Outlook.
Note: Indexes are in U.S. dollars.

FIGURE 1.6   Changes in commodity prices and changes in GDP per capita, terms of trade, and inflation

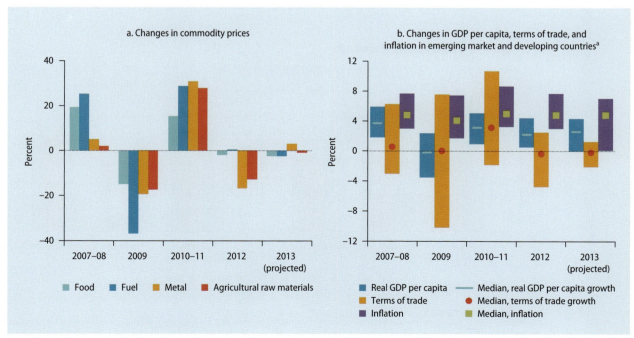

Source: World Economic Outlook.
Note: Bars represent the range between the 25th and 75th percentiles.
a. Annual changes in percent; for 2007–08 and 2010–11, it is the average of annual changes in percent.

FIGURE 1.7 Fiscal deficit

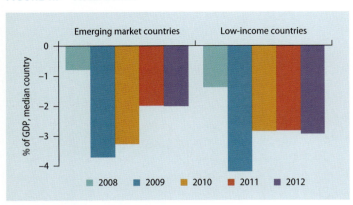

Source: World Economic Outlook.
Note: General government balance (net lending/net borrowing) as defined in IMF Government Finance Statistics Manual 2001.

assessed through annual surveys of IMF country desks.[2] Over the years, significant progress has been made in several areas of economic policy. Low-income countries in Sub-Saharan Africa have registered relatively higher improvements. The number of countries with unsatisfactory policies has declined substantially since 2005 in most categories. However, the quality of policies differs considerably across the different policy areas,

with concerns typically focusing on fiscal issues (figure 1.11). In 2012, the share of countries rated positively on the composition of public spending—an important driver for the attainment of the MDGs—reversed some of the modest gains achieved since 2005. In fiscal transparency, a number of relatively strong-performing countries scored higher in 2012 than they did in 2011, while the number of countries with unsatisfactory policies relating to governance in the public sector declined. Monetary policy and governance in monetary and financial institutions continue to remain relatively strong areas of macroeconomic policies. The assessment of consistency of macroeconomic policies remains mixed. From 2011 to 2012, the number of countries with unsatisfactory policies increased slightly while the number of relatively strong-performing countries fell.

Managing macroeconomic risks in low-income countries

Most low-income countries recovered quickly from the 2009 crisis and have experienced strong growth since early 2010.[3] The continuing recovery was helped by deepening

FIGURE 1.8 Monetary policy loosening

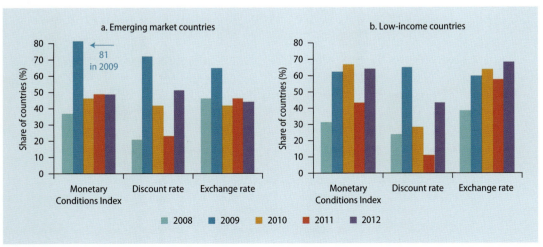

Source: World Economic Outlook.
Note: Monetary policy loosening is based on Monetary Conditions Index (MCI) calculations. MCI is a linear combination of nominal short-term interest rates and the nominal effective exchange rate (with a one-third weight for the latter).

FIGURE 1.9   **Average year-on-year growth in money and the money gap in emerging market countries**

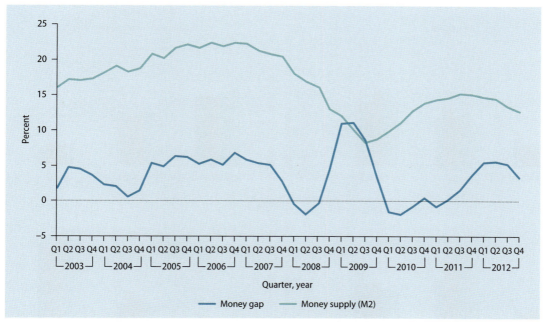

Source: International Financial Statistics.
Note: The money gap is the difference between year-on-year growth rates of the money supply (M2) and nominal GDP. The sample includes emerging market economies that have data on both for the whole sample period shown.

FIGURE 1.10   **Macroeconomic policy mix**

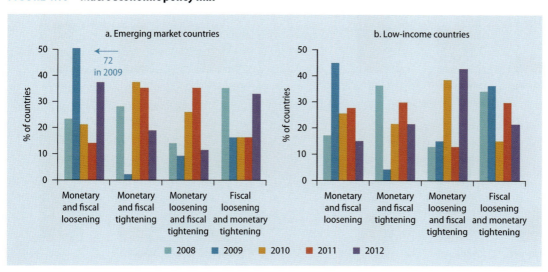

Source: International Financial Statistics.
Note: Fiscal conditions are defined based on annual change in the government balance (net lending/net borrowing) as a percent of GDP in 2008, 2009, 2010, 2011, and 2012. Monetary conditions are based on the change in the Monetary Conditions Index (MCI); changes are calculated Q4 over Q4. MCI is a linear combination of nominal short-term interest rates and the nominal effective exchange rate (with a one-third weight for the latter).

FIGURE 1.11 **Quality of macroeconomic policies in low-income countries**

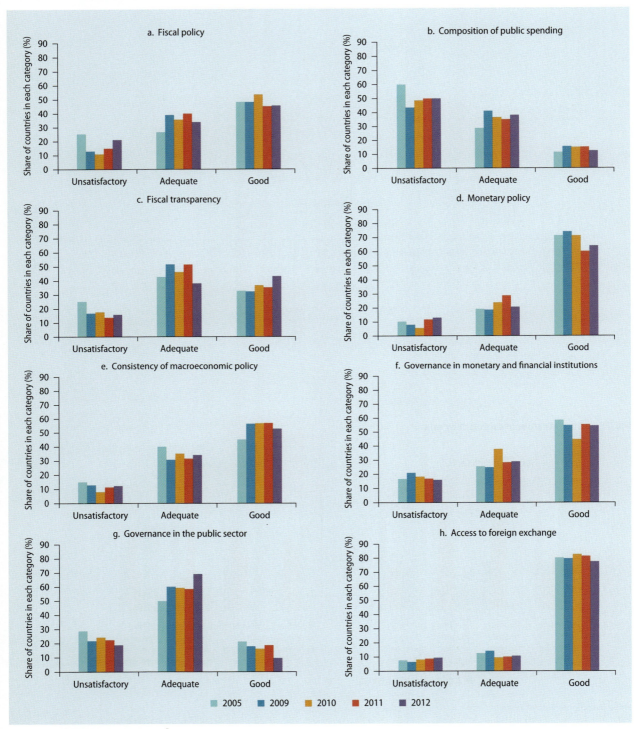

Source: IMF staff estimates.
Note: IMF staff have assessed each low-income country according to a common set of criteria. Policies are assessed as unsatisfactory, adequate, and good for this purpose. For example, a country with an unsustainable level of public debt and a large deficit would be judged to have an unsatisfactory fiscal policy.

links with emerging markets, which complemented traditional export demand from advanced economies. In addition to the traditional trade channels, low-income countries have become linked to emerging markets though remittances and financial linkages (IMF 2011).

Despite sustained economic growth, however, the recent progress in rebuilding policy buffers has been modest for most low-income countries and has been partially reversed in some others over the past two years. The situation varies widely across different country groups (figure 1.12). For example, commodity-exporting countries have relatively high external and fiscal buffers, while small countries seem to be in a somewhat worse position than the rest.[4] Greater emphasis on rebuilding buffers would position low-income countries better to protect spending levels and growth in the event of future shocks. At the same time, the rebuilding of buffers has to be balanced with the need to maintain adequate space for development-enhancing expenditures, particularly for infrastructure and other expenditures aimed at achieving the MDGs.

An analytical framework developed by the IMF that assesses low-income countries' vulnerabilities to global risks was used to simulate the impact of a protracted growth downturn—a low probability event driven by a slowdown in potential growth in advanced and emerging markets (IMF 2012a). Under this scenario, global growth is assumed to be lower than the baseline projection by 0.5 percentage point in 2013, 1.7 percentage points in 2014, and 2.0 percentage points in 2015. The weaker global growth is assumed to lead to weaker demand for commodities, which would depress oil and non-oil commodity prices.

The protracted global growth slowdown scenario is estimated to have a large negative impact on growth in low-income countries, which would get progressively worse over time. The impact stems from below-trend demand for low-income-country exports, as well as a reduction in remittances and inflows of foreign direct investment to low-income countries, particularly from emerging

markets. The cumulative output loss in 2013–15 in the median low-income country could reach 3.2 percentage points, with output losses ranging from 1.9 to 5.7 points across all low-income countries.[5]

Under such a scenario, and before taking account of potential policy responses, fiscal and external buffers in low-income countries would progressively weaken as the permanent output loss accumulates over time (figure 1.13). The cumulative widening in fiscal balances in 2013–15 in the median low-income country could increase by 1.9 percentage points of GDP. This in turn could lead to significant public debt accumulation, compared to the gradual improvement in debt ratios projected in the baseline over the same period. Also, the cumulative deterioration in external balances would increase by 5.1 percentage points of GDP, resulting in sharp declines in reserve coverage across many low-income countries. Such imbalances could not be financed indefinitely. Additional cumulative financing needs could be as large as $26 billion by the end of 2014, and about $61 billion by the end of 2015. This comes against the backdrop of reduced access to traditional sources of financing, reflecting budgetary pressures in donor countries. Therefore, most low-income countries would most likely need to undertake medium-term adjustment in the face of such a protracted shock to global growth, while at the same time the IMF would likely be called upon to provide additional financial assistance.

If the risk of a protracted global downturn materializes, the appropriate policy response would need to reflect the permanent nature of the shock and the existing magnitude of policy buffers:

- *The magnitude of the required fiscal adjustment would depend on available fiscal space and debt sustainability.* Fragile low-income countries and those in Latin America and the Caribbean—especially small states that suffer from high debt and little, if any, fiscal space—may not have room for accommodative fiscal policy. Low-income countries in Asia and

FIGURE 1.12 **Selected macroeconomic indicators for low-income countries, 2007–13**

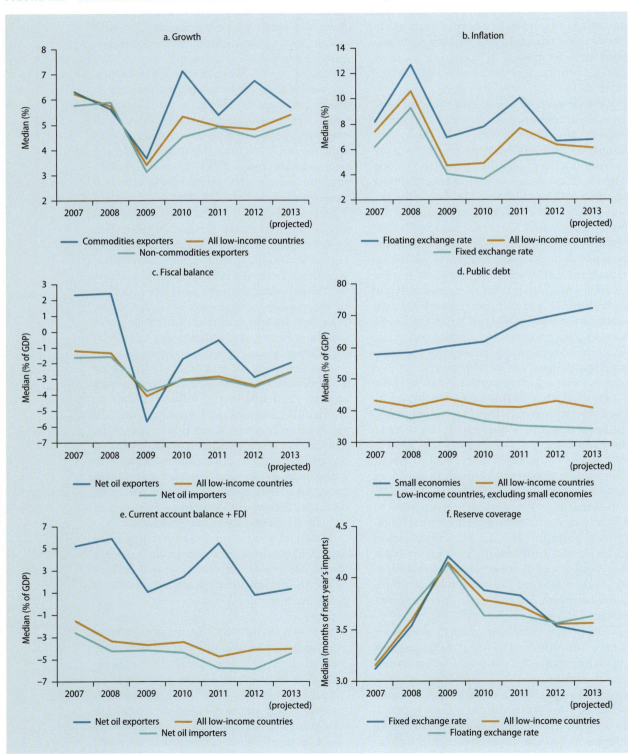

Source: World Economic Outlook.
Note: FDI = foreign direct investment.

FIGURE 1.13   **Low-income countries: Impact of a protracted slowdown in global growth**

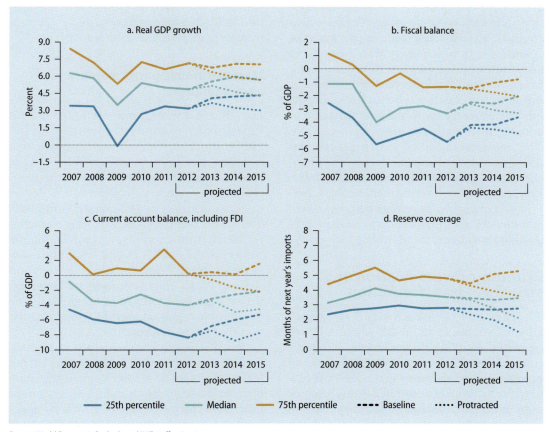

Source: World Economic Outlook; and IMF staff estimates.
Note: FDI = foreign direct investment.

the Pacific would have room for a small increase in deficits to accommodate the shock, given their stronger macroeconomic positions.[6]

- *The magnitude and timing of adjustment would also depend on growth prospects.* Countries with strong cyclical positions (high growth) but weaker macroeconomic positions would benefit from immediate adjustment. In contrast, a more gradual adjustment would be desirable in countries with a weak cyclical position (low growth), because rapid consolidation could depress growth and further weaken the fiscal position.

- *The composition of the adjustment would also need to strike a balance between revenue mobilization and expenditure measures.* Strengthening tax administration

and avoiding ad hoc tax reductions would help limit the burden of adjustment falling excessively on the expenditure side and protect high-priority expenditures (such as infrastructure and social sector spending). Making budgetary spending more growth friendly (by reallocating spending from untargeted subsidies to productive investments, for example) would improve the quality of adjustment and support domestic demand.

Optimally, fiscal adjustment should also be complemented by adjustment in monetary and exchange rate policies and include some important structural measures. The majority of low-income countries would have sufficient policy space to reduce interest rates in response to a protracted global growth slowdown, because weaker domestic demand and commodity prices would lead to moderation in inflation. Some external adjustment could be also implemented, in particular in countries with overvalued exchange rates. In addition, some adjustment in private sector behavior would help to partially offset the impact of lower external demand by reducing imports consistent with the new weaker economic growth path and lower relative prices. The implementation of structural reforms could include measures to deepen the financial sector and develop domestic debt markets, coupled with strengthening the supervisory framework, as well as better-targeted investments in infrastructure to increase productivity and living standards.

Economic diversification and structural transformation

The theme of this year's GMR is "Rural-Urban Dynamics and the Millennium Development Goals." Agglomeration is an important driver of development: as factors of production agglomerate—that is, become geographically more concentrated—they become more productive because it becomes easier to exploit economies of scale and scope (Commission on Growth and Development 2008). Network effects and other positive externalities in turn also positively impact productivity and economic growth. While agglomeration can be immensely beneficial, there are constraints: increasing congestion costs can provide a powerful check on productivity gains.

Agglomeration is part of a broader set of changes—including, for example, the demographic transition—that together constitute the transformation of traditional low-productivity economies into modern high-productivity economies. This transformation also typically encompasses the structural shift to manufacturing and service activities from agriculture. This section includes three different takes on the agglomeration process through a macroeconomic prism. The first explores to what extent differences in the degree of agglomeration across countries can provide insights into differences in

macroeconomic outcomes such as growth. The latter two address economic diversification in low-income countries and structural transformation in Sub-Saharan Africa.

Macroeconomic performance and agglomeration

For *World Development Report 2009: Reshaping Economic Geography* (WDR 2009), Bank staff developed an index that measures on a uniform basis country-specific levels of agglomeration.[7] A recent update of the index provides a snapshot of the degree of agglomeration in 162 countries in 2010. The combined population of the countries for which data are available is 6.8 billion (98 percent of the world's population). The index ranges from a 7 percent urban population share in Papua New Guinea to a 100 percent urban population share in Singapore. The population-weighted average urban population share is 54 percent.[8]

The distribution of the degree of agglomeration across countries is highly uneven, but less so than that of income because the share of population living in urban areas cannot exceed 100 percent whereas there is no upper limit to income levels (figure 1.14). As would be expected, there is a positive and statistically significant correlation between the degree of agglomeration and the level of per capita income. The Pearson and Spearman rank correlation coefficients between the two variables are 0.52 and 0.72 respectively (both statistically significant at the 5 percent level). This positive correlation should, of course, not be interpreted to mean that there is a causal link from agglomeration to income (or vice versa), but rather that a broader underlying development process impacts both agglomeration and income outcomes.

To further explore the interrelationship between countries' level of agglomeration and level of income, countries are divided into low-, medium-, and high-agglomeration/income countries using the methodology of Nielsen (2011 and forthcoming).[9] Countries with an agglomeration share of 40 percent or lower (64 percent or higher) are designated as low-agglomeration (high-agglomeration) countries. Medium-agglomeration countries are those with an agglomeration share between 40 percent and 64 percent. Using the same method, countries with a per capita income of $6,500 or lower ($27,000 or higher) are designated as low-income (high-income) countries. Medium-income countries are those with a per capita income between $6,500 and $27,000 (map 1.1).

There is a large degree of overlap between the categorization of countries as low-, medium-, and high-agglomeration countries and the analytical country categorization of low-income, emerging market, and advanced economies (table 1.4).[10] Most low-income countries are low-agglomeration countries and most advanced economies are high-agglomeration economies. Among emerging market countries about half are medium-agglomeration countries. The correlation between the two country classification systems is statistically significant.[11] Per capita income increases with the level of agglomeration for both low-income and emerging market countries, but the relative increases are more pronounced for low-income countries. Among advanced economies, there is no "return" to agglomeration (the higher per capita income level of the small group of medium-agglomeration advanced economies is because most Nordic countries are included here). These findings suggest that the positive correlation between agglomeration and development is more strongly felt in the poorer countries that are most challenged in attaining the MDGs.

Looking at economic growth over the last 10 years through the prism of agglomeration, growth in medium-agglomeration countries has outpaced that of both low- and high-agglomeration countries (table 1.5). Given the large degree of overlap between countries categorized according to their level of agglomeration or development, this is not a surprising result (compare table 1.5 with table 1.1 and figure 1.1).

Of more interest, therefore, is a comparison of macroeconomic outcomes across levels of agglomeration within different

geographical areas. For example, growth in low- and medium-agglomeration emerging market and developing countries in Europe and Asia has been higher than growth in

FIGURE 1.14   Agglomeration and income distribution, 2010

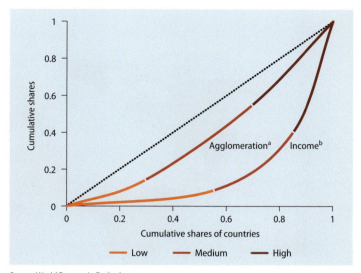

Source: World Economic Outlook.
Note: The Lorenz-curves show the same colors as in Map 1.1.
a. Agglomeration shares are calculated from World Bank agglomeration index data.
b. Income is measured by GDP per capita in U.S. dollars.

TABLE 1.4   IMF and World Bank member countries: Selected indicators, 2010

	Low-income countries	Emerging market countries	Advanced market economies	Total
Number of countries				
Low-agglomeration countries	44	13	0	57
Medium-agglomeration countries	20	42	9	71
High-agglomeration countries	9	28	23	60
Total	73	83	32	188
Population (in millions)				
Low-agglomeration countries	710	104	0	815
Medium-agglomeration countries	525	3,917	57	4,499
High-agglomeration countries	33	477	962	1,473
Total	1,268	4,499	1,019	6,787
GDP per capita (in U.S. dollars)				
Low-agglomeration countries	1,083	6,020	0	1,954
Medium-agglomeration countries	1,415	6,957	43,516	10,263
High-agglomeration countries	4,491	15,258	39,409	23,171
Total	1,608	9,984	40,529	12,306

Source: World Economic Outlook.
Note: Numbers may not add to totals because of rounding.

MAP 1.1   **Do agglomeration and income differences across countries align?**

a. Agglomeration

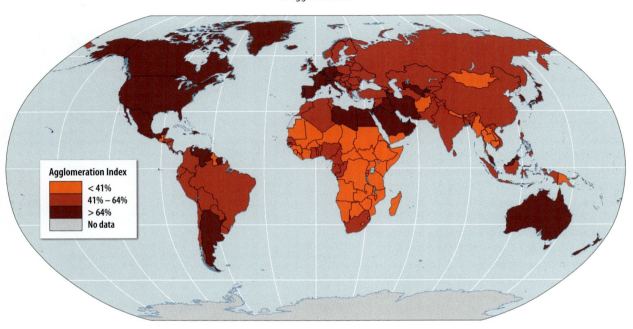

Agglomeration Index
- < 41%
- 41% – 64%
- > 64%
- No data

b. Income

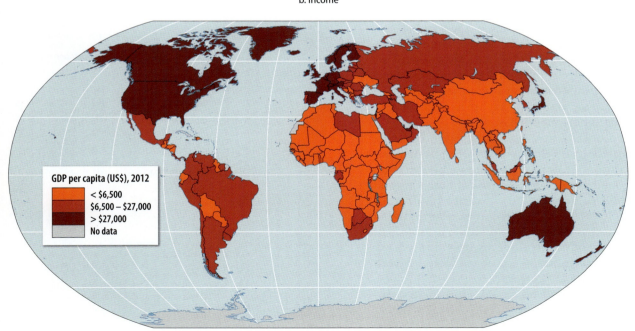

GDP per capita (US$), 2012
- < $6,500
- $6,500 – $27,000
- > $27,000
- No data

TABLE 1.5   Average real GDP per capita growth, 2003–12

	Low-agglomeration countries	Medium-agglomeration countries	High-agglomeration countries	All countries
World	**3.0**	**3.5**	**2.4**	**3.0**
Advanced economies	n.a.	1.2	1.3	1.2
Emerging and developing countries	3.0	3.9	3.2	3.4
Central and Eastern Europe	n.a.	3.8	3.0	3.7
Commonwealth of Independent States	n.a.	6.5	6.5	6.5
Developing Asia	4.7	5.7	3.2	5.0
Middle East and North Africa	0.7	2.5	3.4	2.9
Sub-Saharan Africa	2.6	2.0	3.6	2.5
Western Hemisphere	1.5	3.1	2.3	2.6
Low-income countries[a]	3.0	2.8	5.6	3.1
Of which: Fragile states[b]	1.8	0.7	n.a.	1.7
Emerging market countries[c]	3.2	4.5	3.0	3.8

Source: World Economic Outlook.
Note: For 162 countries for which data on the agglomeration index are available.
n.a. = Not applicable.
a. Low-income countries are those eligible for financial assistance under IMF's Poverty Reduction and Growth Trust, and Zimbabwe.
b. A subset of low-income countries included in the World Bank's list of Fragile and Conflict-Affected States.
c. Emerging market countries are emerging market and developing countries that are not low-income countries.

high-agglomeration countries in Europe and Asia. For emerging market and developing countries in Africa and the Middle-East, the opposite result holds. In these regions, high-growth countries were for the most part high-agglomeration countries.

Turning to low-income countries, average annual per capita economic growth in 2003–12 in high-agglomeration countries was 5.6 percent annually, compared with 3.0 percent and 2.8 percent respectively in low- and medium-agglomeration countries. The large differences in growth outcomes between high-agglomeration low-income countries, on the one hand, and low- and medium-agglomeration low-income countries, on the other hand, are statistically significant (table 1.6). In contrast, the difference in growth outcomes between low- and medium-agglomeration low-income countries (0.2 percent) is not statistically significant.

Agglomeration is an important aspect of development, but it is usually looked at from a microeconomic perspective. Looking at agglomeration differences across countries, however, can provide additional insights into macroeconomic performance. The evidence presented here suggests that there are high

returns to agglomeration, particularly for countries on the lower rung of development. For countries on higher rungs, the relative benefits and costs of concentrating people and other economic factors of production in urban settings is less clear.

Economic diversification in low-income countries

Limited diversification in production is an underlying characteristic of many low-income countries. As countries grow, their economies often become more diverse, but only up to a point: at higher income levels economies again become less diverse. Low levels of diversity in low-income economies

TABLE 1.6   Statistical tests for mean differences

Mean differences between	Low-income countries	Emerging market countries	Advanced market economies	Total
Low/high-agglomeration countries	S	N	n.a.	N
Low/medium-agglomeration countries	N	N	n.a.	N
High/medium-agglomeration countries	S	S	N	S

Source: IMF staff estimates.
Note: n.a. = Not applicable.
S = statistically significant; N = not statistically significant.

can reflect a broad range of market and government failures, and the result can be concentration in sectors with limited scope for productivity growth and quality upgrading, such as primary commodities. In turn, this can lead to less broad-based and sustainable growth, as well as increased exposure to adverse external shocks and macroeconomic instability.

A recent IMF *Staff Discussion Note* (Papageorgiou and Spatafora 2012) sheds more light on the role of diversification in the macroeconomic performance of low-income countries, examining diversification not just in trade but also in the broader domestic economy. Using existing data, as well as a new IMF cross-country dataset covering output in 12 sectors and several new country case studies, this work reviews and extends the evidence pointing to diversification as a crucial aspect of the development process.

For an extended period, many low-income countries enjoyed little success in diversifying exports and production. The situation broadly improved after the mid-1990s, with significant changes in both the type and quality of goods produced and exported. Regions and countries differed greatly, however, in the degree to which they succeeded in carrying out this economic transformation. In particular, Sub-Saharan Africa is far less diversified and produces relatively lower-quality goods than Asia.

Greater diversification is associated with improved macroeconomic performance, including both lower volatility and higher growth. "Diversification spurts," that is, episodes of rapid, sustained diversification, are associated with a 17 percent average reduction in the volatility of output growth in emerging market and developing countries, and a 30 percent decrease in output volatility in low-income countries.

Analogously, diversification spurts are associated with sharp subsequent accelerations in growth. This is especially true for nonfragile low-income countries (figure 1.15). More broadly, initial diversification is, on average, positively associated with subsequent growth, although there is much cross-country heterogeneity.

These findings raise a key policy question: What factors can spur or, alternatively, impede diversification? Both policy and institutional factors can influence the transition to more diverse production structures and thereby affect the pace at which growth can be sustained. For instance, policy barriers and structural rigidities in labor and product markets, or underdeveloped financial systems, may hamper the process of diversification. Likewise, insufficient or low-quality public infrastructure may retard the development of those sectors that rely disproportionately upon it; this factor may prove especially important in low-income countries, where a large portion of investment stems from the public sector.

Case studies provide some tentative evidence in support of findings. First, diversification and structural transformation are often underpinned by reforms and policy measures that are general in scope. Macroeconomic stabilization is a clear example. But even microeconomic measures are often broad-based, focusing on improving the quantity and quality of infrastructure or essential business services, or on setting up a welcoming environment for foreign investors.

FIGURE 1.15   Diversification spurts and growth accelerations

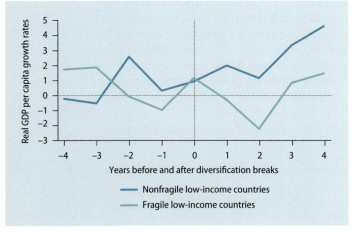

Sources: COMTRADE, World Economic Outlook; and IMF staff estimates.

It remains an open issue to what extent industry-focused and narrowly targeted measures have historically helped underpin diversification efforts.

Second, effective policy measures come in "waves" and aim at exploiting the evolving comparative advantages of the economy in changing external conditions. The types of reforms underpinning diversification and structural transformation in the early stages of development are different from those required at later stages. In general, reforms need to be adapted to the external environment faced by the economy.

Finally, the frequency with which new products are introduced and the rate at which they grow can point to potential policy-driven bottlenecks. Little entry may indicate that barriers deter firms from exporting or experimenting. If survival rates are low, firms may face more obstacles than expected. If surviving firms cannot expand, they may have inadequate access to finance.

Structural transformation in Sub-Saharan Africa

Sub-Saharan Africa has been experiencing an episode of high growth since the mid-1990s. Many of the countries of the region have benefited from relatively high commodity prices. One key question is whether higher growth has been accompanied by structural transformation, defined as the pattern of change in economic activity across sectors—from the primary to secondary and tertiary sectors—and across space—from rural to urban areas.

The IMF's *Regional Economic Outlook: Sub-Saharan Africa* (2012) analyzes one of the dimensions of structural transformation, namely, whether growth has been accompanied by a shift of workers from low to high average productivity activities and sectors. Since on average more than half of the labor force is employed in agriculture in these economies, and agriculture accounts for about one-third of output, average labor productivity in the sector is very low. Thus, structural transformation in Sub-Saharan Africa typically involves increasing the productivity of the agricultural sector, which frees up labor, allowing the shift of agricultural workers to industry and services.

Using data from 1995 to 2010 on agricultural output from the Food and Agricultural Organization (FAO) of the United Nations, GDP by sector from the IMF, and employment by sector from household surveys, the analysis of average labor productivity and the shift of workers across sectors shows that most countries in the region have experienced some degree of structural transformation, although there has been significant variation in its speed and type. In particular, transformation in Sub-Saharan Africa has been slower than that experienced by several countries in Asia: many of the African countries have experienced relatively slow productivity growth in agriculture and a less pronounced shift from agriculture to services and, to an even lesser extent, to manufacturing.

Figure 1.16 compares a sample of Sub-Saharan African countries (Cameroon, Ghana, Mauritius, South Africa, and Tanzania) with a group of low- and middle-income Asian economies that have experienced rapid structural transformation and started their growth takeoffs with similar or lower levels of GDP per capita than the average African country at the time. As can be seen, Ghana and Tanzania have experienced declines in agricultural output and employment shares over time, with Tanzania matching the experience of the comparator Asian economies quite closely. Middle-income countries have experienced declining manufacturing ratios for the past two decades, consistent with the process in more advanced Asian countries, where services play an ever-increasing role in the economy. Relatively few low-income countries in Sub-Saharan Africa have been able to raise their manufacturing output and employment shares on a sustained basis.

An alternative presentation of the data on employment shares shows broad increases in employment in sectors with higher productivity. Figures 1.17 and 1.18 depict annual

FIGURE 1.16 **Sub-Saharan Africa: Sectoral output and employment, 1995–2010**

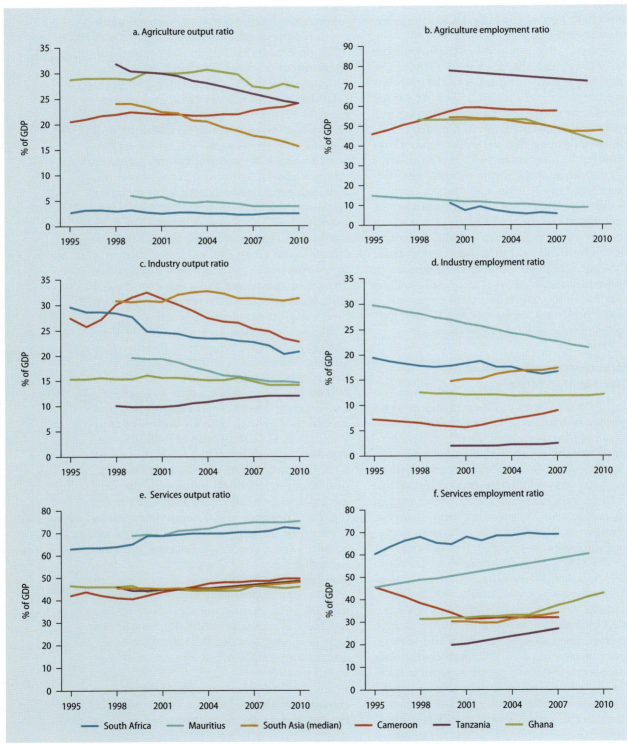

Sources: CEIC database and Haver Analytics database.

FIGURE 1.17   Sub-Saharan Africa: Labor productivity and change in employment shares, 1995–2010

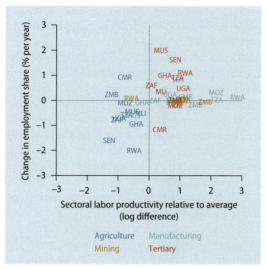

Source: IMF staff estimates.

FIGURE 1.18   South East Asia: Labor productivity and change in employment shares, 1995–2010

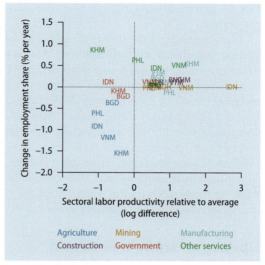

Source: IMF staff estimates.

changes in employment shares against average relative productivity levels for agriculture, manufacturing, mining, and the tertiary sector for Sub-Saharan African and Southeast Asian countries, respectively.[12] Points in the lower left quadrants indicate sectors with below average productivity and declining employment shares, while those in the upper right quadrants indicate sectors with above average productivity and rising employment shares.

Structural transformation has taken place to the extent that the observations for manufacturing and services in most countries are located in the upper right quadrant, corresponding to movements from low to high average labor productivity sectors. In fact, only Cameroon and Zambia show change in the employment share in the opposite direction, namely, from high to low average labor productivity sectors. In all the other Sub-Saharan African countries, workers have moved out of the agricultural sector. This suggests that the findings of McMillan and Rodrik (2011), whose analysis of a smaller subset of countries through 2005 found workers moving into low-productivity sectors, may actually

be reversed when considering a broader set of countries through 2010.

Country groups within Sub-Saharan Africa display important differences. Most oil exporters, middle-income, and nonfragile low-income countries have seen sustained increases in average labor productivity, often underpinned by rising productivity in agriculture and resulting in a declining share of GDP from that sector. Fragile countries, in contrast, have generally experienced low and irregular growth, largely as a result of conflict; this poor growth is reflected in the absence of significant structural transformation in most of these countries.

Most countries in Sub-Saharan Africa that have been growing faster than in the past have not experienced an increase in the share of manufacturing in employment or GDP, in contrast to the experience in Asia. This pattern is not necessarily surprising. To some extent, it is what would be expected given the differences between the two regions in resource endowments and in comparative advantage: when Asia started its takeoff, most countries were abundant in labor, whereas Sub-Saharan Africa is abundant in natural resources. The challenge is that many of those natural resource sectors, such as mining, are capital intensive and will not provide the jobs needed to accommodate the rapidly growing working-age population in the region.

The recent growth in real wage levels in China, together with Sub-Saharan Africa's demographic dividend—implying declining dependency ratios in the future—suggest that manufacturing in Sub-Saharan Africa could become increasingly competitive. But irrespective of whether economies grow through strengthening the manufacturing sector (Mozambique, Tanzania) or services (Kenya, Mauritius), it is unlikely that they can do so without first experiencing a major acceleration of agricultural productivity growth.

Update on trade trends and trade policy developments

Post-crisis recovery in trade has been uneven

Since the outbreak of the financial crisis over four years ago, global interdependency has been underscored by the largely synchronized nature of trade trends between high-income and developing countries. As of November 2012, neither the United States nor the European Union had surpassed pre-crisis levels of imports, although their combined share of world imports remains sizable, at roughly one-quarter of the total. On the other hand, Japan and large emerging economies like Brazil, the Russian Federation, India, China, and South Africa (BRICS) have seen their import levels rise steadily above pre-crisis levels, a trend that began in early 2009 (figure 1.19). These divergent recovery trends have translated into weak trade performance in regions that have traditionally relied on U.S. and EU markets. Exports from Europe and Central Asia, Latin America and the Caribbean, and Sub-Saharan Africa all hover only slightly above pre-crisis levels. The situation is especially dire for countries in the Middle East and North Africa that are not members of the Gulf Cooperation Council; in these nonmember countries, political developments combined with external economic factors

have led to a steady decline in exports since late 2011. Meanwhile, other regions have adjusted with more success. The East Asia and Pacific region has experienced steady positive real export growth, fueled not only by China, but also by smaller economies such as Cambodia, Vietnam, Thailand, and the Lao People's Democratic Republic. In South Asia, positive real export growth in Bangladesh and India helped the region experience the strongest export recovery, peaking in December 2010 at a level one and a half times higher than pre-crisis levels. Since then, however, South Asia's export performance has been lackluster.

Global trade in 2012 was hampered by a mid-year slump in global imports and steadily contracting import demand on the part of high income countries, with the Euro area at the epicenter. Growth rates for world imports of industrial goods during the first half of 2012, year-over-year, were negative (World Bank 2013). At the same time, increased import demand in developing countries helped mitigate the dearth of demand in high income economies. Developing countries' real exports also fluctuated considerably in 2012, with differences across countries and regions.

Protectionist outbreak avoided despite uncertain future for global economy

According to the World Trade Organization's (WTO) monitoring of trade protectionist measures, 190 new trade-restrictive measures were introduced by Group of 20 (G-20) countries between mid-October 2011 and mid-October 2012 (figure 1.20). While this represents a slowdown compared with previous years, the new measures add to the stock of restrictions put in place since the outbreak of the crisis. The growing accumulation of trade restrictions is of concern not only because it undermines the benefits of trade openness, but it also exacerbates the combined effects of the new measures with pre-crisis restrictions and distortions, such as agriculture subsidies and tariff peaks. Nevertheless, in the five months leading up to October 2012, the pace of removal of previous measures was better

FIGURE 1.19 **Trade developments since 2008**

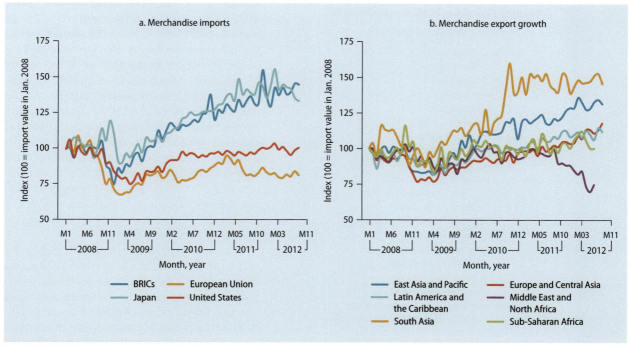

Source: World Bank Datastream.
Note: Data are in constant U.S. dollars, Jan. 2008–Nov. 2012. BRIC = Brazil, Russian Federation, India, China, and South Africa.

FIGURE 1.20 **G-20's new trade-restrictive measures**

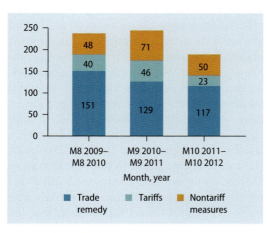

Source: World Trade Organization.
Note: Different methods of codification may lead to small discrepancies between these and other tallies of trade-restrictive measures.

than in previous periods (21 percent overall have been removed since October 2008).

G-20 countries, which have repeatedly committed to refrain from adopting trade-restrictive measures, now account for an increasing share of those measures: 74 percent in 2012, up from 60 percent in 2009 according to the Global Trade Alert (GTA),[13] which provides broader coverage than the WTO in terms of both countries and policy measures included in the database. Argentina, Brazil, the European Union, India, and Russia are among the countries that have implemented the highest number. Globally, the most frequently used trade-restrictive measures are state aids and antidumping, followed by import tariff increases and nontariff measures. Initially, restrictive measures were seen as policy responses to mitigate the temporary effects of the global financial crisis. However, recent measures appear to be more embedded in national industrial plans, and hence longer term in nature (World Bank 2013). G-20 countries are simultaneously responsible for a majority (66 percent) of all trade-liberalizing measures. However, trade-liberalizing measures represent only a quarter of all measures enacted to date (figure 1.21).

FIGURE 1.21 Total number of measures implemented and still in force by each G-20 country, November 2008–December 2012

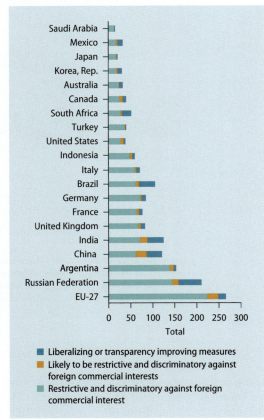

Source: Global Trade Alert database.
Note: Individual measures may cover a very large portion of trade or just one product—these data are therefore not necessarily reflective of trade coverage. For example, Mexico reduced tariffs on 5,000 tariff lines, but this is reflected in just a few "measures."

Limited progress in Doha Round negotiations at the WTO

The need for multilateral agreement remains critical to mitigate the use of trade restrictive measures and promote trade openness. However, the prospects for successfully concluding the Doha Development Agenda (DDA) negotiations—now entering their twelfth year—remain dim, with recent reports that WTO members have turned their attention in 2013 to "realistic" deliverables,[14] rather than a conclusion to the whole round. The deadlock

is costly. In terms of the market access dimension of what has been negotiated to date, there is a potential global welfare boost of some $160 billion at stake (Hoekman 2011). But often overlooked is the opportunity cost of the WTO not being able to deliver on its "legislative" function as an arbiter of new rules of the game in policy matters outside the framework of the DDA. These include "green" industrial policy measures, natural resource- and climate-related trade policies (such as carbon border adjustments), and export restrictions on food products to insulate domestic markets. DDA paralysis carries the risk of countries pursuing unilateral, potentially damaging, responses to the externalities of these policies.

According to experts, much could be gained if a critical mass of the 15–20 or so largest WTO members were to agree to reduce applied barriers to trade and bind current levels of openness, but currently some large countries want more than other large countries are willing to offer (Hoekman 2011). Over the course of 2012, topics including trade facilitation, agriculture, special and differential treatment, least developed country issues, and dispute settlement were advanced—according to the chairs of the various Doha negotiating groups—while others, like services, barely moved at all, and are unlikely to move forward in the months ahead. Successful negotiations at the upcoming December 2013 ninth ministerial conference in Bali are being viewed as a pivotal stepping stone—and necessary precondition—for ending the Doha Round, though there is little optimism that the conference itself will end the round (ICTSD 2012). At the most recent World Economic Forum in Davos, trade ministers from over 20 WTO member countries gathered informally and imposed an unofficial Easter deadline for taking stock of whether "meaningful results" in Bali will be possible. They agreed that success at the conference would have to include gains in the areas of trade facilitation, least-developed country issues, and agriculture (ICTSD 2013).

Aid and international financial institutions

Over the past decade, official development assistance (ODA) steadily increased, reaching its peak in 2010. The general trend of rising annual flows during the 2000s slowed only after the global financial crisis at the end of 2008, with a 1 percent deceleration in growth in 2009. Official development assistance continued to be a stable source of development financing even after the global financial crisis, helping to alleviate the immediate impact of previous financial crises. In 2011 and 2012, however, as the effects of the recession hit donors' aid budgets, the recipients of ODA suffered the first two consecutive years of lower aid disbursements since 1997 (excluding fluctuations affected by exceptional debt relief).

Bilateral and multilateral aid

Members of the Development Assistance Committee (DAC) of the Organisation for Economic Co-operation and Development (OECD) disbursed $128.3 billion (in constant 2011 dollars and exchange rates) in 2012, compared with $133.7 billion the previous year, a decrease in real terms of 4 percent. In current prices, ODA in 2012 equaled $125.5 billion, down from $133.7 billion in 2011 a decline of 6 percent. As a percentage of donors' combined gross national income (GNI), ODA continued to slip from 0.32 percent in 2010 to 0.31 percent in 2011, to end up at 0.29 in 2012 (figure 1.22). The current situation represents some concern, because developing countries have also been affected by the crisis. Within total net ODA, the bilateral share of net ODA decreased from 70 percent in 2011 to 65 percent in 2012, indicating an increase in the share of multilateral aid to close to 35 percent. One of the broad trends in the recent international aid architecture is the rapid increase of "multi-bilateral" ODA, which is defined as bilateral ODA earmarked for a specific purpose and channeled through the multilateral system. According to OECD

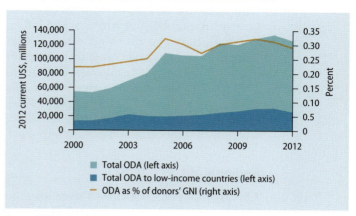

FIGURE 1.22   **DAC members' net ODA disbursements**

Sources: OECD DAC and World Bank.
Note: GNI = gross national income; ODA = official development assistance.

DAC, multi-bilateral ODA increased from $9 billion to $16.7 billion between 2007 and 2010, representing 12 percent of gross ODA excluding debt relief. The World Bank channels over a quarter of such multi-bilateral ODA, becoming the single largest multilateral channel for trust funds.

Gleneagles

At the Group of Eight (G-8) summit in Gleneagles, Scotland, in 2005, important commitments related to ODA and external debt forgiveness were made. Indeed, the international agreement on debt relief (Multilateral Debt Relief Initiative, or MDRI) canceled $56.5 billion in loans owed to the World Bank, the African Development Bank, and the IMF. In addition, DAC donors agreed to increase ODA by $50 billion between 2004 and 2010, at least half of which would be designated for Sub-Saharan and North Africa. This promised increase was made in 2004 prices and exchange rates, and the targeted level of ODA in 2010 prices was estimated to be $152.2 billion. Given the actual amount of $128.5 billion available, a gap of more than $25 billion remains. The DAC's 2012 annual ODA report shows that only a little more than $1.2 billion of the shortfall can be attributed to lower than expected GNI levels stemming from the economic crisis (OECD 2012b). At Gleneagles, the G-8 donors also envisaged an increase in total ODA to Africa of $25 billion in 2004 prices and exchange rates. In current prices and exchange rates, that translates into an increase of an estimated $29 billion in 2010. Yet estimates show that Africa only received an additional $11.8 billion in 2010. Given the decline in ODA in 2011 and 2012, it is clear that this situation has not improved.

Regional aid

Although ODA disbursements were lower in 2011 than in 2010, the trend in regional ODA remained stable. Aid is mainly concentrated in Sub-Saharan Africa, which received 43 percent of net ODA disbursements in 2011, South Asia (21 percent), and the Middle East and North Africa (11 percent) (figure 1.23).

While Sub-Saharan Africa still received most of the aid, this region suffered a further decrease in 2012, with flows of $26.2 billion, or a decline of 7.9 percent in real terms compared with 2011. Europe and Central Asia also saw a fall in net bilateral ODA flows of 17 percent in real terms from 2010; between 2010 and 2011, the decline was around 6

FIGURE 1.24   Net ODA disbursements to low- and middle-income countries

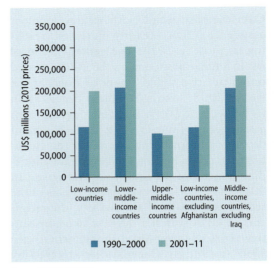

Source: OECD DAC 2012.

percent as the region made strong gains toward poverty alleviation. Latin America sustained a decrease of 3 percent in 2011, while South Asia registered a shortfall of 2 percent. The only region with an increase in net ODA disbursements was the Middle East and North Africa, with the revolutions in this region triggering more aid.

Special groups

Low-income countries received 3 percent more aid in 2011 compared with 2010. Middle-income countries, on the other hand, suffered a decline of 17.2 percent from 2010. For lower-middle-income countries, net ODA disbursements decreased 8.9 percent from 2010, to $5.7 billion (figure 1.24).

When all developing countries are considered, ODA disbursements per capita have increased for countries with no more than two of the MDGs achieved (figure 1.25).

Even though aid fell in 2011, the flows are still being directed to those countries lagging the most (that is, the countries furthest from achieving the MDGs). For example, the group of countries in a fragile situation that have met or are currently on

FIGURE 1.23   Net ODA disbursements to developing regions

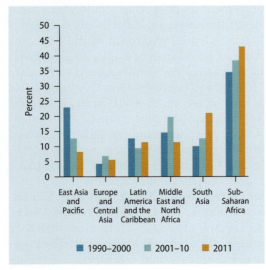

Source: OECD DAC 2012.

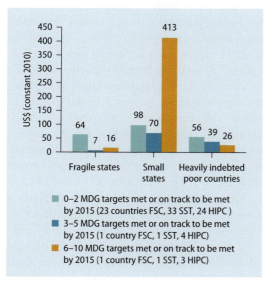

FIGURE 1.25 **Net ODA received per capita by groups of countries ranked by MDG targets met or on track to be met by 2015 (2009–11)**

Source: OECD DAC 2012.
Note: FSC = fragile states; SST = small states; HIPC = Heavily indebted poor countries.

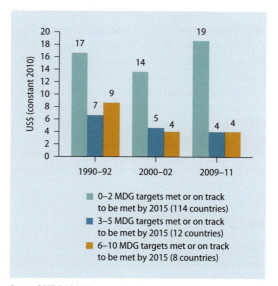

FIGURE 1.26 **Net ODA received per capita by groups of countries ranked by MDG targets met or on track to be met by 2015**

Source: OECD DAC 2012.
Note: FSC = fragile; SST = small states; HIPC = Heavily indebted poor countries.

track to achieve no more than two MDGs received an annual average of $64 per capita in 2009–11 (figure 1.26).

Fragile, small, and heavily indebted poor countries (HIPCs) also suffered the consequences of a smaller amount of ODA disbursements from 2010 to 2011 (figure 1.27). Fragile states and small states received 6 percent less in ODA disbursements than they did in 2010; and the flow to HIPCs decreased by 4.1 percent.

Fragile states—those countries often in internal conflict or with severe political instability—are the developing countries most challenged in meeting the Millennium Development Goals. These countries are typically characterized by weak institutions and macroeconomic instability. For obvious reasons, peace- or state-building activities take priority over economic policy making. Macroeconomic policy advice and implementation are hampered by lack of timely and reliable statistics. Effective engagement by international organizations and development partners requires a recognition of the limited capacity

FIGURE 1.27 **Net ODA disbursements to fragile, small, and HIPC states**

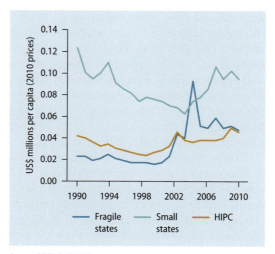

Source: OECD DAC 2012.
Note: HIPC = Heavily indebted poor countries.

and large financing needs of these fragile countries.

Fragile states are vulnerable countries with few if any resources available with which to address vulnerabilities. In a possible protracted slowdown of global growth, these countries would be hard pressed to counteract the accompanying negative shocks to their economies, either by depleting available policy buffers or adjusting macroeconomic policies. With domestic policy space severely limited, these countries would have to turn to the international community for additional assistance if such a downside risk scenario were to materialize. The decline in ODA for these countries is thus especially worrisome because well-targeted external financial aid can be effective in supporting countries exiting from fragile situations (World Bank 2011).

BRICS

ODA DAC resources are not the only resources that countries can use to attain the MDGs; various new donors and philanthropists have become part of the development community, providing resources to countries to use in progressing toward the MDGs and for development in general. In particular, South-South cooperation has become increasingly important, with estimates of financial aid flows from the so-called BRICS to developing countries of up to $4 billion in 2009 (Adugna et al. 2011). These aid volumes do not fully capture the significance and impact of BRICS on the financial inflows of low-income countries, however. For example, since 2000, trade between BRICS and Sub-Saharan Africa has increased 25 percent annually, reaching $206 billion in 2011.

Trade, foreign direct investment, and development aid are often intertwined and come as a package based on the idea of South-South solidarity, shared experiences, and self-reliance (based on the meeting in Yamoussoukro, Côte d'Ivoire, 2008). Even though foreign assistance is diverse among BRICS, development cooperation focuses on trade partners, and consequently, often on neighboring countries and regional integration, to stimulate trade, investments, and growth as the main vehicles for improvement in development outcomes. It also focuses aid on technical rather than financial assistance (EU 2012).

Looking forward: ODA flows through 2015

For the ODA flow to developing countries to remain constant in per capita terms, an increase in total ODA by 2015 of $6.6 billion in 2011 prices and exchange rates is needed. Given the ongoing fragility of the economic recovery in most of the developed world, this increase might be quite a difficult undertaking to accomplish at a time when any additional assistance to facilitate the attainment of the MDGs could prove critical. Continuing at the current level of ODA would result in a fall of 1.3 percent annually until 2015.

Country programmable aid (CPA) is a core subset of ODA, representing about 67 percent of total DAC ODA, with 95 percent of multilateral agencies and 45 percent of bilateral aid agencies reporting on their programmable aid flows. CPA data provide information about the forward spending plans by DAC donors on development.[15] A reliable predictor of actual disbursements, CPA had predictability ratios of 103, 95, and 92 percent in 2009, 2010, and 2011, respectively. A ratio of 92 percent means that, on average, donors disbursed 8 percent less than planned the year before.

The 2013 DAC report on predictability presents the results of the 2013 DAC survey on forward spending plans for 2013 to 2016, including the final year by which the current set of MDGs should be achieved. The survey data indicate that the annual amount of CPA in 2013 is anticipated to jump by 9 percent in real terms compared with 2012. It is then projected to remain constant for the period 2014–16. The result is a slight decline in per capita CPA from $18.18 in 2013 to $17.78 in 2015 (in 2012 prices and exchange rates). The implications of this decline are more pronounced in Sub-Saharan Africa, which received $47.70 per capita CPA in 2012 and will see its allocation decline to $45.08 per capita by 2015. Although the initial recovery bodes well for the availability of ODA to assist with the attainment of the MDGs, the downturn in the outer years does not.

Aid effectiveness

Since the Fourth High Level Forum on Aid Effectiveness in Busan, Republic of Korea, in late 2011, the international community has shifted from concentrating on aid effectiveness to a broader focus on effective development cooperation. Although the aid effectiveness agenda remains important, this shift reflects a recent evolution of the development landscape that includes:

- Support for country-led management of development with a focus on results, in lieu of the traditional discussion focused on donor harmonization and alignment.
- The expanding role in development of new partners, such as middle-income countries, the private sector, and civil society organizations.
- The growing importance of aid as a resource for catalytic change and institutional development.
- The changing global financial base for development, with private financing playing a growing developmental role.
- The emergence of new technologies to increase global connectivity and transparency and accountability.

The Busan Partnership for Effective Development Co-operation calls for the establishment of a "new, inclusive, and representative Global Partnership for Effective Development Co-operation to support and ensure accountability for the implementation of commitments at the political level." At its most recent meeting in June 2012, the Working Party on Aid Effectiveness (which has led the aid effectiveness agenda at the global level since the Paris Declaration on Aid Effectiveness in 2005) formally agreed to establish this Global Partnership. Operational since late 2012, the Partnership brings together developing countries, including major providers of South-South cooperation such as BRICS, together with donor countries, civil society organizations, and private funders, serving as a forum for knowledge exchange and regular monitoring of progress. Its main functions are to maintain and strengthen political support for more effective development cooperation; to monitor the implementation of the Busan commitments; to facilitate knowledge exchange and lesson learning; and to support the implementation of the Busan commitments at the country level (box 1.1) To date, more than 160 countries and 45 organizations from around the world have endorsed the Partnership.

Notwithstanding the changes that will potentially emerge from the new Global Partnership, monitoring of the promised progress by the DAC donor community should continue as a means to improve aid effectiveness as set forth in the Paris Declaration on Aid Effectiveness. The Paris Declaration, which placed country ownership of policies and programs at the center of a reform agenda to make aid more effective, committed donors and developing countries to be mutually accountable for implementing the declaration through a set of thirteen measurable targets (OECD 2012a). By the 2010 deadline, only one of the targets had been met: to strengthen capacity by coordinated support (target 4).

Disaggregating the data for the various multilateral development banks and other international organizations, such as the United Nations and the EU institutions, yields a more nuanced picture, however (table 1.7). For example, the Inter-American Development Bank has met four of the eight indicators for which disaggregated data exist, the World Bank three (see box 1.2 for additional information about World Bank performance in development cooperation), and the EU institutions two. All other multilateral development banks have met one indicator.

Table 1.7 also shows that individual international organizations have made progress in many areas, but each of them has also fallen back on at least one target. The African Development Bank and the Asian Development Bank show deteriorations in four of the eight indicators analyzed. The World Bank is closest to reaching all indicators, with an average gap of 17 percent remaining on five of its unmet indicators, while the Inter-American Development Bank has an average

BOX 1.1   Putting the Busan Partnership for Effective Development Cooperation into operation

During the Fourth High Level Forum, the international community renewed its commitment to moving the effective development cooperation agenda forward while keeping its focus on the unfinished aid effectiveness agenda. Three key vehicles used to bring these agendas forward are the Global Partnership for Effective Development Co-operation, the Global Monitoring Mechanism, and Building Blocks for Post-Busan Implementation.

To follow up, the international community established the Post-Busan Interim Group, which held several meetings in the first half of 2012 and agreed on the Global Partnership mandate and the global monitoring framework. The Global Partnership mandate focuses on maintaining and strengthening political momentum for more effective development cooperation; ensuring accountability for implementing the Busan commitments; facilitating knowledge exchange and sharing lessons learned; and supporting implementation of the Busan commitments at the country level.

The indicators and associated targets of the global monitoring framework (successor to the 2005–10 Paris Declaration Monitoring Survey) intend to promote international accountability for implementing the Busan Global Partnership agreement. Five of the indicators are from the Paris Declaration Monitoring Survey (such as use of countries' public financial management and procurement systems), which ensures continuity with the unfinished aid effectiveness agenda. The remaining five indicators are new and reflect the evolution of the development landscape by including civil society and private sector engagement. The Building Blocks launched at the Busan forum are initiatives to help further progress in eight key areas: conflict and fragility; South-South cooperation; the private sector; climate finance; transparency; effective institutions and policies; results and mutual accountability; and management of diversity and reduction of fragmentation.

To date, 3 minister-level cochairs and 18 steering committee members have been appointed from partner countries, development partners, the private sector, and civil service organizations. The first steering committee meeting to discuss focus areas of the Global Partnership was held in December 2012. The global monitoring framework is being finalized. Given their voluntary nature, the progress on the Building Blocks varies across initiatives. Going forward, a key challenge for the Global Partnership is to connect with other international forums and initiatives, most notably the discussion on the post-2015 MDG goals.

TABLE 1.7   Progress on Paris Declaration survey indicators by multilateral development banks, UN, and EU institutions

	Global target	Overall result	Multilateral Development Banks		World Bank			African Development Bank		
	%	2010 (%)	2010 (%)	Progress since 2005	2010 (%)	Gap	Progress since 2005	2010 (%)	Gap	Progress since 2005
3 – Aid flows are aligned with national priorities	85	72	36	=	79	7%	+	59	31%	+
4 – Strengthen capacity by coordinating support	50	58	50	+	73	Met	+	69	Met	+
5 – How much aid for the government sectors uses country systems	55	35	20	+	55	Met	+	32	42%	–
6 – Strenghten capacity by avoiding parallel PIUs	67	32	49	+	80	Met	+	65	3%	+
7 – Aid is more predictable	71	43	29	–	51	28%	–	50	30%	+
9 – Use of common arrangements or procedures	66	45	32	+	59	11%	+	35	47%	–
10.a – Joint missions	40	19	18	+	29	28%	+	14	65%	–
10.b – Joint country analytical work	66	43	32	=	59	11%	+	50	24%	–

Source: OECD DAC 2012.
Note: PIU = project implementation unit; + = improvement, – = deterioration.

remaining gap of well over 60 percent on its remaining four indicators. The United Nations was only halfway toward reaching its remaining targets in 2010.

Acceleration toward the MDGs

Various other mechanisms exist to accelerate progress toward the MDGs in addition to improvements in aid effectiveness. For example, in 2010, the United Nations Development Programme (UNDP) developed an MDG acceleration framework (MAF) to provide a systematic way of identifying bottlenecks and possible high-impact solutions that could assist countries to pick up the pace on attaining the MDGs. The framework was rolled out in 10 countries across a range of MDGs in 2010 and has been used since then to assist 44 countries across almost all of the MDGs. This work has led to concrete plans of action with coordinated roles for governments and all development partners involved in achieving countries' MDG priorities.

The results from the MAFs completed to date are encouraging and have led to increased collaboration between the World Bank and the UN in this area. The initial lessons learned include the importance of strong national ownership, facilitation of cross-sectoral collaboration, and participation by civil service and nongovernmental organizations. Of critical importance for the countries themselves is actual implementation of the agreed-upon MDG action plan, which includes ensuring that gaps in institutional capacity and sector governance are addressed, that the MDG action plan is adequately incorporated into annual or multiyear partner support plans, and that both intermediate and final indicators of MDG achievement are regularly monitored, all to ensure that efforts are yielding the desired results.

Various other initiatives have been put in place to accelerate progress toward the MDGs such as the Sanitation and Water for All initiative. This is a global partnership between developing countries, donors, multi-lateral agencies, civil society, and other development partners working together to achieve universal and sustainable access to sanitation and safe drinking water, with an immediate focus on achieving the Millennium Development Goals in the most off-track countries.[16] To accelerate progress on MDG 1c (reduction of underweight in children under five), the Scaling Up Nutrition (SUN) global movement was set up to support nutrition sensitive interactions in 33 SUN countries. Investments are supported that are aligned to national nutrition plans and contribute directly to the process of

Asian Development Bank			Inter American Development Bank			United Nations			EU institutions		
2010 (%)	Gap	Progress since 2005	2010 (%)	Gap	Progress since 2005	2010 (%)	Gap	Progress since 2005	2010 (%)	Gap	Progress since 2005
64	25%	–	48	44%	+	31	64%	–	51	40%	+
44	12%	+	65	Met	+	67	Met	+	50	Met	+
29	47%	–	5	91%	+	12	78%	+	47	15%	+
95	Met	+	7	90%	=	1	102%	–	71	Met	+
54	24%	–	48	32%	–	23	68%	+	48	32%	+
50	24%	+	80	Met	–	45	32%	+	52	21%	+
15	63%	+	67	Met	+	38	5%	+	19	53%	–
39	41%	–	75	Met	+	61	8%	=	57	14%	+

BOX 1.2   World Bank performance on development cooperation

The World Bank's performance on development cooperation has continuously improved and is among the strongest of all development partners. Evidence from international assessments, including the Paris Declaration Monitoring Survey, confirms the Bank's sustained commitment to improving its own effectiveness in support of stronger development outcomes. With the Global Partnership for Effective Development Co-operation in mind, the Bank focuses on the following priorities:

Partner Country Leadership and Ownership. The Bank promotes better development cooperation and more effective institutions by:

- Aligning its support with each country's development priorities.
- Focusing on capacity development, investing in human capital, and strengthening stakeholder ownership to facilitate achievement of national development goals.
- Supporting public sector institutions and systems through better diagnostic, analytical, and measurement tools.
- Enabling stronger government-led management of development support and greater integration of aid and other support into national budgets.
- Strengthening and using country systems—for budget and project management, procurement, financial management, environmental and social safeguards, and results measurement—with the ultimate objective of transforming development support into sustainable results.

Results. The Bank adopts results-orientation implementation by:

- Implementing a Corporate Scorecard, an institutional-level IDA Results Measurement System, and an Annual Results Report.
- Mainstreaming a results culture with systematic results frameworks for all lending projects, programs, and country assistance strategies, as well as adopting new results-oriented financing instruments such as the Program for Results (P4R); and increasing impact evaluations and evidence-based decision making through the collaborative Bank–partner country Development Impact Evaluation Initiative (DIME).

- Supporting country capacity to implement results-based approaches; building country statistical capacity to support enhanced and rigorous monitoring and evaluation; and working with regional Communities of Practice for cross-country knowledge exchange and capacity development on results management.
- Using innovative tools such as geo-mapping, beneficiary feedback, third-party monitoring, and other mechanisms to enhance social accountability and improve service delivery.

Transparency. The Bank has made great strides in the area of transparency by:

- Launching an Access to Information Policy, the Open Data and Open Knowledge initiatives, and the Open Access Repository. These initiatives encourage public access, help improve accountability, and link funding to development outcomes and results.
- Being identified as a global leader on transparency by the Aid Transparency Index from Publish What You Fund and the transparency component of the Center for Global Development's QuODA assessment.
- Demonstrating leadership as an active proponent and implementer of the International Aid Transparency Initiative (IATI), which sets a common standard for all development partners to share aid data.
- Supporting recipient country Open Government initiatives and efforts to improve budget management and transparency for domestic accountability.
- Promoting aid predictability to facilitate greater transparency.
- Maintaining AidFlows (http://www.aidflows.org/), a publicly available web-based source of information about aid flows that seeks to better inform the global conversation about development funding. AidFlows began as a partnership between the OECD-DAC and the World Bank. AidFlows provides easy access to country-by-country information in an intuitive visual format. The site has been well received by a range of users, including government officials in donor and recipient countries, aid agencies, MDBs, NGOs, and civil society organizations.

(box continues next page)

BOX 1.2   World Bank performance on development cooperation (continued)

Development partnerships beyond aid. The Bank integrates key themes and opportunities presented by the evolving development landscape through:

- Partnering with lower- and middle-income developing countries to facilitate support through South-South cooperation, including knowledge exchanges, technology transfers, investment, trade, and financial support.
- Leveraging funding from middle-income countries, the private sector, foundations, global funds and programs, and other sources that contribute significantly to development.

Countries in fragile and conflict situations face complex development challenges and are a special area of focus for the Bank. The New Deal for Engagement in Fragile States sets out a collective vision and principles for engagement with these fragile and conflict-affected countries. The Bank is spearheading efforts in several key areas critical to successful implementation of the New Deal, such as supporting technical capacity in the g7+ (the country-owned and -led global mechanism to monitor, report, and draw attention to the unique challenges faced by fragile states), piloting peace-building and state-building Indicators for partner countries, and actively supporting forums for strengthening partnerships among partner countries, donors, MDBs, civil society organizations, and the private sector.

Recognizing that progress on development cooperation at the global, institutional, and country levels is interlinked, the World Bank continues its engagement and leadership in international platforms, initiatives, and partnerships; leads and innovates through institutional reforms, policies, and practices; and promotes support for country-led and -owned development efforts.

---

achieving high coverage of vulnerable target populations (pregnant women and children up to age 24 months) with evidence-based direct nutrition services.[17]

Another example of a special focus to improve achievement of the MDGs is in this case a World Bank initiative. The World Bank's five-year (2010–2015) Reproductive Health Action Plan (RHAP) is accelerating progress on maternal and child health by targeting 57 high priority countries, mostly in Africa and South Asia, with the highest burden of maternal and neonatal deaths, high prevalence of sexually transmitted infections, and high fertility rates. Projects include increasing skilled attendance at births, training health care workers, and expanding girls' education. As of March 2013, more than half (56) of the World Bank's 102 active health projects address high fertility and maternal mortality, and 52 projects address child health. Focusing on health system strengthening and targeting the poor and vulnerable through innovative mechanisms, such as results-based financing, these projects are showing promising results. For example, in Burundi, support from the Burundi Health Sector Development Support Project for the nationwide results-based financing (RBF)[18] program has helped to increase utilization of maternal and child health services including: (a) a rise in births at health facilities by 25 percent; (b) an increase in prenatal consultations by 20 percent; (c) a 35 percent increase in curative care consultations for pregnant women; and (d) a 27 percent increase in family planning services obtained through health facilities—during the just first year of implementation.

Using ICT to improve the effectiveness of projects

The use of information and communication technology (ICT) for economic development was recognized when the official list of MDG indicators was adopted as part of MDG 8, which focuses on the deepening of a global partnership for development. A specific description of this sub-MDG was chosen and indicators identified. Target 8F states that, in cooperation with the private sector, the benefits of new technologies, especially those related to information and communications, will be made available.

An evaluation of these indicators shows that mobile phone subscriptions have risen exponentially across the globe, while growth in the number of fixed telephone lines has stagnated. Impressive increases have also taken place in Internet usage, although here progress is more diverse, with stronger growth in high-income countries than in low- and middle-income countries. Even though access challenges remain, particularly in low-income countries, the extraordinary rise in mobile phone penetration has led to the emergence of a variety of innovations that allow citizens, governments, and international organizations to be more engaged and better informed, and that enable aid providers to identify and communicate more directly with beneficiaries.

In addition to the various business opportunities it has made possible, the evolution of ICT has also opened up a range of opportunities to improve the effectiveness of government programs and associated aid financing, consequently accelerating attainment of the MDGs. Table 1.8 illustrates how mobile telephone technology has assisted countries in making progress toward each MDG. Many more examples demonstrate how ICT can facilitate service delivery. Indeed many governments around the globe, in varying stages of development, are adopting ICT, particularly mobile communication technologies, to assist in this endeavor. At the same time, various international aid agencies are exploring opportunities to deliver aid more effectively using ICT (for example, the Swiss Agency for Development and Cooperation).

What can governments do to foster ICT for development?

Numerous studies have found a positive relationship between ICT adoption and economic development in general. The widespread availability of ICT and mobile phone usage has created opportunities for governments to strengthen service delivery and enhance governance.

An evaluation of initial experiences suggests that the benefits accrue to those countries that put in place policies and programs that not only enable technological transformation but also support institutional reforms and process redesign through which services are delivered (World Bank 2012). Fostering an accelerated diffusion of ICT in developing countries requires undertaking country-specific analysis to take into account local conditions and translating these findings into policy actions that enable and encourage development of the demand and supply sides of ICT. On the demand side, affordability of mobile devices and services is a concern, while on the supply side, common bottlenecks such as spectrum and backbone networks must be addressed.

What can international organizations do to foster ICT for aid effectiveness?

International agencies have been increasingly interested in leveraging the rapid spread of ICT such as mobile phones to better hear the voices of beneficiaries in developing countries. By reducing barriers to accessing information, technology can facilitate transparency and contribute to accountability. Information and communication technology can help solicit, provide, and respond to feedback regarding projects and programs for development. In addition, ICT can also help reduce the transaction costs of, for example, payment systems and improve access to finance.

Introducing new technologies to improve citizens' feedback has significantly reduced the barriers of cost, time, and space that have historically constrained direct interactions with citizens (box 1.3). By using these ever-evolving tools, governments and international aid agencies can improve the success of feedback mechanisms to increase the effectiveness of development programs.

TABLE 1.8   Mobile technology and the Millennium Development Goals

MDG	Example
Poverty and hunger	A study of grain traders in Niger found that cell phones improved consumer welfare (Aker and Mbiti 2008). Access to cell phones allowed traders to obtain better information about grain prices across the country without the high cost of having to travel to different markets. On average, grain traders with cell phones had 29 percent higher profits than those without cell phones. In Niger, demand for cell phones sprang up organically rather than through a specific program.
Universal education	According to a survey of teachers in villages in four African countries, one-quarter reported that the use of mobile phones helped increase student attendance. A main factor was that teachers could contact parents to enquire about their child's whereabouts (Puri et al. n.d.). Mobile phones have also been used in Uganda to track school attendance and detect patterns in attendance, for instance by village, by day of the week, and by season. Tracking pupils' attendance also indirectly tracks absenteeism among teachers (Twaweza 2010).
Gender equality	A study looking at gender differences in the availability and use of mobile phones in developing countries reported that 93 percent of women who had mobile phones felt safer because of having the phone, 85 percent felt more independent, and 41 percent had increased income or professional opportunities (GSM Association 2011).
Child health	A program using text messaging to identify malnutrition among rural children in Malawi is notable for its impact on the speed and quality of data flows.[a] Using a system called RapidSMS, health workers in rural areas were able to transmit weight and height information in two minutes—it took two months with the previous system. The data entry error rate was significantly improved, to just 2.8 percent from 14.2 percent in the old system. The improved information flow enabled experts to analyze data more quickly and accurately, identify children at risk, and provide treatment information to health staff in the field.
Maternal health	One of the earliest uses of mobile technology to improve maternal health took place in rural districts of Uganda in the late 1990s. Traditional birth attendants were provided with walkie-talkies, allowing them to stay in contact with health centers and obtain advice. An assessment of the program found that it cut maternal mortality roughly in half (Musoke 2002).
HIV/AIDS	In Kenya, weekly text messages were sent to AIDS patients to remind them to take their antiretroviral drugs (Lester et al. 2010). Those who received the text messages had significantly higher rates of taking the drugs than those who did not. The study noted that text messaging intervention was less expensive than in-person community adherence interventions on the basis of travel costs alone and could theoretically translate into huge health and economic benefits if scaled up.
Environment	According to one forecast, mobile technology could lower greenhouse gas emissions 2 percent by the year 2020 (GSM Association 2009). This reduction could be met, among other ways, through widespread adoption of various mobile-enabled technologies such as smart transportation and logistics, smart grids and meters, smart buildings, and "dematerialization" (or replacing the physical movement of goods and services with online transmission). Mobile phones can also be used as tools for environmental monitoring. For example, cab drivers in Accra, Ghana, were outfitted with mobile phones with GPS and a tube containing a carbon monoxide sensor to test pollution levels.[b]
Partnership	MDG target 8F states: "In cooperation with the private sector, make available benefits of new technologies, especially information and communications." Mobile phone penetration in low-income economies grew from less than one per 100 people in 2000 to almost one per every three in 2010—largely as a result of private sector investment. Of some 800 telecommunications projects in developing countries with private sector participation between 1990 and 2009, almost three-quarters involved greenfield operations, primarily in mobile telephony.[c]

Source: World Bank 2012.
a. "Malawi—Nutritional Surveillance" on the RapidSMS web site: http://www.rapidsms.org/case-studies/malawi-nutritional-surviellence/.
b. http://www.globalproblems-globalsolutions-files.org/unf_website/PDF/vodafone/tech_social_change/Environmental_Conservation_case3.pdf.
c. World Bank and PPIAF, PPI Project Database. http://ppi.worldbank.org. Date: 04/03/2011.

BOX 1.3   Potential uses of mobile phone surveys

As mobile phone ownership rates have risen dramatically in Africa, interest has increased in using mobile telephones as a data collection platform. Face-to-face household surveys are usually expensive and time consuming, and mobile phone surveys are proving to be a cost-effective, flexible, and rapid way to collect data on a wide range of topics and over time.

South Sudan and Tanzania have both piloted mobile phone surveys, with reasonable success. In South Sudan, 1,000 respondents in 10 urban areas were given cell phones in 2010 and surveyed on a monthly basis. In Tanzania, 550 households were administered a baseline survey in 2010, and an adult respondent was selected for a weekly mobile phone survey (for 25 weeks), later administered every 2 weeks (for 8 weeks). Both surveys collected information on a wide variety of issues, including health, education, water, security, nutrition, travel times, prices, electricity, and governance. The surveys also asked respondents for their perceptions on the most pressing problems to be addressed by the city government and their opinion about a draft constitution, and collected baseline information for large-scale programs on food fortification.

The cost per interview in each round in Tanzania ranged between $4.10 and $7.30, or about $0.42 a question (plus $50–$150 for a baseline interview). Thus for long surveys, face-to-face interviews may be more cost-effective. However, the evidence from South Sudan and Tanzania suggests that mobile surveys can collect quality data in a timely manner that is of use to a wide range of data users. Attrition and nonresponse need to be dealt with at implementation, but the ability to modify surveys easily in subsequent survey rounds is a key benefit.

Last, the data collected in Tanzania were widely disseminated through a dedicated website, with additional help from a local television journalist who ensured that information was widely publicized. Accountability for public services has reportedly increased, suggesting that results need to be disseminated systematically to civil society, the media, and the government to be fully effective.

Source: Croke et al. 2013.

Notes

1. The classification of countries is the one used in the IMF's *World Economic Outlook*. Emerging market and developing countries are those countries that are not designated as advanced countries. Countries that are eligible for financial assistance under the IMF's *Poverty Reduction and Growth Trust* constitute a subset of emerging market and developing countries; these countries are denoted low-income countries although eligibility is based on other considerations in addition to income levels. Emerging market and developing countries that are not eligible for financial assistance under the *Poverty Reduction and Growth Trust* are designated as emerging market countries. Fragile states are countries included in the World Bank's list of Fragile and Conflict-Affected States as of early 2013. Appendix table A1.2 includes the list of all countries and economies.

2. Each low-income country has been assessed according to a common set of criteria. For example, a country with a large fiscal deficit and an unsustainable level of public debt would be judged to have an unsatisfactory fiscal policy stance.

3. Somalia and South Sudan have been excluded from the IMF's vulnerability exercise for low-income countries, because of lack of data.

4. Small low-income countries are those with a population less than 1.5 million.

5. All data under the vulnerability exercise refer to the median observation for 72 low-income countries, unless otherwise noted.

6. Fiscal consolidation would also be needed in some resource-rich countries to build buffers over time that would help manage challenges arising from volatility and exhaustibility of natural resources.

7. The index uses a globally consistent definition of settlement concentration based

on population density, the population of a "large" urban center, and travel time to that large urban center.

8. In comparison, the United Nations *World Urbanization Prospects, the 2011 Revision*, (April 2012) estimates the average urban population share to be 52 percent in 2010. The United Nations database is a more comprehensive and detailed data source; however, the definition of urbanization is not necessarily the same across countries.

9. The methodology provides a way to construct a linear approximation of a Lorenz curve that minimizes the difference between the linear approximation and the actual Lorenz curve. The linear segments represent different categories of countries. In this application, these linear segments represent low-, medium-, and high-agglomeration or -income countries.

10. World Bank and IMF member countries as of early 2013. For the 26 countries for which no agglomeration data are available, countries were assigned agglomeration status based on heuristic comparisons with like countries. GDP per capita income estimates exclude ten countries owing to lack of data.

11. The Spearman rank correlation coefficient is 0.58 (statistically significant at the 5 percent level).

12. The initials appearing in the graphs correspond to the following countries: Bangladesh (BGD), Cambodia (KHM), Cameroon (CMR), Ghana (GHA), Guinea (GIN), Indonesia (IDN), Mali (MLI), Mauritius (MUS), Mozambique (MOZ), Namibia (NAM), Philippines (PHL), Rwanda (RWA), Senegal (SEN), South Africa (ZAF), Tanzania (TZA), Uganda (UGA), Vietnam (VNM), and Zambia (ZMB).

13. www.globaltradealert.org

14. The realistic deliverables refer to the topics in which negotiations saw progress over the past 12 months, including trade facilitation, agriculture, special and differential treatment, least-developed country issues, and dispute settlement.

15. Country programmable aid is total ODA corrected for aid that is inherently unpredictable (humanitarian and disaster relief aid); that entails no flows to the recipient country (such as donor administrative cost); and whose

use is determined through dialogue between the donor agency and partner government. In addition, loan repayments are netted out because they are not normally part of aid allocation decisions by donor governments (OECD 2010).

16. See http://www.sanitationandwaterforall.org for more information.

17. See http://scalingupnutrition.org/ and the 2012 Global Monitoring Report for more information.

18. See http://www.rbfhealth.org/ for more information.

References

Adugna, Abebe, et al. 2011. "Finance for Development: Trends and Opportunities in a Changing Landscape." CFP Working Paper 8, World Bank, Washington, DC.

Aker, Jenny C., and M. Isaac Mbiti. 2008. "Mobile Phones and Economic Development in Africa." *Journal of Economic Perspectives* 24 (3).

Croke, K., A. Dabalen, G. Demombynes, M. Giugale, and J. Hoogeveen, 2013. "Collecting High-Frequency Data Using Mobile Phones: Do Timely Data Lead to Accountability?", Economic Premise Notes Series, World Bank, Washington, DC.

Commission on Growth and Development. 2008. *The Growth Report: Strategies for Sustained Growth and Inclusive Development*. Washington, DC: World Bank.

GSM Association. 2009. "Mobile's Green Manifesto" (November). http://www.gsmworld.com/our-work/mobile_planet/mobile_environment/green_manifesto.htm.

———. 2011. "Women & Mobile: A Global Opportunity." http://www.vitalwaveconsulting.com/pdf/Women-Mobile.pdf.

Hoekman, Bernard. 2011. "The WTO and the Doha Round: Walking on Two Legs." *Economic Premise* 68, World Bank, Washington, DC (October).

ICTSD. (International Centre for Trade and Sustainable Development). 2012. "WTO Members Aim for 'Realistic' Doha Deliverables for 2013." *Bridges Weekly Trade News Digest* 16 (43).

———. 2013. "Trade Ministers at Davos Press for 'Meaningful Results' in Bali." *Bridges Weekly Trade News Digest* 17 (3).

International Monetary Fund. 2011. "New Growth Drivers for Low-Income Countries—The Role of BRICs." Washington, DC: IMF.

———. 2012a. "Global Risks, Vulnerabilities, and Policy Challenges Facing Low-Income Countries." Washington, DC: IMF.

———. 2012b. "Structural Transformation in Sub-Saharan Africa." Chapter 3 in *October 2013 Sub-Saharan Africa: Regional Economic Outlook*. Washington, DC: IMF.

International Monetary Fund and World Bank. 2012. *Global Monitoring Report 2012: Food Prices, Nutrition, and the Millennium Development Goals*. Washington, DC: World Bank. http://site.ebrary.com/id/10556448.

Lester, R., et al. 2010. "Effects of a Mobile Phone Short Message Service on Antiretroviral Treatment Adherence in Kenya (WelTel Kenya1): A Randomized Trial." *Lancet* 376 (9755, November):1838–45. doi:10.1016/S0140-6736(10)61997-6.

McMillan, M. and D. Rodrik. 2011. Globalization, Structural Change and Productivity Growth. NBER Working Paper No. 17143.

Musoke, M. 2002. "Maternal health care in Uganda: leveraging traditional and modern knowledge systems." IK Notes World Bank.

Nielsen, Lynge. 2011. "Classifications of Countries Based on Their Level of Development: How It Is Done and How It Could Be Done." IMF Working Paper 11/31, 2011. International Monetary Fund, Washington, DC.

———. Forthcoming. "How to Classify Countries Based on Their Level of Development." *Social Indicators Research*.

OECD (Organisation for Economic Co-operation and Development). 2010. "Getting Closer to the Core—Measuring Country Programmable Aid." Development Brief Issue 1. OECD, Paris.

———. 2012a. "Aid effectiveness 2005–2010: Progress in Implementing the Paris Declaration." OECD, Paris.

———. 2012b. "Development: Aid to Developing Countries Falls Because of Global Recession." OECD, Paris.

OECD DAC (Development Assistance Committee). Statistics 2012 (database). OECD, Paris. http://stats.oecd.org/Index.aspx?datasetcode=TABLE1.

Papageorgiou, Chris, and Nikola Spatafora. 2012. *Economic Diversification in LICs: Stylized Facts and Macroeconomic Implications*. IMF Staff Discussion Note 12/13, International Monetary Fund, Washington, DC.

Puri, J., Patricia Mechael, Roxana Cosmaciuc, Daniela Sloninsky, Vijay Modi, Matt Berg, Uyen Kim Huynh, Nadi Kaonga, Seth Ohemeng-Dapaah, Maurice Baraza, Afolayan Emmanuel, and Sia Lyimo. n.d. "A Study of Connectivity in Millennium Villages in Africa." http://www.mobileactive.org/files/file_uploads/ICTD2010%20Puri%20et%20al.pdf.

Twaweza. 2010. "CU Tracking School Attendance in Uganda." http://twaweza.org/index.php?i=221.

World Bank. 2011. *Global Development Horizons 2011 Multipolarity: The New Global Economy*. Washington, DC: World Bank.

———. 2012. *Maximizing Mobile: 2012 Information and Communications for Development*. Washington, D.C.: World Bank. http://dx.doi.org/10.1596/978-0-8213-8991-1.

———. 2013. "Global Economic Prospects: Assuring Growth Over the Medium Term." Washington, DC: World Bank.

WTO (World Trade Organization). 2012. "Report on G-20 Trade Measures (Mid-May 2012 to Mid-October 2012)." WTO: Geneva (Ocober 31).

2

Rural-Urban Disparities and Dynamics

In 2011, nearly 50 percent of the population in developing countries lived in areas classified as urban, compared with less than 30 percent in the 1980s (figure 2.1). Urbanization has implications for attaining the Millennium Development Goals (MDGs). Managed with care, it can benefit residents of both urban and rural areas; managed poorly, urbanization can marginalize the poor in both areas. Slums are a symptom of the marginalization of the urban poor. Close to 1 billion people live in urban slums in developing countries, including middle-income countries like Brazil and emerging countries like China and India (UN-Habitat 2010).

Location remains important at all stages of development, but it matters less in rich countries than in poor ones. Estimates from more than 100 Living Standard Surveys indicate that households in the most prosperous areas of developing countries such as Brazil, Bulgaria, Ghana, Indonesia, Morocco, and Sri Lanka have an average consumption almost 75 percent higher than that of similar households in the lagging areas of these countries. In comparison, the disparity is less than 25 percent in developed countries such as Canada, Japan, and the United States (World Bank 2009).

According to various estimates, 40 percent of the increase in the urban population in developing countries comes from migration or reclassification of rural to urban (Chen et al. 1998; UN-Habitat 2008). In China and Indonesia, however, rural-urban migration and reclassification of rural and urban boundaries are estimated to account for more than 70 percent of urban growth in the 1980s and about 80 percent in the 1990s.[1] These migration patterns have vital consequences for the effect of urbanization on poverty as well as implications for policies that can make urbanization a force for poverty reduction.

To better understand these rural-urban dynamics, this chapter looks first at the disparities in attaining the MDGs between rural and urban areas, including small towns and peri-urban areas. The chapter continues with an overview of the pace and causes of urbanization, the role of rural-to-urban migration dynamics, and the consequences for attainment of the eight MDGs discussed in this report.

Trends in rural-urban poverty

Of the 1.3 billion poor in developing countries in 2008, 76 percent resided in rural areas

FIGURE 2.1   **The world is becoming more urban**

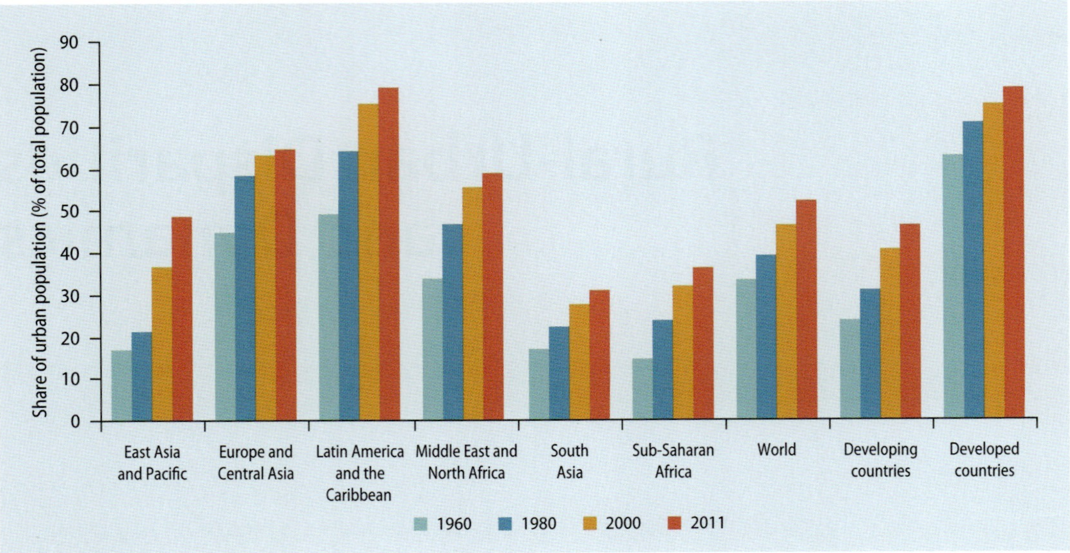

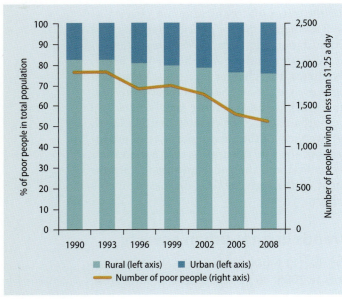

Source: World Bank 2012c.

(figure 2.2). In South Asia, which had the largest number of poor in 2008, poverty was high in rural and urban areas (table 2.1). A ten percentage point difference between rural and urban poverty rates in 1990 persisted until

FIGURE 2.2   **Overall poverty has declined**

Source: GMR team 2013.

2008. In 1990, East Asia had almost 1 billion poor and the highest rural poverty rate of about 67 percent. Its achievement in reducing rural poverty to 20 percent by 2008 is spectacular. East Asia has an equally impressive record in eradicating urban poverty from 24 percent in 1990 to 4 percent in 2008. Sub-Saharan Africa remains the last frontier in the fight to reduce poverty. Nearly half of the rural and one third of the urban population lived on less than $1.25 a day in 2008. For each poor person in an urban area, there were 2.5 as many in rural areas. In South Asia, for each poor person in an urban area, there were three poor ones in rural areas (map 2.1).

Unveiling the face of urban poverty

Urban poverty is not uniformly distributed across a country's cities and towns. Populations are typically conceptualized as being spatially bipolar: people live in either rural or urban places. Poverty, too, is typically seen from this perspective. In reality, people and poverty are located along a continuous "settlement" spectrum ranging from sparsely populated rural areas, to small towns to

TABLE 2.1   Poverty rates are falling in both urban and rural areas but are lower in urban areas

Share of the population below $1.25 a day

	1990		1996		2002		2008	
	rural	urban	rural	urban	rural	urban	rural	urban
East Asia and Pacific	67.5	24.4	45.9	13.0	39.2	6.9	20.4	4.3
Europe and Central Asia	2.2	0.9	6.3	2.8	4.4	1.1	1.2	0.2
Latin America and the Caribbean	21.0	7.4	20.3	6.3	20.3	8.3	13.2	3.1
Middle East and North Africa	9.1	1.9	5.6	0.9	7.5	1.2	4.1	0.8
South Asia	50.5	40.1	46.1	35.2	45.1	35.2	38.0	29.7
Sub-Saharan Africa	55.0	41.5	56.8	40.6	52.3	41.4	47.1	33.6
Total	52.5	20.5	43.0	17.0	39.5	15.1	29.4	11.6

Source: World Bank staff calculations.

MAP 2.1   Poverty is becoming more urban in more urbanized regions

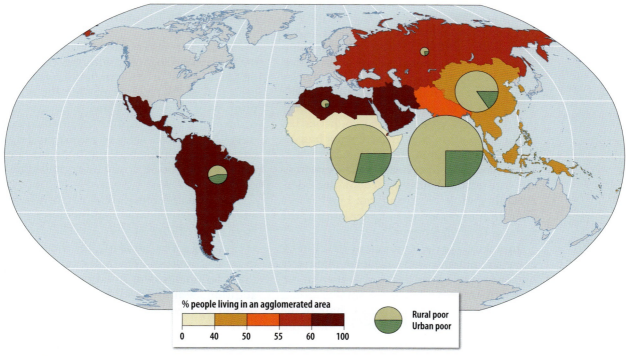

% people living in an agglomerated area

0   40   50   55   60   100

Rural poor
Urban poor

Source: GMR 2013 team.
Note: The agglomeration index was developed by the WDR 2009 team. They define an agglomerated area as having these metrics: a settlement's population size (more than 50,000 people); population density (more than 150 people per square kilometer); and travel time to the nearest large city (60 minutes). The graduated circles are roughly proportional to the total poor population and show the relative share of rural and urban poor.

small cities, to megacities (figure 2.3). In 2010, some 17.5 percent of the urban population in developing countries lived in cities of 5 million or more; 31 percent lived in cities of 0.5 to 5 million, and 51 percent lived in smaller towns (table 2.2) (UN 2011). The distribution of the urban poor follows a similar pattern, with the smallest share living in megacities and larger shares living in medium and small towns. Indeed, the large cities are not necessarily places where the poor are also concentrated (table 2.3).

FIGURE 2.3   Poverty is located along a rural-urban spectrum

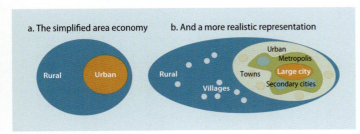

Source: Adapted from World Bank 2009.

With the aid of new analytical techniques that combine census and household survey data, researchers have constructed "poverty–city size gradients" that reveal interesting insights on the relationship between poverty and city size (Elbers, Lanjouw, and Lanjouw 2002, 2003). Recent research for a large number of countries shows that urban poverty is clearly lowest in the largest cities (Ferré, Ferreira, and Lanjouw 2012). In the 1970s and 1980s, better provision of services in urban areas of developing countries led to the perception that governments had an "urban bias" (Lipton 1977). In recent years, researchers who have analyzed the poverty–city size gradient have raised similar questions: Is there a "metropolitan bias" in the allocation of resources to larger cities at the expense of smaller towns?[2]

In a fairly large number of developing countries, not only is the incidence of poverty higher in small cities and towns than in the large urban areas, but these smaller urban centers also account for a larger share of the urban poor. In such countries as Brazil and Thailand, with well-known megacities such as São Paulo, Rio de Janeiro, and Bangkok,

the share of the urban poor residing in small- and medium-size towns exceeds that in the largest cities. In Brazil, one of the most urbanized developing countries, 83 percent of the population is settled relatively evenly along the urban spatial spectrum—22 percent in megacities, 33 percent in intermediate-size cities, and 28 percent in the smallest towns. Brazilian poverty has a predominantly urban face, though not in its megacities: 72 percent of the poor live in urban areas, but surprisingly, only 9 percent reside in the megacities of Rio de Janeiro and São Paulo. The rest of the poor are concentrated in medium (17 percent) and very small towns (39 percent). In Thailand, the share of the urban poor is 17 percent, of which 76 percent resides in extra small towns.

Findings from a study of eight developing countries show that with the exception of Mexico, the urban population was concentrated in the largest cities but the urban poor were dispersed along a continuum of medium, small, and extra small towns (table 2.3). Lower rates of poverty in large cities are consistent with the hypotheses of urban growth being driven by agglomeration externalities.

Many small countries do not have a megacity, and nearly all large countries have many large cities of various sizes as well as one or several megacities. Similarly, the small towns in small countries are significantly smaller than the small towns in large countries. In addition, while official boundaries rarely demarcate them as "slums," the size of urban cityscapes that can be considered slums is significant. Almost by definition, slums are home to many of the urban poor. Asia is

TABLE 2.2   Distribution of urban population by size of urban area

City size class	Number of agglomerations			Population in urban areas (in 1,000s)			Percentage of urban population		
	1975	2005	2010	1975	2005	2010	1975	2005	2010
10 million or more	3	19	23	53,185	284,943	352,465	3.5	8.9	9.9
5 to 10 million	14	33	38	109,426	229,718	266,078	7.1	7.2	7.5
1 to 5 million	144	340	388	291,663	667,652	759,919	19.0	20.9	21.4
500,000 to 1 million	224	463	513	155,770	317,166	353,802	10.1	9.9	9.9
Fewer than 500,000	—	—	—	927,625	1,698,055	1,826,313	60.3	53.1	51.3

Source: UN 2011.
Note: — = not available.

TABLE 2.3   The poor are disproportionately concentrated in smaller cities and towns
Percent

Country	Urban	XL	L	M	S	XS
Albania						
Population share	42	—	—	15	13	14
Share of the poor	31	—	—	11	9	11
Brazil				—		
Population share	83	22	7	24	1	28
Share of the poor	72	9	6	17	1	39
Kazakhstan						
Population share	57	8	—	29	5	15
Share of the poor	43	1	—	21	5	15
Kenya						
Population share	19	7	2	3	2	4
Share of the poor	16	6	2	3	2	4
Mexico						
Population share	6	27	13	11	4	6
Share of the poor	39	16	6	7	3	7
Morocco						
Population share	51	12	9	27	3	1
Share of the poor	34	3	7	2	3	1
Sri Lanka						
Population share	12	—	3	3	2	4
Share of the poor	5	—	1	1	1	2
Thailand						
Population share	31	12	—	3	2	14
Share of the poor	17	1	—	1	1	13

Source: Ferré, Ferreira and Lanjouw 2012.
Note: Population share = percent of the population living in each category; share of the poor = percent of the country's poor living in each category.
XL = > 1m; L = 500k–1m; M = 100k–500k; S = 50k–100k; XS = < 50k.
— = not available.

home to 61 percent of the world's nearly 1 billion slum dwellers; Africa 25.5 percent; and Latin America, 13.4 percent. The number of slum dwellers is projected to grow by nearly 500 million between now and 2020 (UN-Habitat 2010). The proportion of urban residents living in slums is already about 62 percent in Africa. Between 2000 and 2010, the increase in the absolute number of slum dwellers was greatest in Sub-Saharan Africa, southeastern Asia, southern Asia, and western Asia.[3] While southern Asia, southeastern Asia, and eastern Asia have made impressive progress in moving people out of slums, the most significant reductions have occurred in North Africa. During 2000–10, regional differences in the success of addressing the MDG 7.d slum target (achieve, by 2020, a significant improvement in the lives of at least

100 million slum dwellers), were self-evident, with some 227 million people moving out of slum conditions.[4]

The effects of urban poverty can be as dehumanizing and intense as those associated with rural poverty. Various MDG indicators showed remarkable similarities between slum and rural areas. For instance, in low-income countries such as Bangladesh, Ethiopia, Haiti, India, Nepal, and Niger—countries where poverty is seen as primarily a rural phenomenon—4 of every 10 slum children are malnourished, a rate comparable to that found in the rural areas of these countries. Likewise, in cities such as Khartoum and Nairobi, the prevalence of diarrhea is much higher among slum children than among children in the rural areas of Kenya and Sudan. In slums, child deaths result less from infectious diseases and more from unhealthy living conditions, such as indoor air pollution or lack of access to safe water and sanitation, which lead to water-borne and respiratory illnesses among children (UN-Habitat 2008).

Sub-Saharan Africa: Low urban poverty concentrated in the largest cities

An ongoing study of 12 Sub-Saharan African countries shows that although the poverty–city size gradient observed in African countries is similar to that seen in developing countries elsewhere, the African experience is different (Coulombe and Lanjouw 2013). Not surprising, poverty is a rural phenomenon in the region, with the share of the poor in rural areas ranging from 68 percent in the Central African Republic to 90 percent in Mali and Swaziland to 95 percent in Malawi. The urban poor are a small share of the total urban population, but unlike other regions, they are concentrated in large cities. Sub-Saharan Africa thus reflects a "largest city" model: the largest city accounts for a disproportionately large share of the total urban population and hence also for the bulk of the urban poor. For example, in the Central African Republic, Gabon, and Malawi, more than half of each country's urban poor live in the largest city, which is usually the capital. In Guinea, Niger, Senegal, Sierra Leone, and Swaziland, 40 percent of the urban poor live in the largest city. In most African countries, "urban" is synonymous with "largest city." In Malawi, Mali, and Togo, the combined population of the towns with 5,000–100,000 inhabitants account for just 2–6 percent of the total population. This pattern is different from other predominantly "rural" developing countries such as India and Vietnam. The primary reason for urban poverty's relative concentration in the capital city is the paucity of better-paying, nonfarm jobs in smaller towns. Rural migration to urban areas in Sub-Saharan Africa has stalled in large part because the structural transformation from agriculture to industry (manufacturing and services) has been slow to emerge. Manufacturing, especially agro-industry, and related service sectors account for only 10 percent of the economy in the region, and industries related to them generally locate in the largest city.

South and East Asia: High urban poverty concentrated in small towns

Despite their megacities and sprawling slums, urban poverty in South and East Asia is firmly located in smaller towns, not in big cities. The majority of the poor in South Asia reside in rural areas where the poverty rate was 38 percent in 2008. At 30 percent, the urban poverty rate was only 4 percentage points below that in Sub-Saharan Africa in the same year. But unlike Africa, poverty rates in smaller towns are significantly higher than in megacities.

Recent research in India, for example, indicates that poverty is still primarily a rural phenomenon at the aggregate level, but that urban poverty is growing and, within urban areas, is concentrated in smaller towns. The poverty rate in India in 2004–05 was 28 percent in rural areas and 26 percent in urban areas. As figure 2.4a shows, among urban areas, the poverty rate in small towns (population less than 50,000) was double the rate in large towns with a population of 1 million or more (30 percent to 15 percent) (World Bank 2011; Lanjouw and Marra 2012).

The poverty–city size gradient is steep in India, however, so even a "medium" city has close to 1 million residents. In Vietnam, in contrast, the population of an average medium-size town is about 85,000. In Vietnam, the nexus between urban population and urban poverty is mirrored in a remarkable U-shape (figure 2.4b). Two megacities, Hanoi and Ho Chi Minh, with a population of over 4 million each, are home to about 30 percent of urban residents but only about 10 percent of the poor. In comparison, the 634 smallest Vietnamese towns, with an average population of about 10,000, are home to more than 55 percent of the urban poor (World Bank 2011; Lanjouw and Marra 2012).

Small towns can play an important role in arresting the "urbanization" of poverty if

FIGURE 2.4   **In India and Vietnam, poverty in small towns is worse than in large cities**

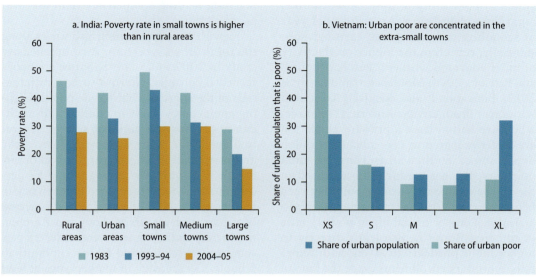

Source: World Bank 2011.
Note: Poverty rates based on Uniform Recall Period (URP) and official poverty lines.

Source: Lanjouw and Marra 2012.
Note: XS = > 4k – 50k; S = 50k – 300k; M = 300k – 500k; L = 1m–5m for centrally governed and 0.5m–1m for locally governed; XL = > 5m.

policies that nurture economic activity and improve residents' access to basic services are implemented. The reality of the poverty–city-size gradient shows that policies that improve service delivery and foster nonfarm job creation in small towns and peri-urban areas can offer rural migrants better livelihoods, thus helping to reduce both urban and rural poverty. In countries where population density is high in smaller towns, the scale economies may be sufficiently large to make service delivery, including infrastructure-related services, cost-effective.

More than 200 cities and towns dot Bangladesh and Pakistan, yet urbanization in both of these countries is dominated by a few large metropolitan cities with a population of more than 1 million. Chittagong and Dhaka account for 43 percent of Bangladesh's urban population; in Pakistan, eight cities each with a population of more than 1 million account for 58 percent of the urban population. Another 24 percent of the urban population in Pakistan resides in 48 cities with populations of 100,000 to 1 million. Evidence from these countries reveals that the incidence of poverty is highest in rural areas (43 percent),

followed by smaller towns and cities (38 percent), and then metropolitan areas (26 percent) (Deichmann, Shilpi, and Vakis 2009).

The MDGs, human capital, and disparities along the rural-urban spectrum

Not all MDG-related services have similar characteristics. Investments in primary education, nutrition, and health care lay the foundations for the human capital endowed in individuals, who can carry it with them when they move and add to it if they migrate to places where related secondary and tertiary services are available. In this sense, primary education and health care are portable.

Together, education, nutrition, and health care, combine to form human skills and abilities that have been powerfully linked to productivity growth and poverty reduction in the medium to longer run (Hanushek and Woessmann 2008; Commander and Svejnar 2011). As such, human capital is a fundamental ingredient for desirable job outcomes, in both rural and urban areas (World Bank 2013).

Primary education improves an individual's opportunity to join the workforce, regardless of location. An additional year of schooling can raise wage earnings substantially, reflecting the higher productivity of more educated workers (Psacharopoulos and Patrinos 2004; Montenegro and Patrinos 2012). Education is also positively associated with farm productivity. And rural migrants who have had at least a primary education are better prepared to take advantage of job opportunities in urban areas. For many rural migrants, the basic education acquired in the village can be the turning point between being prepared for a better-paying job upon arrival in a city or remaining in poverty once in the city. Better health leads directly to higher labor productivity. Gender differentials in primary enrollments erode the human capital foundations of women, putting them at a disadvantage compared with men in all aspects of human welfare but especially economic empowerment. Lack of gender equality in one dimension can multiply the negative effects on other dimensions. *World Development Report 2012: Gender Equality and Development* (WDR 2012) noted that in Mozambique low levels of maternal education are strongly related to high levels of child malnutrition and low use of health services.

Quality of primary education matters

East Asia and Pacific, Europe and Central Asia, and Latin America and the Caribbean have either already achieved or are close to achieving the MDG target of universal primary school completion by 2015. The differentials in primary school completion rates in rural and urban areas are surprisingly low across these regions (based on data from 46 countries) but mask enrollment shortfalls (see box 2.1). Gender differences in education, however, are also large in rural areas. In Sub-Saharan Africa, where rural enrollments are already low, gender differentials of 8–15 percentage points prevail in Cameroon, Côte d'Ivoire, Kenya, and Zambia.

The differentials in the *quality* of education, on the other hand, are greater: Urban

areas have a higher percentage of pupils reaching reading competency than do rural areas.

As with poverty, learning also varies along the rural-urban spectrum. A comprehensive study in 2007 in 15 Sub-Saharan countries recorded considerable rural-urban differentials in the share of sixth-grade pupils reaching competency levels in reading and mathematics relative to national scores. Several findings of the study were both noteworthy and worrisome. First, the rural-urban differentials were vast. On average, only 57 percent of rural students reached competency in reading levels 4–8 compared with 75 percent of urban students. In Malawi and Zambia, the corresponding figures were under 25 percent in rural schools and 40 percent in urban schools. Competency in mathematics at level 4 was discouragingly low: only 18 percent of children in rural schools and 24 percent in urban schools reached this level. Worse, only 1.2 percent of all pupils reached competency in mathematics level 8. Clearly, governments need to pay as much, if not more, attention to the quality of schooling in Sub-Saharan Africa as they do to completion rates (SACMEQ 2010).

Poor literacy (reading and writing) scores in rural Sub-Saharan Africa highlight the risk of overestimating the schooling benefits associated with urban living (figure 2.5). In a study of 12 Sub-Saharan African countries, the differentials in urban-rural literacy rates range from 32 percent–39 percent in 7 countries, and around 22 percent in another 2 countries. The differences between the small towns and large cities are small in several countries and are explained by the fact that the poverty city-size gradient is not as pronounced in Sub-Saharan Africa as in other regions (Coulombe and Lanjouw, 2013).

Children attending primary school in rural areas are often disadvantaged because it is difficult to attract teachers to rural areas. One study finds that many parents in rural schools complain that the schools do not have enough teachers. Parents also complain about high rates of teacher absenteeism (Wodon 2013a).

BOX 2.1   The link between primary enrollment and completion

A recent study permits a closer examination of progress toward primary school completion (Nguyen and Wodon 2013a). It demonstrates that completion rates need to be evaluated with more care. One way to look at differentials in education attainment structures between various households consists in calculating an attainment ratio for the completion of primary school, which is itself the result of a two-step process: starting primary school, and completing primary school for those who started it. This type of simple decomposition helps in assessing where exactly differences in attainment between gender, quintiles of well-being, or urban and rural areas take place. Rural-urban ratios estimated at each step of the process help to identify exactly where the main attrition takes place in the education system. The decomposition has been applied to a large number of African countries and in South Asia using Demographic and Household Survey (DHS) data (Nguyen and Wodon 2013b, 2013c).

Data for urban-rural enrollment in Bangladesh, India, Nepal, and Pakistan are set out in table B2.1. The share of those starting primary education is higher in urban areas, and the gap widens for the completion of primary school. As an example, the completion rate in rural Pakistan is 87 percent of the proportion of students who actually started primary school. This number may not seem overly worrisome until one considers that only 59 percent of the rural

TABLE B2.1.1   Measuring primary education, selected countries

Country	Share of children who start primary school	Share of starting children who complete primary school
Bangladesh		
Urban	90	84
Rural	84	75
India		
Urban	92	96
Rural	79	90
Nepal		
Urban	93	93
Rural	83	86
Pakistan		
Urban	82	95
Rural	59	87

Source: Nguyen and Wodon 2013b.

child population started school. The actual proportion of rural children completing primary school is 51 percent (0.59 x 0.87). Of the two steps that relate to primary education completion, which matters the most for disparities between urban and rural areas? Data on Indian states show that in about half of the states, the largest determinant of the gap is fewer students starting primary school in rural areas, while in the other half, completion is the issue.

Source: Nguyen and Wodon 2013b.

Rural-urban differentials in health indicators

"Successful development is so intimately related to health—to measures that directly or indirectly help individuals, households, or communities avoid or prevent disease, injury, and inadequate food intake" (Satterthwaite 2011). The foundations of good health start even before birth. Like basic education, the human capital formation of good health is cumulative and continues to be formed throughout childhood and young adulthood. Of crucial importance are adequate health and nutrition during "the first 1,000 days," from conception to two years of age (World Bank 2012a).

While many factors underlie the differences in rural and urban mortality rates, including differences in income, consumption, and wealth between urban and rural households, fertility rates and access to safe water, sanitation, and health services play a critical role.

Rural-urban differentials in access to primary health care are significant across all regions. Evidence from DHS surveys for a large number of developing countries indicates that urban infant mortality rates are 8–9 percentage points lower than the rural

FIGURE 2.5   Literacy rates in rural areas and smaller towns are worse than in large cities

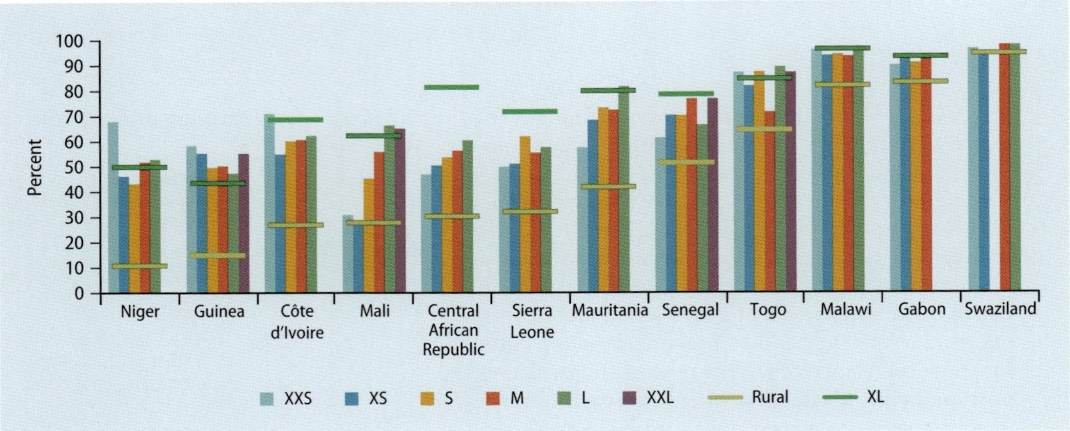

Source: Coulombe and Lanjouw 2013.

rates in Latin America, Europe and Central Asia, and 10–16 percentage points in the Middle East and North Africa, South Asia, and Sub-Saharan Africa. East Asia has the highest differential, at 21 percentage points. Individual country differences are more informative (figure 2.6).

A study of 40 Sub-Saharan African countries based on DHS data indicates that the infant mortality rate is 65 (per 1,000 live births) in urban areas and 80 in rural areas.

The percentage of deliveries in health facilities in urban areas is about 78 percent on average across the countries, compared with 43 percent in rural areas, in a sample of 28 Sub-Saharan Africa countries. The largest rural-urban differences are in some of the poorest countries (Wodon 2013b). Similar patterns are observed for measures of child malnutrition. Countries with the worst indicators for infant and child mortality also have the largest absolute differences between rural and urban areas. The average share of stunting in children is 42 percent in rural areas compared to 30 percent in urban areas (Wodon 2013b).

It is sometimes argued that other dimensions of poverty—health outcomes, for example—tend to be better in large cities. Analysis of anthropometric health outcomes for children across cities of different sizes in Mexico (based on small-area estimation

methods) suggests that the prevalence of child stunting in Mexico tends to be higher in small towns than in the largest cities (Ferre, Ferreira, and Lanjouw 2012). This corresponds with findings regarding poverty, which is more pronounced in smaller cities than in larger cities.

Understanding the broader economic consequences of closing health gaps in low-income countries

Most countries are lagging behind in all three health-related MDGs. It is therefore useful to quantitatively evaluate the broader economic consequences of closing health gaps in low-income countries. In a simulation exercise conducted for this report, the broader economic consequences of closing health gaps in low-income countries were explored by adapting maquette for MDG simulations (MAMS), a computable general equilibrium (CGE) model for country strategy analysis, to address the rural-urban aspects of MDG achievement (Lofgren 2013). The database used was designed to capture characteristics typical of low-income countries, including their MDG outcomes, sectoral shares in value-added of agriculture, manufacturing and services, degree of urbanization, and population growth. Annex 2A.1 presents the results of this exercise. The main results

FIGURE 2.6   Rural-urban differentials in infant mortality rates remain substantial

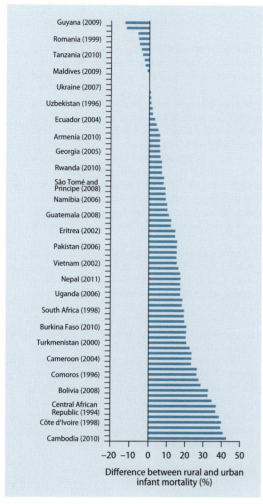

Source: GMR team 2013.

indicate that if the government can finance increased access to rural health care through a combination of borrowing and greater efficiency in health sector spending, it can considerably reduce rural under-five mortality. If the financing is a combination of grants and greater efficiency in health sector spending, government can do even more—it can reduce rural under-five mortality and contribute to other MDGs, including poverty reduction. If the government has to rely solely on domestic resources, however, then the trade-off is lower poverty reduction and less progress in

other MDGs. These trade-offs are especially difficult for governments in low-income countries.

Increasingly, governments are becoming interested in collaborating with the private sector or nongovernmental organizations (NGOs) to deliver services to the poor. Such partnerships can be instrumental in improving the delivery of health care, especially in South Asia, East Asia and Pacific, and Sub-Saharan Africa, where over 90 percent of the poor live (box 2.2).

Affordable access to sanitation and water: Infrastructure needs scale economies

In comparison to basic education and health care whose benefits are embedded in an individual's human capital, infrastructure needed to increase access to safe water and sanitation must be provided at a fixed spatial location. New or old connections in a rural area cannot be moved costlessly to an urban area. The initial fixed costs of establishing these services are high; routine maintenance is also costly. Because sparsely populated areas do not have sufficient population density, they are unable to benefit from scale economies that reduce the unit costs of network infrastructure services. As a result, residents in less agglomerated areas (typically, rural populations, very small towns, and less densely populated peri-urban areas) often receive a lower level of service (map 2.2).

The greatest rural-urban disparities in the delivery of MDG-related infrastructure services are in South Asia and Sub-Saharan Africa. In these two regions, access to sanitation among the rural population, which accounts for between 60–80 percent of the total population, is significantly lower than in most urban areas. This disparity would appear to be a combination of extreme poverty in the rural areas combined with the lack of network scale economies. In regions with higher proportions of their populations in urban areas, access to sanitation is higher in both urban and rural areas and the rural-urban differentials are much smaller.

BOX 2.2   Leveraging the private sector to reach the health-related MDGs

More than 90 percent of the poor live in South Asia, East Asia and Pacific, and Sub-Saharan Africa. In these three regions, the private sector provides at least 50 percent of the health services that the poor receive. Furthermore, delivery of priority health services by the private sector has been growing rapidly. For example, the proportion of women who delivered children in private facilities increased from 8 percent in 1990 to 22 percent in 2008.[a] Indeed, the private sector already plays and must continue to play an important role in many countries if they are to meet their health-related MDGs.

Some of the innovative mechanisms being pioneered around the world to leverage the private sector are:

- **Smart policies and regulations** with a dual approach to reaching the poor. On one hand, marketwide reforms such as simplifying licensing of health facilities and establishing enforceable patient safety and quality standards are expected to disproportionately benefit the poor. On the other, interventions explicitly target the poor and those private providers that serve them. In Kenya, for example, the World Bank and the International Finance Corporation (IFC) are helping the National Health Insurance Fund introduce poverty-targeted subsidized coverage. They are also working with the Ministry of Health to introduce the legal and regulatory framework for newly established local

governments to contract services from faith-based organizations and other nongovernmental organizations located in the hardest-to-reach areas of the country.

- **Public-private partnerships** that tap the capital, management capacity, and creativity of the private sector to improve public services. In India, the IFC helped the state of Meghalaya design an innovative insurance scheme whereby the government, a private sector insurer, and hundreds of surveyed public and private health care providers cooperated in a large-scale partnership to enhance financial protection and access to quality health care for the population of one of the lowest-income states in the country.

- **Capital finance** that fuels expansion of access to quality health services and products from the private sector. The IFC is investing in and advising health care companies seeking to expand access to quality health services and products to those at the "bottom of the pyramid."[b] In Africa, the IFC helped establish an innovative private equity fund that not only focuses on health but is also given explicit incentives to finance companies that serve the poorest. One such company is the Nairobi Women's Hospital. An independent assessment shows that about three-fifths of its patients are at the bottom of the pyramid. In India, IFC investee Apollo Hospitals is seeking to expand its top quality services to smaller cities and rural areas.

FIGURE B2.2.1   Percent seeking care in private versus public facilities by region

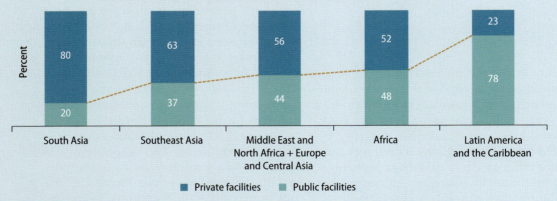

Source: Demographic and Health surveys.
Note: The figure shows the shares of health care facilities funded by public and private providers for the poorest quintile.
a. Karen Grepin, http://ps4h.org/ihea2011.
b. The bottom of the pyramid is defined as those with an annual household income of less than $3,000.

MAP 2.2   **Access to sanitation across regions**

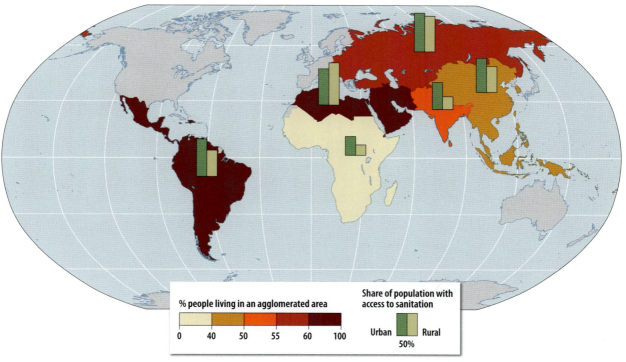

Source: GMR team 2013.
Note: The bars show the percent of regional urban and rural populations (developing countries only) with access to sanitation; the bars are not proportional to population size. For a definition of agglomeration, please see the note to map 2.1.

To the extent that infrastructure availability acts as a determinant of urban growth and poverty reduction, the imbalance of service availability could help explain lower welfare outcomes in smaller towns. For many of the 12 Sub-Saharan African countries shown in figure 2.7, the differences in access to sanitation between the largest cities and smaller towns are as stark as those between urban areas as a whole and rural areas. In Côte d'Ivoire, Guinea, Mauritania, and Sierra Leone, access to sanitation in the smallest towns is significantly lower than in larger cities. In Gabon, Malawi, Niger, and Swaziland, access in smaller towns is as good as it is in larger towns (Coulombe and Lanjouwe 2013).

All regions offer better access to safe drinking water in urban than in rural areas, although rural-urban differentials are shrinking (see MDG 7 in the report card, which

follows the overview). In 2010, 96 percent of the urban population in developing countries had access to safe drinking water compared to 81 percent of the rural population. In general, the rural-urban differentials in access to water diminish with the level of urbanization in most regions. The largest differentials (about 70 percent or higher) are in Ethiopia, Gambia, Niger, and Sierra Leone, which are mostly rural.

Through their density, urban areas make public services more accessible and affordable. For example, on average a cubic meter of piped water costs $0.70–$0.80 to provide in urban areas compared with $2 in sparsely populated areas (Kariuki and Schwartz 2005). As a result, the poor often pay the highest price for the water they consume while having the lowest consumption levels. For example, in Niger, the average price of a cubic meter of water cost CFAF 182 when it

FIGURE 2.7   **Small towns have generally poorer service delivery than large cities**

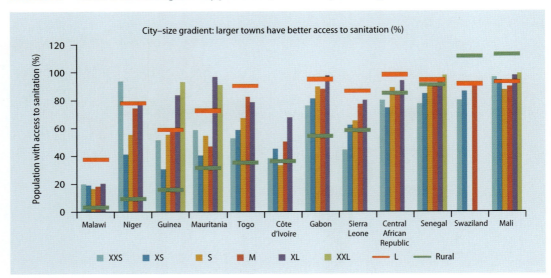

Source: Coulombe and Lanjouw 2013.
Note: XXS = < 5k; XS = 5k–10k; S = 10k–25k; M = 25k–50k; L = 50k–100k; XL = 100k–1m; XXL = > 1m.

was piped from a network, CFAF 534 when it came from a public fountain, and CFAF 926 when it came from a vendor (Bardasi and Wodon 2008). This means that the urban poor without access to the network often pay the highest price for the water they consume while having the lowest consumption levels. More than 55 percent of households did not have access to piped water in their dwelling. Having a private connection was strongly correlated with wealth: among the poorest 20 percent of households, none had a private connection, while 65 percent of households in the top quintile were connected.

Poor access to basic infrastructure disproportionately affects rural women by directly reducing the time they have available for income generating activities because they perform most of the domestic chores and often walk long distances to reach clean water. WDR 2012 on gender noted that in rural Guinea, women spend three and a half times more than men in fetching water. In several rural and small towns in Sub-Saharan Africa, where network connections are often not economically viable, public private partnerships

have been designed to leverage innovative means for delivering safe water (box 2.3).

Why urbanization matters for the MDGs

Urbanization matters for the MDGs. It can facilitate several factors that play an important role in attaining those goals. It can reduce poverty in two main ways: through the benefits of agglomeration, cities potentially generate higher living standards for all their residents and reduce urban poverty; and through the benefits of scale economies, public services, including those related to the MDGs can be provided in urban areas at a lower fixed unit cost. Cities are also a source of revenues that governments need to foster agglomeration economies for firms and households, and to finance services for rural and urban migrants. But when the positive forces driving cities are strained by urban congestion, service delivery is unable to keep pace with demand and slums can emerge. An important negative externality of excessive urban congestion is pollution.

BOX 2.3   Water in Africa: Strong public sector leadership is key to sustainable PPPs in rural and small towns

Public-Private Partnerships (PPPs) in nontraditional markets. Nontraditional markets, such as those in sparsely populated and dispersed settlements, present a challenge to making private sector participation a commercially viable proposition because of economies of scale and affordability issues. The experiences of Cambodia, Mali, Mozambique, the Philippines, Rwanda, Senegal, and Uganda have shown, however, that given the right allocation of risks among participants in the PPP, interest can be generated in the private sector. In many African countries, the private sector's role is mostly confined to operating rural water supply schemes, and generally small piped water schemes, serving households through a combination of private connections and standpipes. In India, the private sector is involved in higher value-added services, such as processing and disposal of solid waste. Success comes not just by helping develop PPP arrangements but also by strengthening the enabling legal, regulatory, financial, and institutional environment. In Sub-Saharan Africa, a number of governments have explicit policies for the delegation of water supply services to private operators, as in Benin, Burkina Faso, Mali, Mauritania, Mozambique, Niger, Rwanda, Senegal, and Uganda. Lease and management contracts are the most common types of contract today, whereby operators take commercial and operational responsibility, including for small repairs.

Key lessons from the field: Financial viability suggests the need to lower the cost of services in rural areas to drive consumption. Evidence suggests that a growing number of privately operated schemes are just able to achieve operating cost recovery, with a few making comfortable margins. What separates financial winners and losers? Analysis in Uganda found that the number of active connections was a strong positive determinant of financial cost recovery. More active connections translate to higher volumes of water sold, given that consumption tends to be higher from private house connections than standpipes. This observation captures the common issues across countries: the price of water and connections, rates of consumption, and economies of scale. In rural growth centers outside of small towns, the cost of service tends to be higher than in urban areas. Lowering the cost of service requires approaches that are usually not easy to coordinate or navigate politically and hence, they are typically not undertaken. These include subsidizing the densification of standpipes to bring them closer to household settlements or subsidizing the cost of house connections; and clustering schemes across different political/administrative boundaries to be managed by a single operator.

Holding local institutions accountable matters for the success of the partnership and for rehabilitation. Private sector participation in Africa is often an accompaniment to political devolution, which saw the responsibility for water services decentralized to the local level. This is the case in Benin, Burkina Faso, Mali, and Uganda. The role of local governments as the focal point between the state, consumers, and the private sector is critical. Often, however, transfer of authority for water services is incomplete and not well thought out. Uganda is unique as it has set up a dedicated and autonomous local body that represents the public sector in water services delivery. In contrast, most West African countries, such as Benin and Burkina Faso, expect the local communes (mayors) to take on oversight for water services as an additional mandate.

Source: Water and Sanitation Program, http://www.wsp .org/topics.

Agglomeration economies arise when there is a confluence of people, or population density, and firms, or economic density. The main outcome is the creation of jobs, which are central to poverty reduction and reaching MDG 1. According to the *World Development Report 2013: Jobs* (WDR 2013), in 26 countries across all regions, more than 50 percent of the reduction in poverty can be attributed to an increase in labor income (World Bank 2013).

Higher economic and population densities of urban areas are also good for governments. They generate tax revenues that are essential for financing the public goods necessary for poverty reduction.

Successful urbanization is reflected in dynamic cities that foster agglomeration economies. The latter thrive on large numbers of businesses and create plenty of jobs. Urbanization is a "win-win" recipe for poverty reduction when it generates higher incomes than workers would earn elsewhere, provides access to services essential for a decent livelihood, and creates opportunities for workers to enjoy higher standards of living.

The effects of urbanization on prosperity and poverty

According to *World Development Report 2009: Reshaping Economic Geography* (WDR 2009), it is not a coincidence that the high-income countries are more urbanized: "Place is the most important correlate of a person's welfare. . . . The best predictor of income in the world today is not *what* or *whom* you know, but *where* you work." Economic history shows that this has always been true. Before the Industrial Revolution, the world was a "rural" place, where

the differences in living standards between countries were minimal. England's Industrial Revolution unleashed a wave of industrialization that was necessarily grounded in cities or urban spaces. The mechanization of production was powered by economies of scale and a concentration of population available only in cities. Rapid industrialization was accompanied by increasing urbanization, which, in turn, nurtured agglomeration economies.

There is a nexus between urbanization, poverty, and prosperity (figure 2.8). Urbanization in developing countries can offer similar benefits to its citizens. Income per capita tends to rise as the share of the urban population rises. Urbanization rates above 70 percent are typically found in high-income countries, whereas those in poorer countries, such as Chad Ethiopia, Laos, and Uganda, are closer to 20–30 percent.

The relationship between the level of urbanization and poverty is negative. Countries with low levels of urbanization have significantly higher poverty rates than countries with high levels of urbanization (map 2.3). Rising urbanization is also positively related to increases in the share of gross domestic

FIGURE 2.8   **Nexus between urbanization, poverty, and prosperity**

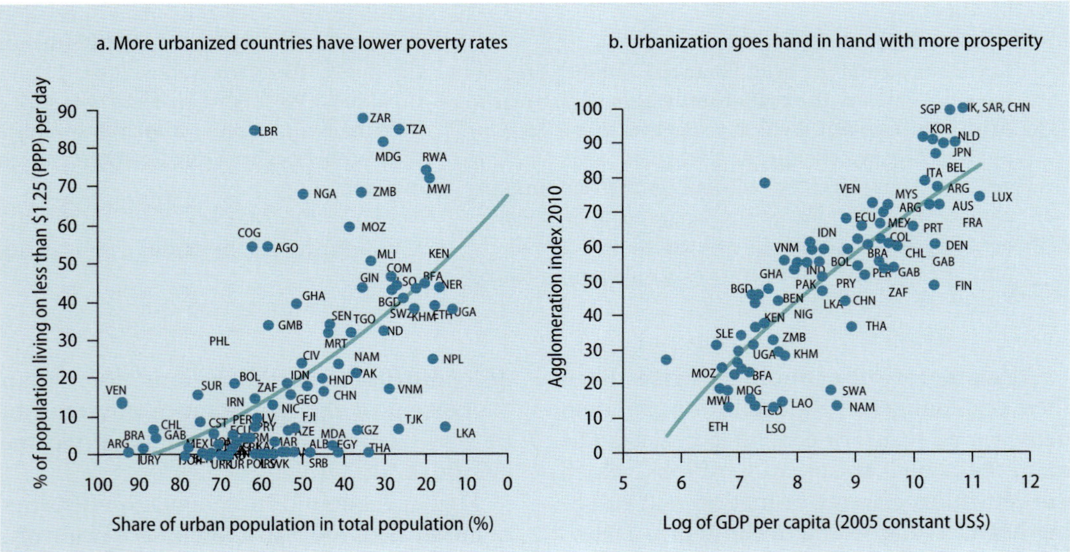

Source: GMR team 2013.
Note: PPP = purchasing power parity.

MAP 2.3   The poor are mostly concentrated in less urbanized countries

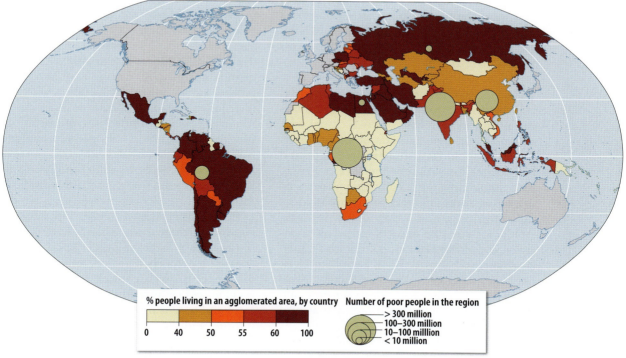

% people living in an agglomerated area, by country	Number of poor people in the region
0 40 50 55 60 100	> 300 million 100–300 million 10–100 milllion < 10 million

Source: GMR team 2013.
Note: For a definition of agglomeration, please see the note for map 2.1.

product (GDP) generated by industry and services as well as with the share of the labor force working in those sectors (Satterthwaite 2007). Indeed, together with complementary macroeconomic policies and an investment and business-friendly climate, urbanization is one of the important ingredients of a policy mix that fosters economic growth and prosperity.

The potential of urbanization to close the gender gap in earnings and enhance women's empowerment is enormous and rests to a large extent on women's access to education. Women earn less than men everywhere—in the informal sector, paid work, and farm and nonfarm jobs. WDR 2012 reports that wage differences by gender range from 20 percent in Mozambique and Pakistan to more than 80 percent in Jordan, Latvia, and the Slovak Republic. The emergence of agglomeration economies benefits poor women with basic education

through large-scale job opportunities in light manufacturing. The feminization of export industries that produce labor-intensive goods is prolific in countries such as Bangladesh, Cambodia, China, India, Laos, Lesotho, Nepal, and Vietnam. While the average share of female employment in manufacturing is 30 percent, it is as high as 56–66 percent in apparel and accessories, leather tanning and finishing, retail bakeries, and garments (Do, Levchenko and Raddatz 2011) that are also less skill intensive. In Bangladesh, Kabeer and Mahnud (2004) find that 1.5 million of the 1.8 million jobs created in export-oriented garment industries in 2000 went to women. According to WDR 2013, in the urban areas of India, the abundance of call center jobs for women is another source of women's economic empowerment but more than primary education is required for these jobs (World Bank 2012d). South Africa provides similar evidence (Levinsohn 2007). On average, women are more reliable remitters than men and form the backbone of rural household support in many cases (Vullnetari and King 2011; Piotrowski and Rindfuss 2006; Tacoli and Mabala 2010).

Urbanization has not always led to poverty reduction. In most countries, structural transformation from agriculture to manufacturing and services has been in lockstep with urbanization. Industrialization often begins in a light manufacturing export sector and has created large numbers of better-paying jobs, stimulating the urbanization process by attracting rural migrants to the urban areas (Chandra, Lin, and Wang 2013). In Latin America, where the share of the urban population is over 80 percent, quantitative analysis confirms that in 10 of 18 Latin American countries, changes in labor income explain more than half the reduction in poverty, and in another five countries, more than a third (World Bank 2013).

Sub-Saharan Africa's higher poverty rates and lower income levels have created a perception that African cities have grown larger without enjoying the attendant benefits of urbanization—better-paying jobs, prosperity, and higher standards of living. It appears that the advantages of urbanization set in only after it has reached a critical level: countries with urbanization rates of 40 percent or less have distinctly lower income levels and higher poverty rates (maps 2.4 and 2.5). They also have the largest rural-urban differentials, especially in access to basic services.

Links between urbanization and rural poverty

Urbanization and poverty reduction are linked in numerous ways. Rural-urban migration and nonfarm economic activity are two of them. Other intricate links between rural and urban sources of growth generate additional potential for poverty reduction.

The concentration of the rural population in agriculture has gone hand in hand with poverty in most developing countries. In developed countries, about 20 percent of the population lives in rural areas and 5 percent is dependent on agriculture for employment. In South Asia and Sub-Saharan Africa, more than half the labor force is employed in agriculture, mostly as unpaid family workers (figure 2.9). Indeed, in the absence of adequate safety nets, agriculture is an important fallback option for family members who lose their job to economic shocks or other crises. A consequence of limited job opportunities outside agriculture in low-income countries is that agriculture, by default, absorbs extra labor, which leads to underemployment, low labor productivity, and thus low farm incomes.

Economic growth is another link between rural and urban areas, where what happens in one area affects the other. Rural growth contributes to urban growth and vice versa, but rural growth cannot occur without good access to (urban) markets and vibrant farm and nonfarm activities. Successful land reforms and the green revolution in agriculture preceded East Asia's rapid population and economic growth in urban areas (with some exceptions, such as the Republic of Korea) (Gollin 2009; Mellor 1996). Rural growth helped to lower food prices and real wages for urban areas and created demand for urban goods. Rising income in rural areas allowed rural households to invest in their own businesses and in their children's health and education, better preparing them for their future. This cycle is not happening as fast in Sub-Saharan Africa and South Asia, where rural poverty is most pervasive.

A large literature documents how lack of market access adversely affects agricultural productivity as well as commercialization and specialization. Da Mata et al. (2007) found that the growth of cities in Brazil was positively associated with market potential in surrounding rural areas (measured by rural per capita income weighted by distance). Using household data from Nepal, Emran and Shilpi (2012) analyzed the relationship between market size, defined as the size of the population in a certain area, and the distance of that area to the closest market. They found that the crop portfolio of a village becomes

MAP 2.4   Level of urbanization in 1990

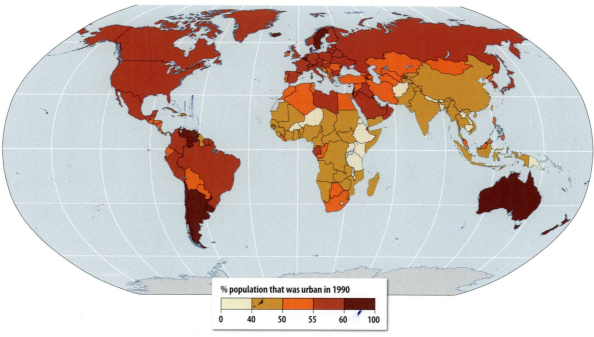

% population that was urban in 1990

0   40   50   55   60   100

Source: GMR team 2013.
Note: For the definition of "urban" please see UN 2011.

MAP 2.5   Level of urbanization in 2010

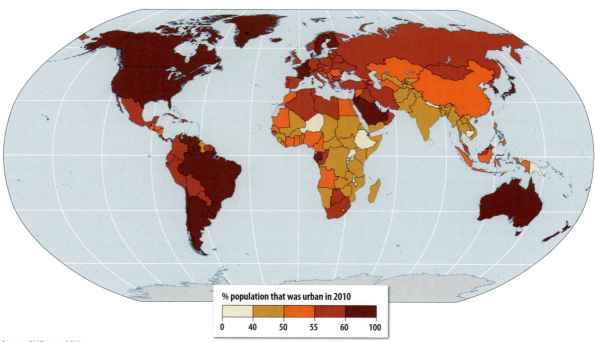

% population that was urban in 2010

0   40   50   55   60   100

Source: GMR team 2013.
Note: For the definition of "urban" please see UN 2011.

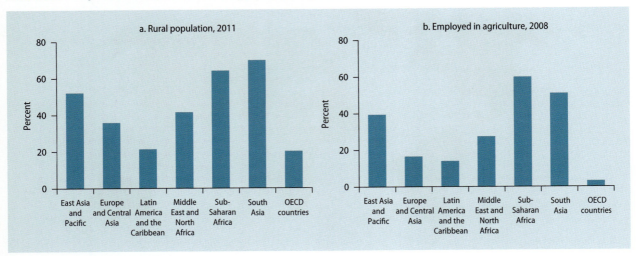

a. Rural population, 2011 / b. Employed in agriculture, 2008

Source: GMR team 2013.
Note: OECD = Organisation for Economic Co-operation and Development.

more diversified with a decrease in the size of the market up to a threshold, after which it becomes specialized. They also found that agricultural commercialization increased with a decline in the distance to a market.

Rural-urban migration

In most developing countries, especially low-income ones, urban areas symbolize many good things. They offer better jobs, sufficient food for children, a respite from toiling on a farm without a decent income, safe drinking water, and shorter distances to doctors and other health care facilities. These attributes explain why people from rural areas are "pulled" to cities. The "pull" effects, which work through the dynamics of rural-urban migration, are an important source of reductions in rural poverty. Through the natural movement of people, migration has the potential to move large numbers of poor people to urban areas where they have better economic opportunities and access to basic services. In countries where urban areas have benefited from structural transformation, rural-urban migration has been instrumental in moving large numbers of the rural poor to the cities. The extent to which migration

alleviates rural poverty depends upon a variety of factors.

In Sub-Saharan Africa, poverty remains for now a predominantly rural phenomenon, but rural to urban migration is playing a prominent role in reducing overall poverty. In Kagera, a region in northwestern Tanzania, between 1991–94 and 2010, more than 50 percent of the rural population migrated to urban areas (Beegle, De Weerdt, and Dercon 2011). For more than 45 percent of male but only 15 percent of female migrants, the main motivation was to find better-paying work. In the same study, Beegle, De Weerdt, and Dercon (2011) looked at consumption levels of residents of the Kagera region, where agricultural production of food and a few cash crops are the mainstay for more than 80 percent of rural residents. On average, they found that over 19 years, consumption increased by more than 40 percent for residents who remained in Kagera, but for those who left, consumption tripled. Nearly all migrants escaped poverty, but poverty declined only modestly for those who remained in rural Kagera.

Several studies have estimated the magnitude of rural-urban migration for one or more regions but a global study that provides consistent estimates for all regions is not available. Demographic and Health Surveys indicate that in 26 of the 46 countries with data on female migrants, rural-rural migration is the most common type and tends to be highest in Africa. Rural-rural migration is also most common among male migrants in another seven countries, mostly located in Africa (UN-Habitat 2008). These results are supported by the Kagera region study, which puts a 50 percent estimate on rural-urban migration. New research from long-term longitudinal data for India finds evidence of migration rates of about 34 percent in comparison to rates of 55–80 percent in the past 20 years for China (Dercon, Krishnan, and Krutikova forthcoming).

Poor people are willing to move to gain access to basic services. Poor people already pay for access to services in rural areas, and they are also willing to pay for them in urban areas. Their desire to access better education and health services to enrich their families' human capital and future income is a motivation for moving to urban areas. Lall, Timmins, and Yu (2009) combined a rich data set of public services at the municipality level with individual records from four decades of Brazilian census data to evaluate the relative importance of wage differences and public services in migrants' decisions to move. Their findings showed a clear distinction in preferences according to income level: for relatively well-off people, basic public services were not important in the decision to move, but for the poor, differences in access to basic public services did matter. In fact, Brazilian minimum wage workers earning an average R$7 an hour (about US$2.30 in February 2008), for example, were willing to pay R$420 a year to have access to better health services, R$87 for a better water supply, and R$42 for electricity.

One reason for not migrating or migrating only to the nearest small town is the desire to remain close to rural support systems. Informal barriers such as language, ethnicity, and religious differences also impede migration. For example, Munshi and Rosenzweig (2009) found that strong mutual assistance networks among subcaste groups in the place of origin strongly discourage migration in India. Much of the migration in India is from rural to rural areas because more than half the migrants are women who move primarily for family reasons (marriage). Work is the primary reported motivation for migration for men. In some countries, higher costs of living in the larger cities can be a deterrent.

Two important factors that can facilitate rural-urban migration, as well as benefit the overall economy, are investment in education and health and the removal of direct and indirect restrictions on labor mobility. Education helps give workers the skills they need to compete for well-paying jobs; good health helps workers be their most productive; and labor mobility helps balance the supply of and demand for labor. Other factors that can encourage migration include proximity to paved roads and areas with higher housing prices or rents which reflect a premium for the provision of better services.

When migrants move to cities primarily for better access to services ("push effects"), congestion in cities can worsen urban poverty, and lead to the creation or expansion of slums. Migrants who move in the hope of finding better jobs ("pull factors"), and who have the human capital necessary to find a better job make a positive contribution to the process of urbanization. In this context, if people are migrating from villages to gain access to services (such as electricity or sanitation), policy makers can prioritize provision of these services in areas where it is less costly to provide them. In Nepal, where limited agricultural potential in the hills and mountains makes migration an important livelihood strategy, migrants also value proximity to paved roads because it is easier for them to travel back and forth between their families in rural areas and their jobs in urban areas (map 2.6). Paved roads reduce the time and costs of accessing schools, health facilities, and markets. Migrants are willing to accept lower wages to get access to better services (Fafchamps and Shilpi forthcoming; Lall, Timmins, and Yu 2009).

Many governments have placed restrictions on rural-urban migration in an effort

MAP 2.6   Travel time to the nearest city in Nepal

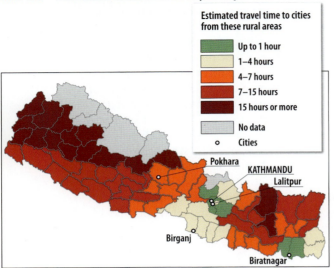

Source: GMR team 2013.
Note: Migrants in villages and small towns (population less than 100,000; orange, red, and bur-
gundy) migrate to markets in cities (population greater than 100,000, marked with a black circle).
The map shows the travel time to the closest city; travel time is calculated using the existing road
network (travel speed can vary by road type and terrain). When there are no roads, informal tracks
or trails are used for foot travel.

to preempt overcrowding in cities. These restrictions prevent the rural poor from benefiting from the advantages of urbanization. However, migration cannot be leveraged uniformly by policy makers to equalize the benefits of urbanization between rural and urban areas in every country. Higher population density in cities can accelerate scale economies that make the extension of basic network services (piped water, sewers) more affordable for resource-constrained governments. However, in countries in South Asia, where rural-urban migration is low, its equalizing potential will be limited.

The removal of official direct and indirect restrictions on labor mobility can help to reduce poverty and improve access to the basic services emphasized in the MDGs. Restrictions in the land market are detrimental not only to agricultural productivity growth but also hinder diversification into nonfarm activities that have higher returns. Evidence from Mozambique and Uganda suggests that free mobility of labor can eliminate

welfare differences between rural and urban areas for unskilled and poorer workers and households (Dudwick et al. 2011). Many developing countries have in place land market policies in rural areas to discourage migration to urban areas but these tend to worsen poverty. Migration is officially restricted in a large number of developing countries, including Ethiopia and Vietnam. In China, the free movement of people from the countryside to the city was restricted under the hukou system that was established in 1958 (Au and Henderson 2006a, 2006b). In 2012, restrictions on migration to all urban areas except the large cities of China were abolished. To discourage migration from rural areas, many countries simply do not provide basic water and sanitation services to poorer urban areas, often the first destination of rural migrants. For example, governments in the richer and larger localities in an urban area in Brazil reduce provision of water and sewerage connections to the smaller houses in which poorer migrants would live to discourage in-migration and deflect migrants to other localities (Feler and Henderson 2011).

Economic growth is often concentrated geographically and described as being located in a leading region complemented with a lagging region where growth is stagnant. MDGs' related issues in leading and lagging regions are quite similar to those for rural and urban areas. In Uganda, where the leading lagging region issue surfaces in policy discussions, the test the government faces is to allow, if not encourage, the concentration of economic activity while achieving a convergence of living standards and delivery of basic services like the MDGs across a geographical area (box 2.4).

Nonfarm employment and rural poverty

Rural areas also undergo profound transformation as rural workers move out of agriculture to nonfarm activities. Indeed, throughout the developing world, nonfarm sectors have been becoming increasingly important

BOX 2.4   Is the policy agenda different for leading-lagging regions? The case of Uganda

Economic growth, often concentrated geographically, can lead to specialization, and can induce migration. Certain regions thus lead economically, while other regions lag, creating a challenge for economic and social development. Governments face a test to allow, if not encourage, the concentration of economic activity while achieving a convergence of living standards and delivery of basic services like the MDGs across space.

Uganda realized that its development path is dominated by these types of challenges. Uganda has made commendable progress in reducing income poverty at the national level, but there are gaps with some geographical pockets (lagging regions) not improving as much as others (leading regions). The Midnorth, Northeast, and West Nile regions are lagging behind in the incidence of poverty compared to the national average. Kampala is well ahead of other regions, with the poverty head count declining from 14 percent to 4 percent between 1992 and 2010. Similar differentials are observed for other measures of welfare. Consequently, in collaboration with the World Bank, the government of Uganda is trying to prioritize policies that generate the highest payoff for economic efficiency and provide geographic equity at the same time (World Bank 2012b).

The process began by identifying four policy areas that can make possible the integration of lagging and leading regions. The first is facilitating integration through *better labor mobility,* which emphasizes equipping people with a minimum level of education and skills so they are able to take on the more demanding jobs in the leading regions. The second one is *making land, a physically immobile asset, more fluid* and its tenure more secure, allowing farmers to raise productivity within agriculture and to facilitate labor movement from agriculture to nonagricultural activities, as leasing and renting of land becomes feasible. One important policy action identified in Uganda is the development of a well-functioning system of conflict and dispute resolution through a clear legal and institutional framework to promote security and encourage development of the rental market. The third policy area is to support integration through *improved connectivity,* which allows for improved mobility of people, products, and technology. Isolation can confine producers to small markets and restrict them to inputs available in their geographic location. By enhancing connectivity, producers and firms can increase market size and consequently their ability to exploit economies of scale, draw from a larger pool of workers, and have greater access to raw materials and equipment. Finally, underpinning effectiveness of these areas of focus is *broadening coverage, quality, and accessibility of MDG-related social services across leading and lagging regions.* This will empower people seeking economic opportunity and reduce congestion costs resulting from migration in search of access to social services in leading areas.

Not surprisingly, the expected impact of public expenditure on development needs to guide Uganda's policy makers in their decisions on prioritizing and sequencing the various policies competing for the limited resources available. For instance, geographical prioritization of investments in (social and physical) infrastructure is complicated if the trade-offs between economic efficiency and welfare gains are taken into account. On one hand, economic returns suggest that investing in physical- or place-specific economic infrastructure should be prioritized in leading areas to exploit economies of scale and agglomeration, build density, and accelerate growth. As in many other countries, Uganda firms locate where they can benefit from agglomeration economies, suggesting prioritization of investments in infrastructure where these clusters are already forming in the southern-eastern corridor of Uganda. On the other hand, investments in social infrastructure yield positive returns across all regions, emphasizing the need for equitable provisions of social services across geographical space.

This policy focus is not much different from the policy agenda advocated in this GMR; that agenda facilitates progress toward the MDGs through better use of policies that assist the urbanization process given the advantages that urban areas have regarding income and thus poverty and MDG-related outcomes that are linked to better service delivery in urban areas.

sources of employment and income in rural areas (Lanjouw and Lanjouw 2001; Haggblade, Hazell, and Dorosh 2007). The nonfarm sector accounts for 25–50 percent of rural employment in South Asian countries. In eight Sub-Saharan African countries, Fox and Sohnesen (2012) estimated that the nonfarm sector accounted for 20–33 percent of total rural employment.

On average, returns to labor are higher from nonfarm activities than from farming, and the incidence of poverty is lower among households with access to nonfarm employment than among households wholly dependent on agriculture (for an example, see Foster and Rosenzweig 2004).

The agglomeration economies associated with urbanization strongly affect the location of nonfarm activities. Manufacturing and salaried nonfarm jobs in developing countries usually follow specialization patterns (von Thunen 1966). Salaried and wage jobs, including administrative work (such as clerks and managers), are concentrated within and around large cities and decline precipitously within 3–4 hours travel time from the city (Fafchamps and Shilpi 2003, 2005). The concentration of better paid nonfarm activities near larger cities is confirmed for Bangladesh (Deichmann, Shilpi, and Vakis 2009) and Indonesia (Yamauchi et al. 2011).

Growth of nonfarm activities is often driven by growth in agricultural productivity in the initial stage because of production, consumption, and labor market links between the farm and nonfarm sectors (Haggblade, Hazell, and Dorosh 2007). Smaller towns in the vicinity of rural areas are usually the most popular locations for nonfarm activities. However, nonfarm economic opportunities that can alleviate rural and small town poverty fail to emerge if access to markets in large urban centers do not exist. Deichmann, Shilpi, and Vakis (2009) found that lack of connectivity is doubly damaging for areas with higher agricultural potentials in Bangladesh. It not only depresses growth in agricultural productivity but also discourages growth of better-paying nonfarm activities directly and indirectly (because of

agricultural linkages). Other factors that foster nonfarm activity include education (Lanjouw and Lanjouw 2001; World Bank 2007; Haggblade, Hazell, and Reardon 2007; Fox and Sohnesen 2012) and access and reliability of electricity. Lack of reliable electricity is found to be among the topmost constraints to nonfarm activity in rural areas and small towns in Bangladesh, Indonesia, Sri Lanka, Tanzania, and many more countries, according to the World Bank–International Finance Corporation Investment Climate Surveys.

Closing the gender gap in basic education can boost rural women's empowerment by increasing agricultural incomes. Farm productivity rises when farms are managed by more educated and experienced individuals (Alene and others 2008; Kumar 1994; Moock 1976; Saito, Mekonnen, and Spurling 1994). WDR 2012 indicates that the potential to leverage women's education to boost productivity on female-managed farms is large. Relative to male farmers, female farmers have lower productivity which can be measured in crop yield gaps that average around 20–30 percent in Benin, Ethiopia, Ghana, Kenya, Malawi, and Nigeria. In Europe and Central Asia and Latin America and the Caribbean, productivity differentials of about 34 percent between female- and male-managed farms prevail.

Land market restrictions deter diversification into nonfarm activities. Do and Iyer (2008) reported that land reforms in Vietnam had a positive and significant effect on long-term investment in agriculture and on the time devoted to nonfarm activities. Ethiopia (Deininger et al. 2003) and Sri Lanka (Emran and Shilpi 2011) are examples of countries where land sales are restricted and where rural employment has not diversified into nonfarm activities.

Research in India suggests that urbanization is associated with rural nonfarm employment and thereby with rural poverty reduction. Earlier studies showed that urban growth had an impact on urban poverty but no discernible impact on rural poverty (Datt and Ravallion 1996). A recent study found that while rural growth remains vital for rural poverty reduction, urban economic growth has also been good for rural and hence aggregate poverty reduction since 1991 (Datt and Ravallion 2009; Cali and Menon 2012). Multiple mechanisms can account for this link. The first and obvious channel is the first-round effects of urban growth that induce migration of poor people in rural areas to urban areas. A second channel is that in rural areas population density can increase such that they become classified as urban. If these rural areas had significant concentrations of poor people before reclassification, then rural poverty becomes automatically urban poverty. The incidence of rural poverty in a district decreases by some 2–3 percent with an increase of 200,000 urban residents in the district (Cali and Menon 2012). This effect stems from reclassification, not migration. Numerous other second-round effects are possible when urban growth increases the demand for rural goods or leads to growth in marketing, transport, and agricultural trade or to remittance incomes from urban to rural areas. Diversification out of agriculture in rural areas may also raise agricultural wages as rural labor markets tighten. The World Bank (2011) reports that growth in per capita consumption in urban areas in India is associated with growth in rural nonfarm employment.

Policy makers can leverage nonfarm activities that typically connect rural areas to small towns to reduce poverty in both. For this, they need to focus on the provision of connectivity between rural areas, small towns and large cities, electricity provision in rural areas and small towns, and establishment of an efficient land market.

Small towns and delivery of MDG-related services

The role of small towns in urbanization is of importance in achieving progress toward the MDGs. Urbanization is usually equated with better access to basic services that enable the poor to have a decent livelihood. But, as discussed earlier in this chapter, urban areas

are not homogenous and the advantages and disadvantages of urbanization are not distributed evenly: some city locations are better served than others. In general, megacities and large cities offer the best services, smaller towns have the next best, and slums and rural areas tend to have the worst access as well as the lowest quality of services. Both slums and small towns contribute to the urbanization of poverty. Attention to the small town-large city differentials in urban poverty has shed light on small town poverty as a critical challenge to poverty reduction.

The presumption has long been that poverty-reducing policies should focus on urban growth in cities. However, if urban poverty is more concentrated in smaller towns, then the singular use of poverty-alleviating measures in larger towns may be neutralized or even overwhelmed by worsening poverty in smaller towns. The places where the poor live may not necessarily be the least-cost locations for extending coverage of piped water and sanitation, or for building a school or hospital or health clinic. These differentials can play a pivotal role in determining the coverage, efficiency, and costs of MDG related service delivery.

Urbanization, congestion, and slums

Typically, slums emerge in cities when the demand for services outpaces supply. That can happen through natural increases in the urban population, in rural-urban migration, or both. Slums can be a transient home for some, and a permanent one for others.

There is no technical definition of a slum, but in 2002, the UN-Habitat Expert Group put forth a description of slums that included several indicators: "a group of individuals living under the same roof in an urban area with at least one of the following four basic shelter deprivations: lack of access to improved water supply; lack of access to improved sanitation; overcrowding (three or more persons per room); and dwellings made of nondurable material." A fifth indicator is insecurity of tenure, but insufficient data

FIGURE 2.10 **Proportion of urban population living in slums, 1990–2010**

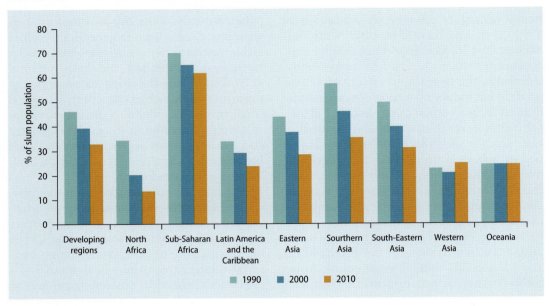

Source: UN-Habitat 2010.

prevents this dimension from being formally included in estimates of slums.[5]

In developing countries, where all five indicators are often found together, extreme deprivation occurs. Given that the two poorest regions, Sub-Saharan Africa and South Asia, are the farthest behind on access to safe water and sanitation, it is no surprise that they also house a large proportion of their urban population in slums (figure 2.10). Poorly functioning land and housing markets, lack of urban planning, and exclusionary attitudes toward the urban poor are the main reasons why the urban poor are forced to reside in low-quality housing on insecure land with few or no basic services (Baker 2008). Insecurity of tenure takes on complex forms in situations where slum populations represent a mix of owners, squatters, and renters.

Slum settlements may have differing degrees of marginalization depending on the recognition of their status by the government. Slums may actually serve the urban poor by offering low-cost housing and potential proximity to work. Slum settlements can also be the basis for self-employment and operation of small home-based businesses.

Lack of basic services in cities is often tied to insecure tenure. According to the United Nation's *MDG Report 2012*, slum evictions without due legal process are the most visible violation of housing rights confronted by the urban poor. Slum evictions have increased significantly since 2000. For example, in Jakarta in 2003/04 more than 100,000 people were either evicted or threatened with eviction as part of an effort to clear various areas of informal occupation. In Beijing, an estimated 300,000 people lost their homes as a result of preparations for the 2008 Olympic Games (Du Plessis 2005).

While slum and informal settlements may provide an entry point into cities in the short run, they are likely to have negative impacts on the conditions of the urban poor in the medium and long term. A lack of government intention to provide basic services in slum settlements does not necessarily deter urban poor and rural migrants for whom slums are the only entry point into urban areas. It does, however, negatively affect their

---

BOX 2.5   Costs of coping with lack of water service

In Bangladesh, in the absence of state-provided services, a parallel network of service providers known as *mastaans* provides the needed services for high fees, with patronage from politicians and law enforcement agencies. Based on interviews with government agencies and nongovernmental organizations, a World Bank (2007) report noted that the *mastaans* exploited slum residents not only by demanding high rates for the provision of basic services but also by using physical force and threats of eviction when pay-offs were not made.

Such instances are not limited to Bangladesh. Water sold at water kiosks in informal settlements in Eldoret, Kenya, costs more than five times what residents in the formal urban areas of Eldoret pay the municipal council for water (Kimani-Murage and Ngindu 2007). Karuiki and Schwartz (2005) analyzed data from 47 countries (93 locations) and found that the average water prices charged by private vendors compared with the public network were four and a half times higher for point sources (ranging from a simple connection to a standpost or kiosk and tap to a borehole with tank, pipe and tap) that are most commonly found in peri-urban or unplanned settlements with unclear tenure.

These higher costs of access to water associated with the use of informal providers not only increase expenditures of slum households but may also increase costs related to ill health. In Indonesia, the use of low-priced drinking water of lesser quality from informal providers by slum families was associated with considerably higher infant and under-five mortality as well as child morbidity (Semba et al. 2009). The lack of safe water provision in urban slums has far-reaching implications and threatens the progress of MDGs related to poverty eradication and child health.

---

economic situation if they have no choice but to rely on private and informal providers for provision of basic services at higher cost than those provided by the government to other strata of the society (box 2.5). Eviction from slums can drastically affect the livelihood of the residents by spatially displacing them from the proximity of their livelihoods, creating higher transportation costs. Because slums are also sites of economic production for small business enterprises, slum evictions and demolitions can also destroy livelihoods (Mehra, Maik, and Rudolf 2012; Du Plessis 2005). Given the lack of access to insurance or secure savings, such losses can create dire economic conditions for the urban poor. Slum dwellers often cope with these problems by discontinuing the education of children, especially girls.

More significantly, the lack of legal recognition of slum settlements translates into poor access to basic services, especially water and sanitation, for those living in slums. For example, more than 50 percent of the slum population in South Asia and 40 percent in Sub-Saharan Africa lack access to sanitation services (UN-Habitat 2010). In the slums of Nairobi, there is one toilet for every 500 people on average. (There are, however, some encouraging though rare examples to redress the lack of toilets, including an initiative in Agra, India, described in box 2.6). Governments are reluctant to provide basic services to slum settlements with insecure tenure, for fear such actions will encourage further urban poor settlement on unoccupied lands and invite rural migrants to migrate to cities in expectation of better services (Durand-Lasserve 2006). According to the *World Population Policies Report* (UN 2011), in 1976, 44 percent of developing countries reported having implemented policies to restrict or retard rural-urban migration; by 2011, that proportion had increased to 72 percent. Further, the inability of migrants to prove urban residence via water or electricity bills or formal rental leases in slums, along with their informal employment, makes their situation even more precarious. In some countries, proof of urban residence is needed to

BOX 2.6   Catalyzing citywide development though toilet design in the slums of Agra, India

The city of Agra is making news with a community-driven, nongovernmental organization (NGO)-facilitated, and local government-supported initiative that has made toilets an entry point for catalyzing housing, slum, and city development. In the slums of Agra, the user-toilet ratio is as high as one seat for every 345 to 1,000 users. Personal toilets are a luxury for several reasons. Poor families with little savings or access to affordable formal credit are unable to invest in building a toilet (the initial investment is estimated to be equivalent to up to six months of a poor household's earnings in Agra). Lack of space in small and temporary slum structures makes it impossible to construct a toilet using conventional technology. Plus, technical knowhow is lacking to make the connection to a sewer line (usually far away from a slum) or to a safe underground septic tank connected to a conveyance system. Women, who are disproportionately affected by the lack of toilets, have little influence on spending decisions to construct a toilet. But the biggest constraint is the insecure tenure of slums. Local bodies are reluctant to permit construction of permanent structures for the fear of legitimizing their stay.

The Centre for Urban and Regional Excellence (CURE), an Indian NGO, has approached the lack of private toilets for slum dwellers using a four-cornered strategy: enabling women to be the decision makers; creating access to credit and technical knowhow; designing, improving, customizing, and stabilizing the technology with last mile connections; and enhancing local capacities to address organizational, governance, and scaling-up restraints. Toilet Savings Groups of CURE enable women to save and set aside money for construction. The balance comes from a Community Credit Fund, repaid in small installments, and the money revolves to other toilet-less families. While the plumbing and collection and conveyance system is mandatory, women can choose to make the housing, such as walls, roof, and doors,

from less permanent materials to save costs. State permissions and reformed local bylaws are encouraging more families to invest in toilets.

Toilet designs were customized to suit the slum environment; for example, septic tanks were retrofitted and strengthened in partnership with a local manufacturer that was also trained to install the full toilet on a turnkey basis for long-term sustainability. Surface drains were improved to convey septic tank overflows to the city drain, where the city's first Decentralized Waste Water Treatment System (DEWAT) was built with support from international donors and the Agra Municipal Corporation. This model is being replicated in the Savda Ghevra resettlement colony in Delhi. To simultaneously ensure environmental safety and convey toilet waste away from homes, cluster septic tanks were designed below neighborhood parks and linked to DEWAT to treat the water, which could then be recycled for flushing. The community in Savda Ghevra contributes a small monthly amount to pay for annual maintenance of common septic tanks but also profit by way of sale of composted sludge, money that is reinvested in the community.

The success of these toilets in Agra has begun to catalyze housing upgrades. For temporary shacks, a core house design using columns is enabling the poorest to have a toilet and build a stable structure around it incrementally from small savings or housing finance. Local government in Agra has seen this as an opportunity to improve the city's overall sanitation and has developed an inclusive city development strategy to help build and retrofit 4,000 slum toilets, intercepting their direct sewage discharge into drains, and transporting it through appropriate channels. Ultimately, this will restore Agra's now sewage-choked storm water drainage system.

Source: Dr. Renu Khosla, Director, Centre for Urban and Regional Excellence (CURE), India.

access basic services. A qualitative study of the Kyrgyz Republic found that without proof of urban registration status, rural migrants faced difficulty accessing treatment at health clinics, and many no longer seek

health services assuming that they will not be treated (Nasritdinov 2007).

Substandard housing or illegal and inadequate building structures are another housing-related marker of slums. Overcrowding and high density worsen service delivery when the one tap or toilet supplied to a dwelling has to be shared by many. Overcrowding is associated with a low space per person, high occupancy rates, cohabitation by different families, and a high number of single-room units. Many slum dwelling units have five or more persons sharing one room used for cooking, sleeping, and living.

Slums dwellings may be built in hazardous locations or on land unsuitable for settlement, such as floodplains, in proximity to industrial plants with toxic emissions or waste disposal sites, or in areas subject to landslides. The layout of the settlement may be hazardous because of a lack of access ways and high densities of dilapidated structures. Lack of basic services is manifested by visible, open sewers, a lack of pathways, uncontrolled dumping of waste, and polluted environments.

Slums and child morbidity and mortality go hand in hand. A slum household can be one or two times more at risk when it is extremely deprived than when it is affected by only one deprivation. For example, in Ouagadougou, the proportion of children with diarrhea in slum areas is 20 percent, whereas those children living with three shelter deprivations are two times more exposed (37 percent) and those with four shelter deprivations are two and a half times more at risk. Likewise in Harare, the capital of Zimbabwe, children in slum households suffering from two shelter deprivations are five times more exposed to diarrhea than children in slum households with only one shelter deprivation (UN-Habitat 2008).

A Nairobi Urban Health and Demographic Surveillance Site study indicates that slum children bear the biggest burden of poor environmental sanitation and housing conditions and poor quality health services. Data from this study show that diarrhea and pneumonia are the leading causes of death among children under five and that the mortality burden among these children is four times higher than in the rest of the population (Kyobutungi et al. 2008). High mortality levels are not

surprising given that children in slums have exceptionally low levels of vaccination—only 44 percent are fully immunized) (Mutua and Kimani-Murage 2011). These slum children were also found to have exceptionally high levels of malnutrition and a high prevalence of infectious diseases, with little access to curative health care (Ndugwa and Zulu 2008).

In overcrowded and underserviced urban slums, the lack of basic sanitation and safe water is an acute problem for women and girls. Migration from rural to urban areas can increase women's opportunities to access better reproductive health care, education, and livelihoods, but these benefits need to be weighed against the negative consequences of the possibility of living in a slum (Mora 2008). Many wait until dark to relieve themselves, often confronting harassment and even sexual assault when defecating in public. Because women carry a heavier burden of household chores (including cleaning, washing, and caring for children), the lack of water and sanitation provision in slums affects them disproportionately more than men (Tacoli and Mabala 2012).

This disproportionate burden on women has important implications for attaining the MDGs. A recent study of 5,033 migrant women living in makeshift slum settlements in India found a strong relationship between reproductive tract infections and lack of access to proper sanitation (Singh, Kandpal, and Roy 2011). A lack of gender-balanced approaches to sanitation also has significant impact on MDGs related to the education of adolescent girls. Poor sanitation is a leading determinant of adolescent girl dropouts (MoE Kenya 2011; FAWE 2006; Obonyo 2003). A UNICEF study in urban Bangladesh found that a simple school sanitation intervention to provide separate facilities for boys and girls helped boost girls' school attendance 11 percent a year, on average, from 1992 to 1999 (UNICEF 2003a). Similar results were found in Mozambique (UNICEF 2003b).

Slums often surface on the periphery of a city, but the problems are the same as those in the city center. As Satterthwaite (2007) observes, settlements are formed on the urban periphery of many cities including megacities like Buenos Aires, Delhi, Manila, Mumbai, Phnom Penh, Santiago, and Seoul, when evicted inhabitants were forced out to these areas by local government slum clearance schemes. The social and environmental consequences include the segregation of low-income groups in the worst located and often most dangerous areas as well as a lack of access to water, sanitation, health services, and educational facilities. That is particularly the case for recent rural-urban migrants who may not be able to afford rentals within a slum, and have to squat on sites that may not be fit for habitation. Unfortunately, these sites are also prone to significant environmental risks.

Heath, Parker, and Weatherhead (2012) used Rapid Climate Adaptation Assessment methods to assess how changes to the climate interact with existing vulnerabilities in peri-urban and informal areas in a manner that is likely to affect safe water and sanitation supplies for the urban poor. The model was tested in Naivasha (Kenya); Antananarivo (Madagascar), and Lusaka (Zambia) in the eleven communities studied, eight were found to be vulnerable to flooding and four to water shortages, with especially severe negative effects for the peripheral sites prone to flooding. For example, in the peri-urban slum settlement of Kanyama on the outskirts of Lusaka, the 2009/10 flood lasted for three months, causing water kiosks and buildings to collapse, contaminating water supplies (particularly the shallow wells used in the areas unserved by the kiosks), and affecting livelihoods, education, and health. Satterthwaite (2007) argues that in several cities, extreme overcrowding in informal settlements (including the unserviced ones on urban peripheries) is viewed as a result of serious housing shortages and acute shortages of infrastructure and services in particular areas. Yet large amounts of land in cities are often left vacant or only partially developed; planning for low-income housing with proper basic services and infrastructure could result in lower costs than those incurred in upgrading existing

dense settlements, resettling slum dwellers, and undertaking slum clearance projects.

In a few countries disillusioned with government's lack of interest in their plight, slum dwellers are taking the initiative to make their voices heard. Two examples are insightful and encouraging. In Agra, India, a community-driven initiative has made toilets an entry point for catalyzing housing, slum, and city development (box 2.5). In Uganda, where more that 60 percent of the country's urban population lives in slum communities, the purported benefits of urban agglomeration are not being felt. Rather than waiting passively for better service provision, Uganda's slum dwellers have adopted a proactive strategy that is harnessing the potential of collective action to drive a shared agenda for better service delivery in slums (box 2.7).

Policy challenges and implications

The MDGs are about meeting the basic needs of all citizens in developing countries. The two facets of urbanization that matter the most for attainment of the MDGs in general and poverty reduction in particular are managing the factors that affect urban population growth and expand the boundaries of urban areas; and understanding the spatial location of poverty. Because these facets vary significantly between countries, country specificity should not be ignored in the design of any country policies aimed at attaining the MDGs.

The key relevant factors identified in this report that can inform policy makers and others addressing these challenging facets are:

- The natural increase in the urban population accounts for approximately 60 percent of urban population growth in all countries. Urban population growth is also affected by the reclassification of rural boundaries. Migration is a third factor in urban population growth. The weight of each of these factors in affecting urbanization depends on country circumstances.

BOX 2.7   Agglomeration of collective capacity among Uganda's slum dweller communities

In the slum dweller communities of Uganda, where over 60 percent of the urban population lives, the purported benefits of urban agglomeration are not being felt and many urban areas are characterized by rising unemployment and inadequate access to basic services. Rather than waiting passively for the benefits of urban agglomeration, Uganda's slum dwellers have adopted a proactive strategy that is harnessing the potential of collective action. The strategy is one that has evolved within the Shack/Slum Dwellers International (SDI) network. It involves the clustering, or federating, of community saving groups into urban poor federations. The National Slum Dwellers Federation of Uganda (NSDFU) is one of 33 federations in the SDI network. Founded in 2002, the NSDFU today comprises almost 500 savings groups and approximately 38,000 members. Savings are used to bring people together, build their capacity to act as a collective, and build organizational capacity and trust.

When savings groups begin, they often focus solely on livelihood issues and income generation. But with time and greater exposure to SDI rituals such as enumeration and peer-to-peer exchange, communities formulate an urban agenda that looks beyond group members and toward transforming the settlements in which they live. This is when benefits to service delivery begin to accrue as part of a collective upgrading agenda. The spatial proximity of urban savings groups allows for the agglomeration of collective capacity necessary to create a critical mass of urban poor to hold public officials accountable and to collaborate with municipalities and leverage their savings. This critical mass is required to make community participation more than a platitude and aid more effective, and it is uniquely possible in the urban setting.

The positive externalities of this agglomeration of collective capacity are not hard to see. The NSDFU is the key community mobilizer in the government of Uganda's Transforming Settlements of the Urban Poor in Uganda (TSUPU) program. The NSDFU has capitalized on the opportunities of this Cities Alliance–funded program to expand from Jinja and Kampala to Arua, Kabale, Mbale, and Mbarara. Within this national program, the NSDFU has demonstrated that organized communities can improve urban governance by organizing citizens to demand accountability; improve urban planning by generating information on slum populations; improve living conditions for members and nonmembers alike through slum upgrading projects; and improve the environment by upholding their responsibilities to keep cities clean and maintain public services. Over the past 10 years, the NSDFU has constructed sanitation units and community halls in slums throughout the country. Last year the NSDFU began extending clean water and improving drainage, while in Jina it has begun construction of a low-cost housing project. In almost every case, projects were built upon land provided by municipal councils, demonstrating true partnership.

The increasing returns to scale for the agglomeration of collective capacity are also evident. The more the federation grows, the easier it becomes to negotiate with government, mobilize members and savings, leverage funds, and implement projects. Because the NSDFU is part of SDI, the returns to scale also benefit tremendously from the growth of the global urban poor movement.

Source: Skye Dobson, Uganda Program Officer, Shack/Slum Dwellers International.

- All else being equal, rural-urban migration can lead to a reduction in rural poverty, but migration is not uniform across regions or countries. It is highest in Latin America and East Asia and lowest in South Asia; Sub-Saharan Africa falls somewhere in between. Governments play an important role in urban poverty reduction when they facilitate migration. Whether rural-urban migration increases or reduces urban poverty depends on whether migrants contribute to the positive or negative aspects of urbanization.
- Poverty is not spatially bipolar but distributed along a spectrum. Rural areas are the poorest; megacities and large cities are the

richest, and smaller towns of varied sizes and slums in larger cities lie in between. The implications of the spatial location of poverty along a spectrum are nontrivial. The challenge for the MDGs is to design poverty-reducing and service delivery strategies that take into account the spectrum along which poverty is located.

- In a large number of countries, the majority of the urban population resides in the larger cities, as for example in India and Vietnam, but the majority of the urban poor lives in smaller towns that are often as poor as rural areas. Ignoring the growth of urban poverty in smaller towns can undermine efforts to reduce overall urban poverty as well as overall poverty.

- The spatial distribution of poverty in Sub-Saharan Africa is distinct from that of other regions. This region's poor are disproportionately concentrated in rural areas. Most of the small proportion located in urban areas live in the largest city, usually the capital. Population density in Sub-Saharan Africa is sparse, making it difficult and costly to deliver network-based services that benefit from scale economies.

- Rural poverty is distinct from urban poverty, but there is a strong interdependence between rural and urban economies. Three-fourths of the poor worldwide still reside in rural areas, making the role of rural poverty-reducing policies central to any policy approaches aimed at attaining the MDGs.

- The necessary ingredients for strong and sustainable links between rural areas and smaller towns are a rich rural hinterland that can supply urban areas and that has access to urban markets where rural households can trade. In short, rural-urban migration can be an equalizer with the potential to bridge rural-urban disparities in incomes and access to basic services, alleviating rural poverty, as illustrated in Tanzania. Rural growth also has a positive impact on urban poverty reduction. Policies that spur this process include an increase in rural productivity through the introduction of new farm technologies and investment in the human capital development of

rural residents; removal of land market distortions; improved connectivity with urban markets; and a fostering of nonfarm activity and rural-urban migration.

- At least seven of the MDGs are related directly to the delivery of basic services, and the poverty–city size gradient is a strong marker of access to services. Invariably, rural areas are the worst off and smaller towns and slums have poorer access to basic amenities than do larger cities. Problems in service delivery are related to both quantity and quality.

- To shrink persisting gender differentials in educational attainment and earnings, discrete policies need to improve girls' access to education when poverty, ethnicity, or location (rural, small town) excludes them. WDR 2012 notes that economic development is not enough to shrink all gender disparities. It recommends that corrective policies focused on persistent gender gaps are essential. A priority is reducing the gender gaps in human capital, specifically those regarding female mortality and education. Conditional cash transfers to encourage girls to attend school have been successful in increasing primary school enrollments in various countries.

- Other policies that have a disproportionately positive impact on women's economic empowerment are ones that improve rural livelihoods by increasing female farmers' access to markets. Policies that increase rural women's access to water reduce the time they spend in fetching water and free up the time they can spend in income-generating work that increases their economic empowerment. There is also a clear need for policy that prioritizes not only the provision of sanitation in slums on the whole, but mainstreams gendered needs in the design of sanitation policies.

The implications of urbanization for the provision of MDG-related services to all individuals in developing countries are complex and need to be considered in a framework that appropriately recognizes the factors described here. Governments have two main policy levers with which to achieve the

MDGs: the suite of macroeconomic policy instruments that spur agglomeration economies and job creation; and public investment in MDG-related services.

The first-best solution is to facilitate access to *all* MDG-related services for *all* poor through expert management of the urbanization process. This implies either accelerating investments in the factors that fuel the urbanization process (the subject of chapter 3) and attract the poor to cities; or equalizing service delivery wherever the poor are located—that is, in rural areas and small towns as well as slums. The implications are different, however, in highly urbanized countries such as in Latin America, where, compared with other regions, rural areas offer greater income-earning opportunities. Indeed, recent experience in Latin America shows that when agricultural production (via higher prices, higher productivity, and the like) allows rural workers to obtain decent incomes, the propensity to migrate fades. However, because rural-urban poverty differentials remain large, Latin America continues to register one of the highest migration rates.

Not surprisingly, the first-best solution is unviable for several reasons: Resource and capacity constraints must be overcome. Not all of the rural poor who want to move to urban areas can migrate to cities at once, and even if they could, congestion effects would likely worsen urban poverty and undermine the urbanization process. Even if ideal cities were created, not all of the rural poor would be willing to forgo their rural assets and migrate. Finally, it is unrealistic to presume that the rural poor who do want to migrate would be able to find productive jobs if they did not arrive endowed with at least some basic human capital.

The second-best approach is to prioritize the type of services provided, their delivery location, and their timing. Three types of policies could be leveraged:

- In areas where migration is significant and poverty is more bipolar, boosting the urbanization process in large cities through better delivery of MDG-related services and provision of incentives for job creation would make large cities more attractive and would motivate rural-urban migration. Migrants would enjoy the benefits of urban living and would presumably step out of poverty and toward greater prosperity. For this to happen, poor migrants need human capital—that is, they need to be healthy and have a basic education. Thus public investment in primary education and health care should be directed to the poor both in small towns and in rural areas.

- In countries where migration is limited and reclassification and natural population growth dominate the expansion of urban boundaries, where population density is high, and where the poverty–city size gradient is dominant, the poverty differentials between poorly served areas and larger cities are unlikely to shrink sufficiently to foster the attainment of the MDGs. In these situations, policies that encourage migration will help. Progress toward the MDGs would be accelerated by delivering services wherever the poor are concentrated, otherwise both rural and urban poverty will remain grounded wherever it is.

- In situations where poor people are concentrated in small towns, policies should focus on improving connectivity with other urban centers. Poverty in small towns is often high, and the quantity and quality of services in these places differ little from those in rural areas and lag behind those in more mature urban settlements. In these cases, measures to better connect the activities in small towns with the economies of larger cities become paramount.

In all three cases, investment in portable services (education and health care) would optimally be provided wherever the poor are. But in countries with high migration and low population density in rural areas, delivery of nonportable infrastructure services in larger cities would be more cost-effective and more supportive of urbanization and industrialization and could be prioritized as such. Countries in Sub-Saharan Africa would typically fall in this group.

Finally, a reduction in the number of slum dwellers is a dedicated MDG and needs a dedicated approach. To address the unique challenges associated with slums, policy solutions must:

- Tie land tenure policies for slums to those of the city as a whole, particularly in terms of land pricing, connectivity of residential and commercial urban space, and, above all, the appropriate balance between economic and population density. A "silo" approach will lead to a lose-lose solution for cities and their slums.

- Take advantage of slums' proximity to the city so that the unit costs of extending access to basic health and education services to slum dwellers are relatively low.
- Expand the supply of public toilets and water to slum dwellers in creative ways (such as putting water fountains in public places) in the short term, recognizing that permanent solutions to water and sanitation provision is tied to the land issue.
- Make use of the fact that in most cases, slum dwellers are willing to pay a small fee to access basic services.

Annex 2A.1   Equalization of health service delivery and its expected impacts on the MDGs: A simulation exercise

Closing the rural-urban MDG and service gaps may represent a major challenge for many countries, especially if these gaps are large and the unit costs of services for rural populations are higher than for their urban compatriots. In the simulation exercise presented in this annex, the broader economic consequences of closing health gaps in low-income countries are explored by adapting MAMS, a CGE model for country strategy analysis, to address rural-urban aspects of MDGs. The database used was designed to capture characteristics typical of low-income countries, including their MDG outcomes, sectoral shares in value-added.

The base simulation assumes an annual growth rate of 5.6 percent, following the trend of low-income countries since 2000; and "business as usual" in government policies and spending, including borrowing that is consistent with debt sustainability. In the comparator simulations, for the period 2014–30, it is assumed that the government gradually scales up its health services, either by closing the gap in the levels of per capita health services reaching rural and urban residents, or by closing the rural-urban gap in the under-five mortality rate (U5MR), the outcome indicator of interest here. These efforts are undertaken using alternative sources for required additional financing (foreign grant aid, domestic borrowing, taxes, and reduced spending on infrastructure).

Under the base scenario, the major macroeconomic indicators (GDP, government and private consumption, and investment) all grow at annual rates of around 5 percent; in per capita terms, household consumption grows at an annual rate of around 3.1 percent, with a slightly more rapid rate for rural households (3.2 versus 3.0 percent). As shown in figure 2A.1, significant progress

is realized for both poverty and the U5MR, while the rural-urban gaps narrow but still remain substantial.

In the first simulation (denoted *mdg4u+fg*), the government gradually raises per capita rural health services to the urban level while maintaining a growth rate for urban services that is sufficient to maintain the same reduction in the urban U5MR as under the base; in other words, the improvement in the rural population does not come at the expense of the health outcome of the urban population; additional foreign grant aid provides needed financing. As shown in figure 2A.2, this set of actions reduces the 2030 rural U5MR by slightly more than 5 points, closing roughly half of the rural-urban gap. Both rural and urban poverty rates are virtually unchanged. At the macro level, growth in government consumption increases by 0.6 percentage points (Figure 2A.3), accompanied by a similar increase for government investment, with the increases directed to the health sector and financed by foreign grant aid; by 2030,

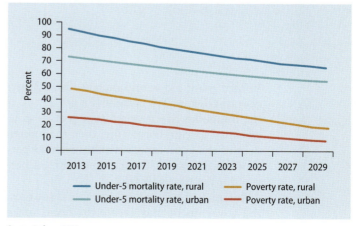

FIGURE 2A.1   Poverty and under-5 mortality for base simulation

Source: Lofgren 2013.

FIGURE 2A.2   Poverty and under-5 mortality—deviations from base in 2030

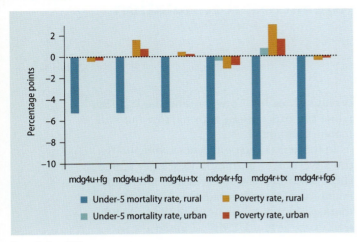

Source: Lofgren 2013.

FIGURE 2A.3   Macro indicators—deviations from base annual growth

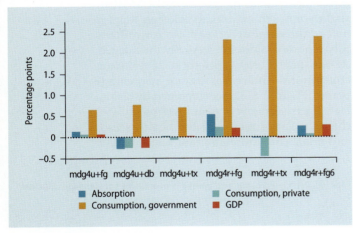

Source: Lofgren 2013.

foreign grant aid would increase by 1.2 percent of GDP, to 5.1 percent (Figure 2A.4). If the financing gap instead were met by concessional foreign borrowing, then the foreign debt of the government would reach 43 percent of GDP in 2030 compared with 32 percent for the base scenario.

Instead of relying on foreign resources, the government may create the fiscal space needed for this increase in health spending

by turning to domestic resources, including borrowing or higher taxes (scenarios denoted as *mdg4u+db*, and *mdg4u+tx*, respectively). While the outcomes are very similar or the same in terms of the rural and urban U5MRs, these scenarios lead to higher urban and rural poverty rates (see figure 2A.2), accompanied by slower growth in private consumption; for the borrowing scenario, the poverty reduction and consumption outcomes are more negative, and GDP and absorption growth rates also decline, because the private sector is deprived of investment funding (see figure 2A.3). For both scenarios, the macro slowdown reflects the opportunity costs of reallocating resources to government health spending: less funding for domestic private investment and capital accumulation (*mdg4u+db*), or reduced real disposable income for households, leading to losses spread over private consumption, investment, and capital stock growth (*mdg4u+tx*).[6]

Under the preceding scenarios, the rural U5MR remains above the urban level, indicating that lack of government health services is only one factor behind the gap between rural and urban health outcomes. Alternatively, the government may decide to be more ambitious and gradually raise government health services in rural areas to such an extent that by 2030 the U5MR of the rural population will have declined to the urban U5MR level in 2030 simulated under the base scenario; that is, the government would try to make up for the other gaps suffered by the rural population by providing them with additional targeted health services while, at the same time, maintaining the same per capita real health spending for the urban population as under the base scenario. On the margin, the increase in real services per capita (or per avoided death) is higher under this scenario, reflecting the need to reach more disadvantaged population groups and to turn to more costly interventions, in effect reversing the initial discrimination against the rural population in health service provision. If foreign grants provide the marginal financing (*mdg4r+fg*), then in 2030, these will have to increase by 5.6 percent of GDP compared to the base, to 9.7 percent of GDP. Compared with the base outcome in 2030, the intended reduction in the rural U5MR is realized, together with small reductions in the urban U5MR and poverty in both rural and urban areas (see figure 2A.2). A strong growth increase is recorded for government consumption, along with more modest increases for private consumption, GDP, and absorption, the latter enlarged by the increase in grant aid (see figure 2A.3).

It is difficult to reallocate this amount of resources to government health spending without negative repercussions. If the government relies on higher taxes (*mdg4r+tx*), the increases in which reach 7.6 percent of GDP in 2030 compared with the base, these repercussions are felt in the form of a slightly higher urban U5MR and higher poverty rates, especially in rural areas (see figure 2A.2), as well as in slower growth for private consumption (see Figure 2A.3). The reason behind a relatively strong rural poverty increase (for this and some of the preceding scenarios) is that government services, which were scaled up, are relatively intensive in the use of the more educated labor supplied by urban households, whereas private spending, which was scaled down, disproportionately reduces the demand for land and less educated labor, factors that provide a relatively large share of the incomes of the rural population.[7]

From a different angle, given inefficiencies in the government health sector in many low-income countries, it is possible to reduce the need for extra financing by raising efficiency. For a set of scenarios that raise the rural U5MR to the urban level by 2030, figure 2A.5 maps out combinations of average per capita foreign grant increases (in constant 2009 dollars) for 2014–30 and additional annual growth in government health service efficiency (covering efficiency of new investments, as well as of labor and capital use but excluding material inputs such as medicines). In the absence of a gain in efficiency, the grant increase in an average year is around $26 per capita (at 2009 prices; from the scenario *mdg4r+fg*). The need for additional

FIGURE 2A.4   Additional foreign grants to finance health spending

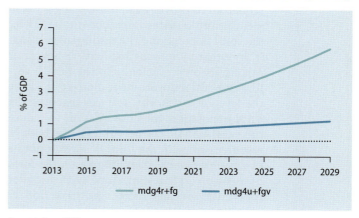

Source: Lofgren 2013.

grant aid would be eliminated if efficiency grew by an additional 6.2 percent a year. While such rapid gains may be infeasible, additional growth of at least 1–2 percent a year may be within the realm of possibility.[8] Interestingly, the gains in reduced aid per additional percentage point of efficiency growth are diminishing—that is due to real exchange rate effects: at high levels, grant aid leads to strong marginal appreciation, with strongly reduced domestic purchasing power as the result.

FIGURE 2A.5   Trade-offs between more grant aid and domestic efficiency gains

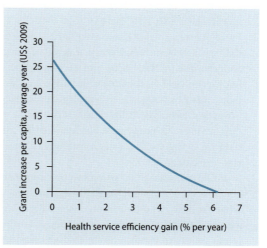

Source: Lofgren 2013.

In sum, these simulations explore the consequences of providing and financing government health services to reduce the U5MR of the rural population. The results suggest that if, by either mobilizing required resources or raising its own efficiency in the health sector, or both, a government manages to raise the level of real health services reaching the rural population, then it is possible to reduce the rural U5MR considerably. If the bulk of resources come in the form of foreign grants or efficiency gains, then progress in the form of a lower U5MR can come with broader repercussions that have a positive impact on other development indicators, including poverty reduction. But if most additional resources have to be mobilized from domestic sources, then progress on reducing U5MR would threaten to come at the expense of less progress in poverty reduction and other indicators, illustrating the difficult trade-offs facing low-income countries and their governments.

Notes

1. Because the estimates are derived from census information and because the definitions of "urban" used in the Chinese censuses have been changing, this finding should be interpreted with caution. Estimates for Indonesia indicate that the contribution of natural increase to urban growth declined steadily, from nearly 70 percent in the 1960s to 32 percent in the 1990s (UN 2011).
2. Ferré, Ferreira, and Lanjouw (2012) suggest that while "urban bias" was a much discussed concern during the 1970s and 1980s, following Lipton (1977), the idea of a "metropolitan bias" has not been widely emphasized in the poverty measurement literature. This is likely due, at least in part, to scant availability of data on living standards across finely defined city-size categories.
3. It should be noted that estimation of a complex concept such as "slum" will always be somewhat arbitrary and definition driven. By using a consistent definition in the same places at different points in time, genuine changes may be observed—particularly when broad averages

are "drilled down" to examine the underlying changes in real conditions in individual cities.
4. The original target to improve the lives of at least 100 million slum dwellers by 2020 was based on an estimation of close to 100 million slum dwellers in the world. Upon measurement of the slum population using the internationally agreed upon UN-Habitat definition of slums following the UN Expert Group Meeting of October 2002, it was learned that the global estimate of the slum population was in fact close to 1 billion (924 million). As a result, even though the slum target has been globally achieved, and in fact significantly surpassed 10 years ahead of schedule, there is little room for complacency given the existing magnitude of populations currently living in slums.
5. In April 2011, however, the UN Habitat Governing Council adopted a resolution to improve the measurement of tenure security and to generate globally comparable estimates. Observations using this method are being implemented in 25 cities around the world.
6. As a result of more rapid private consumption growth for *mdg4u+fg* than for the other scenarios, the health objectives can be achieved with a slightly smaller acceleration in government health spending and government consumption growth for *mdg4u+fg*.
7. Additional simulations showed that the domestic resources that could be mobilized through increased government borrowing were insufficient to finance the health policy of the last two scenarios (*mdg4r+fg* and *mdg4r+tx*).
8. For example, on the basis of surveys in six low- and middle-income countries, Chaudhury et al. (2006) found that, on average, primary health workers were absent 35 percent of the time. Other things being equal, a moderate gradual reduction in their absenteeism to 17.5 percent of their time by 2030 would correspond to an annual increase in their productivity by around 1.5 percent a year.

References

Alene, A, V. Manyong, G. Omanya, H. Mignouna, M. Bokanga, and G. Odhiambo. 2008. "Economic Efficiency and Supply Response of Women as Farm Managers: Comparative

Evidence from Western Kenya." *World Development*. 36 (7): 1247–1260.

Au, Chun-Chung, and J. Vernon Henderson. 2006a. "Are Chinese Cities too Small?" *Review of Economic Studies* 73 (3): 549–76.

———. 2006b. "How Migration Restrictions Limit Agglomeration and Productivity in China." *Journal of Development Economics* 80: 350–88.

Baker, J. L. 2008. *Urban poverty: A global view.* Washington, DC: The World Bank.

Bardasi, E., and Q. Wodon. 2008. "Who Pays the Most for Water? Alternative Providers and Service Costs in Niger." *Economics Bulletin* 920: 1–10.

Beegle K., J. De Weerdt, and S. Dercon. 2011. "Migration and Economic Mobility in Tanzania: Evidence from a Tracking Survey." *Review of Economics and Statistics* 93: 1010–33.

Bell, M., and S. Muhidin. 2008. "Cross-National Comparison of Internal Migration." Report prepared for the *2009 Human Development Report,* New York.

Cali, M., and C. Menon. 2013. "Does Urbanisation Affect Rural Poverty? Evidence from Indian Districts." *Policy Research Working Paper* 6338, World Bank, Washington, DC.

Chandra, V., J. Y. Lin, and Y. Wang. 2013. "Leading Dragon Phenomenon: New Opportunities for Catch-up in Low-Income Countries." *Asian Development Review* 30 (1): 1–32.

Chen, N., P. Valente, and H. Zlotnik. 1998. "What Do We Know about Recent Trends in Urbanization?" In *Migration, Urbanization, and Development: New Directions and Issues,* edited by R. E. Bilsborrow. New York: United Nations Population Fund and Kluwer Academic Publishers, 59–88.

Commander, S. and J. Svejnar. 2011. "Business Environment, Exports Ownership, and Firm Performance." *Review of Economics and Statistics* 93 (1): 309–37.

Coulombe, H. and P. Lanjouw. 2013. "Poverty, Access to Services and City Size in a Selection of African Countries," *Mimeo.* World Bank, Development Research Group, Washington, DC.

da Mata, Daniel, U. Deichmann, V. Henderson, S.V. Lall, and H. G. Wang. 2007.

"Determinants of City Growth in Brazil." *Journal of Urban Economics* 62 (2): 252–72.

Datt, G., and M. Ravallion. 1996. Why have some Indian states done better than others at reducing rural poverty? *Policy Research Working Paper* 1594, World Bank, Washington, DC.

———. 2009. "Has India's Economic Growth Become More Pro-poor in the Wake of Economic Reforms?" *Policy Research Working Paper* 5103, World Bank, Washington, DC.

Deichmann, U., F. Shilpi, and R. Vakis. 2009. "Urban Proximity, Agricultural Potential and Rural Non-farm Employment: Evidence from Bangladesh." *World Development* 37 (3): 645–60.

Deininger, K., J. Songqing, B. Adenew, S. Gebre-Selassie, and M. Demeke. 2003. "Market and Non-market Transfers of Land in Ethiopia: Implications for Efficiency, Equity, and Non-farm Development." *Policy Research Working Paper* 2992, World Bank, Washington, DC.

Dercon, S., P. Krishnan, and S. Krutikova. Forthcoming. "Migration, Risk-Sharing and Subjective Well-being: Some Eevidence from India 1975–2005." *Mimeo,* Oxford University, Oxford, UK.

Do, Q. T., and L. Iyer. 2008. "Land Titling and Rural Transition in Vietnam." *Economic Development and Cultural Change* 56, pp. 531–79

Do, Q. T., A. Levchenko and C. Raddatz. 2011. "Engendering Trade." Background paper for 2012. *World Development Report: Gender Equality and Development,* Washington, DC: World Bank..

Dudwick, N., K. Hull, R. Katayama, F. Shilpi, and K. Simler. 2011. *From Farm to Firm: Rural-Urban Transition in Developing Countries.* World Bank, Washington, DC. http://site.ebrary.com/id/10477343.

Du Plessis, J. 2005. "The Growing Problem of Forced Evictions and the Crucial Importance of Community-based, Locally Appropriate Alternatives." *Environment and Urbanization* 17 (1): 123–34.

Durand-Lasserve, A. 2006. "Informal Settlements and the Millennium Development Goals: Global Policy Debates on Property Ownership and Security of Tenure." *Global Urban Development* 2 (1): 1–15.

Elbers, C., J. O. Lanjouw, and P. Lanjouw. 2002. "Micro-Level Estimation of Welfare Policy." Research Working Paper 2911, World Bank, Development Research Group, Washington, DC.

———. 2003. "Micro-level Estimation of Poverty and Inequality." *Econometrica* 71 (1): 355–64.

Emran, M. S., and F. Shilpi. 2012. "The Extent of the Market and Stages of Agricultural Specialization." *Canadian Journal of Economics* 45 (3): 1125–53.

EU (European Union). 2012. The Role of BRICS in the Developing World. Directorate-General for external policies, Brussels.

Fafchamps, M., and F. Shilpi. 2003. "The Spatial Division of Labour in Nepal." *Journal of Development Studies* 39 (6): 23–66.

———. 2005. "Cities and Specialisation: Evidence from South Asia." *Economic Journal, Royal Economic Society* 115 (503): 477–504.

———. Forthcoming. "Determinants of Choice of Migration Destination." *Oxford Bulletin of Economics and Statistics*. Also Policy Research Working Paper 4728, World Bank, Washington, DC.

FAWE. 2006. "Experiences in Creating a Conducive Environment for Girls in School." FAWE Centre of Excellence, Nairobi, Kenya.

Ferré, C., F. H. G. Ferreira, and P. Lanjouw. 2012. "Is There a Metropolitan Bias? The Relationship between Poverty and City Size in a Selection of Developing Countries." *World Bank Economic Review* 26 (5508): 1–32.

Feler, L., and V. Henderson. 2011. "Exclusionary Policies in Urban Development: Under-servicing Migrant Households in Brazilian Cities." *Journal of Urban Economics* 69 (3): 253–72.

Foster, A., and M. Rosenzweig. 2004. "Agricultural Development, Industrialization and Rural Inequality." Brown University, Providence, RI, US.

Fox, L. and T.P. Sohnesen. 2012. "Household Enterprises in Sub-Saharan Africa: Why They Matter for Growth, Jobs, and Livelihoods." Policy Research Working Paper 6184, World Bank, Washington, DC.

Gollin, D. 2009. "Agricultural Productivity and Economic Growth." In *Handbook of Agricultural Economics,* vol. 4 (June). Gardner, Bruce L. 2009. *Handbook of agricultural economics.* 4. Amsterdam u.a: Elsevier.

Haggblade, S., P. Hazell, and P. Dorosh. 2006. "Sectoral Growth Linkages between Agriculture and the Rural Nonfarm Economy." In *Transforming the Rural Nonfarm Economy,* ed. S. Haggblade, P. Hazell, and T. Reardon, ch. 7. Baltimore: Johns Hopkins University Press.

Haggblade, S., P. B. R. Hazell, and T. A. Reardon, eds. 2007. *Transforming the rural nonfarm economy: opportunities and threats in the developing world.* Baltimore, Md: Johns Hopkins University Press.

Hanushek, E. A., and L. Woessmann. 2008. "The role of cognitive skills in economic development." *Journal of Economic Literature (Stanford),* 46, 3, 607–88.

Heath, T. T., A. H. Parker, and E. K. Weatherhead. 2012. "Testing a Rapid Climate Change Adaptation Assessment for Water and Sanitation Providers in Informal Settlements in Three Cities in Sub-Saharan Africa." *Environment and Urbanization* 24 (2): 619–37.

Kabeer, N., and S. Mahmud. 2004. "Rags, Riches and Women Workers: Export-oriented Garment Manufacturing in Bangladesh." In *Chains of fortune: linking women producers and workers with global markets.* Ed. Carr, Marilyn. 2004. London: Commonwealth Secretariat.

Karuiki, M., and J. Schwartz. 2005. "Small Scale Private Service Providers of Water and Electricity Supply: A Review of Incidence, Structure, Pricing and Operating Characteristics." *Policy Research Working Paper* 3727, World Bank, Washington, D.C.

Kimani-Murage, E. W., and A. M. Ngindu. 2007. "Quality of Water the Slum Dwellers Use: The Case of a Kenyan Slum." *Journal of Urban Health* 84 (6): 829–38.

Kumar, S. K. 1994. *Adoption of hybrid maize in Zambia: effects on gender roles, food consumption, and nutrition.* Washington, D.C., International Food Policy Research Institute.

Kyobutungi, C., A. Ziraba, A. C. Ezeh, and Y. Yé. 2008. "The Burden of Disease Profile of Residents of Nairobi's Slums: Results from a Demographic Surveillance System." *Population Health Metrics* 6 (1): 1.

Lall, Somik V., C. Timmins, and S. Yu. 2009. "Connecting Lagging and Leading Regions: The Role of Labor Mobility."

Brookings-Wharton Papers on Urban Affairs: 151–74.

Lanjouw J., and P. Lanjouw. 2001. "Rural Nonfarm Employment: Issues and Evidence from Developing Countries." *Agricultural Economics* 26 (1): 1–24.

Lanjouw, P., and M. Marra. 2012. "Urban Poverty and City Size in Vietnam." World Bank, Washington, DC.

Levinsohn, J. A. 2007. "Globalization and the Returns to Speaking English in South Africa." In Globalization and Poverty. Ed. A. Harrison. Chicago: University of Chicago Press.

Lipton, M. 1977. "Why Poor People Stay Poor: Urban Bias and World Development." London: Temple Smith.

Lofgren, H. 2013. "Closing Rural-Urban MDG Gaps in Low-Income Countries: A General Equilibrium Perspective." Policy Research Working Paper 6390. Development Prospects Group. World Bank.

McMillan, Margaret, and Dani Rodrik. 2011. "Globalization, Structural Change and Productivity Growth." NBER Working Paper 17143, National Bureau of Economic Research, Cambridge, MA.

Mehra, R., Maik, M. and Rudolf, G. 2012. "Traditional Livelihoods and Community Centre for Urban Development." *Journal of the Development and Research Organization for Nature, Arts and Heritage*. Winter/Spring edition, pp. 85–90.

Mellor, John W. 1996. "Agriculture on the Road to Industrialization." In *Development Strategies Reconsidered*, edited by John P. Lewis and Valeriana Kallab. New Brunswick, NJ: Transaction Books for the Overseas Development Council.

Ministry of Education, Republic of Kenya. 2011. "Keeping girls in school." Nairobi, Kenya.

Montenegro, C. E., and H. A. Patrinos. 2012. "Returns to Schooling around the World." Background paper for *World Development Report 2013*. World Bank, Washington, DC.

Montgomery, M. R. 2008. The urban transformation of the developing world. *Science*, 319 (5864), 761–764.

Moock, P. R. 1976. The Efficiency of Women as Farm Managers: Kenya. *American Journal of Agricultural Economics*. 58.

Munshi, Kaivan, and Mark Rosenzweig. 2009. "Why Is Mobility in India so Low? Social Insurance, Inequality, and Growth." NBER Working Paper 14850, National Bureau of Economic Research, Inc., Cambridge, MA.

Mutua, M., and E. Kimani-Murage. 2011. "Childhood Vaccination in Informal Urban Settlements in Nairobi, Kenya: Who Gets Vaccinated?" *BMC Public Health* 11 (1): 6.

Nasritdinov, E. 2007. "Discrimination of internal migrants in Bishkek." Unpublished manuscript, Social Research Center, American University of Central Asia Bishkek, Kyrgyzstan. Available at: http://auca.kg/uploads/Migration_Database/Discrimination%20of%20internal%20migrants%20in%20Bishkek.pdf. Last Accessed 03/29/2013.

Ndugwa R. P., and E. M. Zulu. 2008. "Child Morbidity and Care-seeking in Nairobi Slum Settlements: The Role of Environmental and Socio-economic Factors." *Journal of Child Health Care* 12 (4): 314–28.

Nguyen, M. C., and Q. Wodon. 2013a. "Analyzing the Gender Gap in Education Attainment: A Simple Framework with Application to Ghana." *Journal of International Development*, 48.

———. 2013b. "Educational Attainment in Sub-Saharan Africa." *Mimeo*.World Bank, Washington, DC.

———. 2013c. "Educational Attainment in South Asia." *Mimeo*. World Bank, Washington, DC.

Obonyo, S. A. 2003. "A Study of Knowledge and Practices of Slums in Nairobi." Kenyatta University, Nairobi, Kenya.

Piotrowski, M., and R. R. Rindfuss. 2006. *Migration and household demography in Nang Rong, Thailand*. UNC Electronic Theses and Dissertations Collection. Chapel Hill, N.C.: University of North Carolina at Chapel Hill. http://dc.lib.unc.edu/u?/etd,393.

Psacharopoulos, George, and Harry Anthony Patrinos. 2004. "Returns to Investment in Education: A Further Update." *Education Economics* 12 (2): 111–34.

Ravallion, M., S. Chen, and P. Sangraula. 2007. "New Evidence on the Urbanization of Global Poverty." *Population and Development Review* 33 (4): 667–701.

SACMEQ (Southern and Eastern Africa Consortium for Monitoring Educational Quality). 2010. "SACMEQ III Project Results: Pupil Achievement Levels in Reading and Mathematics." Working Document 1.

Saito, K. A., H. Mekonnen and D. Spurling. 1994. *Raising the productivity of women farmers in Sub-Saharan Africa.* Washington, D.C., World Bank.

Satterthwaite, D. 2007. *The Transition to a predominantly urban world and its underpinnings.* London: International Institute for Environment and Development, London, UK..

———. 2011. "Why Is Urban Health so Poor Even in Many Successful cities?" (editorial). *Environment and Urbanization* 23: 5. http://eau.sagepub.com/content/23/1/5.

Semba, R. D., S. Pee, K. Kraemer, K Sun, A. Thorne-Lyman, R. Moench-Pfanner, M. Sari, N. Akhter, and M. W. Bloem. 2009. "Purchase of Drinking Water Is Associated with Increased Child Morbidity and Mortality among Urban Slum-dwelling Families in Indonesia." *International Journal of Hygiene and Environmental Health* 212 (4): 387–97.

Singh, S, S. D. Kandpal, and D. Roy. 2011. "Menstrual Hygiene Practices and RTI among ever-married women in rural slum." *Indian Journal of Community Health (IJCH)* 22.2, 1: 41–43.

Tacoli, C., and R. Mabala. 2010. "Exploring mobility and migration in the context of rural-urban linkages: why gender and generation matter." *Environment and Urbanization.* 22 (2): 389–395.

UN-Habitat. 2008. *State of the World's Cities 2008/2009: Harmonious Cities.* London: Earthscan.

———. 2010. State of the World's Cities 2010/2011: Bridging the Urban Divide. London: Earthscan.

United Nations Children Fund (UNICEF). 2003a. "Sanitation for All." United Nations: New York.

———. 2003b. "At a glance: Mozambique." See: http://www.unicef.org/infobycountry/mozambique_2231.html.

United Nations. 2011. "*World Urbanization Prospects: The 2011 Revision.*" United Nations Department of Economic and Social Affairs/Population Division. United Nations: New York.

United Nations Population Division (UNDP). 2011. *World Population Policies, 2011 Revision.* New York: UN.

von Thünen, J. H. 1966, *Isolated State: an English Edition of Der Isolierte Staat.* Oxford: Pergamon Press.

Vullnetari, Julie, and Russell King. 2011. *Remittances, Gender and Development: Albania's Society and Economy in Transition.* London: I.B. Tauris. http://public.eblib.com/EBLPublic/PublicView.do?ptiID=830137.

Wodon, Q. 2013a. Faith and Human Development: Education and Health Services in Africa, New York: Palgrave MacMillan.

———. 2013b. Note on Urban-Rural Differentials in Health Indicators. *Mimeo,* Human Development Network, World Bank, Washington, DC.

World Bank. 2007. "Dhaka, Improving Living Conditions for the Urban Poor." Dhaka: World Bank Office.

———. 2010. *World Development Report 2009: Reshaping Economic Geography.* Washington, DC: World Bank.

———. 2011. *Perspectives on Poverty in India: Stylized Facts from Survey Data.* Washington DC: Oxford University Press.

———. 2012a. *World Development Indicators.* Washington, DC: World Bank.

———. 2012b. "Uganda Promoting Inclusive Growth." Synthesis report 67377-UG, Poverty Reduction and Economic Management, Unit 2, World Bank, Washington, DC.

———. 2012c. *Global Monitoring Report: Food Prices, Nutrition and the Millennium Development Goals.* Washington, DC: World Bank.

———. 2012d. World Development Report: Gender Equality and Development, Washington, DC: World Bank.

———. 2013. *World Development Report: Jobs.* Washington, DC: World Bank.

Yamauchi, F., M. Muto, S.Chowdhury, R. Dewina, and S. Sumaryanto. 2011. "Are Schooling and Roads Complementary? Evidence from Income Dynamics in Rural Indonesia." *World Development* 39 (12): 2232–44.

3

How Can Urbanization Accelerate Progress toward the MDGs?

Summary and messages

Urbanization matters. In the past two decades, developing countries have urbanized rapidly, with the number of people living in urban settlements rising from about 1.5 billion in 1990 to 3.6 billion (more than half of the world's population) in 2011. Some 2.7 billion people in the developing world now live in urban areas. Citizens in urban areas have an advantage over their rural brethren in that urban poverty rates are significantly lower than rural poverty rates and urban populations also have far better access to the basic public services defined by the Millennium Development Goals (MDGs), including access to safe water and sanitation facilities (chapter 2).

In the next two decades, developing countries will become even more urbanized. Between 2011 and 2030, the population of the developing world is expected to grow by 1.4 billion—and 96 percent of them will live in urban areas. If the forces of urbanization are not managed speedily and efficiently, slum growth can overwhelm city growth, exacerbate urban poverty, derail MDG achievements and reduce, if not eliminate, cities' comparative advantage regarding attainment of the MDGs.

Nor will urban growth be limited to the megacities of today. Secondary cities such as Huambo in Angola, Fushun in China, and Surat in India—cities that few would be able to pinpoint on a map—are likely to grow rapidly into large cities in their own right. The good news is that many of these emerging urban centers are still taking shape, providing policy makers with a unique but rapidly closing window of opportunity to get their cities "right" to enhance economic, social, and environmental outcomes.

In many respects, the move to cities is entirely rational. Cities are the hubs of prosperity—more than 80 percent of global economic activity is concentrated in cities (McKinsey Global Institute 2011). The densities that cities offer can create scale economies that enhance job opportunities and productivity, as well as make it cheaper to expand services. Cities, through their density, make public services more accessible. For example, providing piped water costs $0.70–$0.80 per cubic meter in urban areas, but $2 in sparsely populated areas (Kariuki and Schwartz 2005). Schooling and health care can be delivered at scale in dense environments, close to where people actually live.

Urban densities can pull up rural areas. Research in India has shown a growing link between urban development and a reduction of rural poverty following India's economic liberalization in the early 1990s, with urban development linked to higher demand for rural products and more options for rural nonfarm diversification (World Bank 2013b).

Unregulated markets are unlikely to get densities "right," however, because the productivity of firms and the job-opportunity-generating aspects of increased density are positive externalities accruing freely to all, whereas the increased costs of construction, such as buildings, roads, and network utilities, necessary for higher density to remain efficient are not often fully internalized by firms and households. This situation leads to lower levels of investment than would be optimal and ultimately to less productivity improvement, less job creation, and lower wages (Collier and Venables forthcoming). Yet, higher-quality construction material and more sophisticated buildings are required to support greater densities, and complementary physical infrastructure is critical: roads, drainage, street lighting, electricity, water, and sewerage, together with policing, waste disposal, and health care. More, not less, public policy is needed to ensure that the productivity gains and services that cities can deliver are not overwhelmed by crime, disease, and squalor.

While a fully market-driven process could possibly gradually increase densities through land values over time, the long-lived and lumpy nature of urban investment inhibits such a process. A city's physical structures, once established, may remain in place for more than 150 years (Hallegatte 2009). The alarming news is that the doubling of the urban population in the developing world will be accompanied by a tripling in the built-up area of cities, from 200,000 to 600,000 square kilometers. As an example, consider map 3.1, which shows Shanghai's spatial expansion over the past 20 years. Such rapid population growth accompanied by an even faster spatial expansion of cities is likely to lead to low-density development dominated by individual-vehicle transportation—a largely irreversible pattern (World Bank 2012b). Low-density expansions run the risk of dampening density-induced productivity and service delivery efficiencies. An additional consequence of rapid urban growth is worsening air quality; a recent study of the 189 largest cities using satellite data found that air quality worsened between 2002 and 2010, particularly in the largest cities of the Indian subcontinent, parts of Africa, the Middle East, and north China, all places

MAP 3.1   Shanghai's spatial expansion as shown by average nighttime light intensity

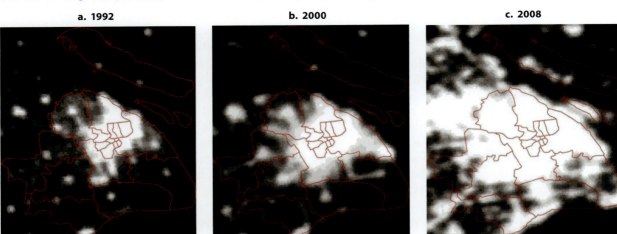

Source: China Data Center at University of Michigan.

experiencing rapid urban growth (Alpert, Shvainshtein, and Kishcha 2012).

Emissions from burning fossil fuel include fine particulate matter (PM10 and PM2.5), carbon monoxide, nitric oxides, and sulfur dioxide, which can cause allergies, respiratory problems, cardiovascular disease, and cognitive deficits. The impacts are significant. In the Russian Federation, a conservative estimate suggests that annual health damages from fossil-fuel burning amount to $6 billion (Markandya and Golub 2012). The social cost of transport in Beijing is equivalent to 7.5–15 percent of its gross domestic product (GDP), with about half of that stemming from air pollution (Creutzig and He 2009). The largest share of these costs comes from increased mortality. Globally, acute respiratory infections associated with air pollution cause about 20 percent of all under-five mortality (Mehta et al. 2011). In the former Yugoslav Republic of Macedonia, a country of about 2 million people, an estimated 1,300 premature deaths are caused by air pollution every year. Beijing, Cairo, Delhi, Dhaka, and Karachi each see an estimated 3,500 to 7,000 premature deaths annually from cardiovascular disease stemming from air pollution (Gurjar et al. 2010). Karachi has the highest overall mortality related to air pollution, at 15,000 a year. That is close to the excess mortality of 13,000 deaths caused by the "Great Smog" in London in 1952, evidence that many cities in today's advanced countries have gone through similar stages of excessive pollution. Managing environmental quality alongside enhancing urban productivity is critical as a means of avoiding significant costs down the road.

Cities can accelerate both economic and social progress when complementary improvements are made along two fronts:

* *Job creation, investment, and growth*, which depend on the density of cities and their links with the rural economy. Enhancing job opportunities in cities requires careful thought about coordinating improvements in land management, housing, transport, communications,

and infrastructure (World Bank 2013b). Urbanization generates an increase in the demand for land, and a clear definition of property rights along with robust systems for assessing land values is key for land redevelopment. Urbanization has to be combined with the development of reliable and affordable public transit to physically connect people with jobs. Complementary improvements in communication and interregional transport can make it easier to integrate neighboring rural areas into the urban economy.

* *Expansion of basic services, such as those reflected by the MDGs, across cities and rural areas*, so that people are "pulled" to cities by the opportunities there, rather than being pushed from the countryside in search of basic services they have been denied. Improvements in basic services such as water, sanitation, education, and health are essential for improving living standards and workers' health and education everywhere, as Colombia did when it systematically improved basic service levels across the country in rural and urban areas alike. In 1964, only half the residents of Bogotá and other large cities had access to water, electricity, and sanitation; today there is nearly universal access in cities of all sizes, a convergence that took more than 40 years (Samad, Lozano-Gracia, and Panman 2012).

Many developing countries have been unable to provide a coordinated package of physical infrastructure and social services (box 3.1). In part, that is because many of these services are network goods that households and communities cannot provide on their own. Even where the service can be supplied by each individual household or a community, as with sanitation, there are substantial externalities, where the benefits of service improvements spread beyond the household or community that made the investment. As a consequence, individual households and communities are likely to underinvest in these services, setting up a classic role for public policy of ensuring that basic services

---

BOX 3.1   Bangalore has nurtured skills but must now tackle infrastructure

Bangalore's economic growth has been rapid and successful. In 1998, the Indian city's incomes were 24 percent higher than the national average. In 2005, they were nearly 70 percent higher.

An analysis shows that the skills of the city's residents are the bedrock of that success. These skills have long been valued in Bangalore, with the maharajas of the princely state of Mysore instituting compulsory education and building the University of Mysore and Bangalore's engineering college. This was the starting point for the cluster of educated engineers that persists to this day. Building on an initial corpus of engineering expertise, firms such as Infosys were attracted to Bangalore, jumpstarting a virtuous circle where smart companies and smart workers came to Bangalore to be close to one another.

Bangalore's economic success is creating infrastructure problems, however, including poor water quality, traffic congestion, and housing shortages. The water system is strained—30 percent of city residents use polluted groundwater; the sewer system does not reach a large part of the city; and average commute times are more than 40 minutes because jobs are dispersed from the city core. If the water problems or commuting times get worse, skilled people—the city's main asset—will leave for cities that offer better amenities. How Bangalore improves the quality of life for its residents will have a considerable bearing on how bright Bangalore continues to shine.

Source: Glaeser 2010.

---

are adequately provided. While each infrastructure sector and service can be addressed by appropriate government policies, addressing only one or two of them has little payoff if the others remain unresolved (Collier and Venables forthcoming). Getting the highest level of political support to enable cross-sectoral and intergovernmental coordination is critical for getting urbanization right.

Framework for urbanization policy

The policy framework used here draws heavily on the *World Development Report 2009: Reshaping Economic Geography* (WDR 2009) (World Bank 2008) and subsequent country level diagnostics under the World Bank's Urbanization Review Program, whose lessons are synthesized in *Planning, Connecting, and Financing Cities—Now* (World Bank 2013a). WDR 2009 looked at urbanization trends and policies worldwide and proposed a three-part policy framework for urbanization. First, institutions should provide the foundations for liberalizing the movement of people and goods and easing the exchange and redevelopment of land,

enabling vast economic gains. Second, investments should respond to the needs of residents and businesses, especially for basic and connective infrastructure. Third, targeted interventions should respond to the needs of the poor and people in marginal locations or address individual behaviors that endanger health, safety, or the environment. Applying this policy framework, the World Bank's Urbanization Reviews offer policy makers diagnostic tools to identify policy distortions and analyze investment priorities.

Each review starts by assessing a country or region's spatial transformation: how the urban economy is evolving; how urbanization is changing the demand for services within the city; the pace of new arrivals; and where these new arrivals are finding places to live and how they are commuting to their jobs. It then compares the city's observed patterns with benchmarks in other cities or with past conditions. Such comparisons help reveal how policy distortions constrain urbanization and how investment shortfalls limit the benefits from it. Once the review has identified the possible constraints and shortfalls, it proposes policy options. It aims to show how a city can harness economic and social

FIGURE 3.1   **A framework for urbanization policy: planning, connecting, and financing**

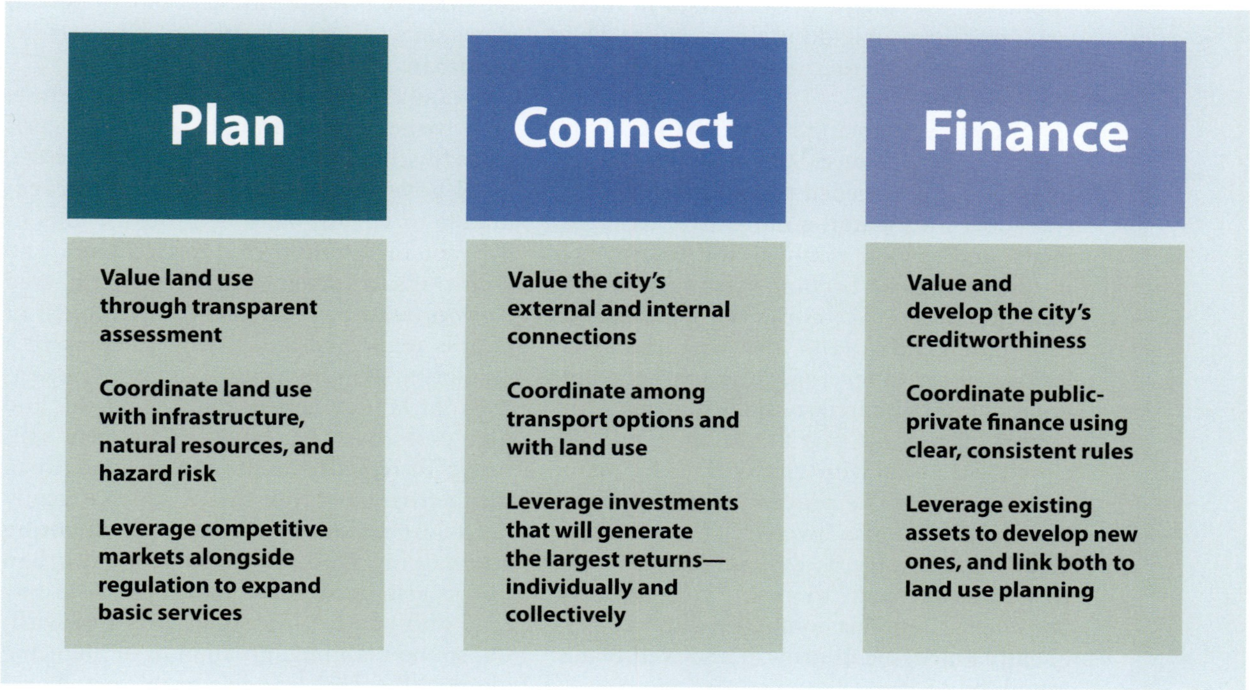

Plan	Connect	Finance
Value land use through transparent assessment	**Value the city's external and internal connections**	**Value and develop the city's creditworthiness**
Coordinate land use with infrastructure, natural resources, and hazard risk	**Coordinate among transport options and with land use**	**Coordinate public-private finance using clear, consistent rules**
Leverage competitive markets alongside regulation to expand basic services	**Leverage investments that will generate the largest returns— individually and collectively**	**Leverage existing assets to develop new ones, and link both to land use planning**

Source: This framework draws on World Bank 2013a and the findings from various country pilots under the Urbanization Reviews.

benefits not just today, but in the future as economies grow, technologies change, and institutions are strengthened. Urbanization Reviews have been piloted in some dozen countries at varying stages of urbanization, including Sri Lanka and Uganda (where urbanization is nascent), China, India, Indonesia, and Vietnam (where it is rapid), and Brazil, Colombia, the Republic of Korea, and Turkey (where it is mature).

At the heart of the diagnostic approach used in the Urbanization Reviews are three main dimensions of urban development (figure 3.1):

- *Planning*—charting a course for cities by setting the terms of urbanization, especially policies for using urban land and expanding basic infrastructure and public services.
- *Connecting*—making a city's markets (labor, goods, and services) accessible to other cities and to other neighborhoods

in the city, as well as to outside export markets.
- *Financing*—finding sources for large capital outlays needed to provide infrastructure and services as cities grow and urbanization picks up speed.

Planning, connecting, financing—these are terms that policy makers use on a daily basis. Of the three, a major finding from the Urbanization Reviews is that regardless of the level or speed of urbanization, planning for land use management must be the top priority. By clearly defining property rights, and putting in place effective systems for land use that are coordinated with infrastructure, transport, and natural resources, policy makers can help their cities attract private investment, connect people with jobs, and reduce environmental, social, and natural hazard risks. With much of urban growth in developing countries likely to take place in secondary cities, strengthening land management provides a unique, albeit rapidly closing, opportunity to shape urban design in these cities so that people do not have to spend a significant part of their day traveling to and from work.

Of course financing rapid urban growth is challenging, because large up-front capital investments are needed to build systems for transport and water, solid waste management, and sewage removal and treatment. But financing can become more sustainable through taxes that come with increased economic growth, and also with the ability of mayors to leverage land markets and approach local currency debt markets. An important point is that financing should be closely integrated with a city's plans for managing growth. The process of urban management should also involve as many private actors as necessary, as well as address women's empowerment, to ensure that the city becomes or remains competitive and consequently an engine of growth and well-being for all (box 3.2).

Policy makers, however, often place financing first without fully considering a city's plans and connections. And the lack of such coordination will be regretted by later urban generations. For example, in Hanoi, a projected new mass transit system will extend in several directions from today's central business district, but it will not reach an emerging second central business district southwest of the city, where dense housing developments called New Urban Zones are already being built (World Bank 2011).

Similarly, Colombia's urban development challenges arise from problems of policy and planning. One of Latin America's most decentralized countries, Colombia has more than 1,000 municipal governments with parallel responsibilities—basic infrastructure and service delivery, land use and economic development, and social service provision. Urban areas comprise multiple municipalities: Bogotá, for example, contains seven. These municipalities lack mechanisms to coordinate policy and planning across their boundaries. As a result, Colombia's metropolitan areas are crippled by inertia—unable to coordinate their land use policies, or plan for strategic investments, at the metropolitan or regional scale that is demanded by a growing urban economy.

Uganda's 1995 constitution created private land ownership and abolished land leases vested with local urban bodies. As a result, local governments were fiscally starved, unable to acquire land or protect rights of way for infrastructure improvement. And land transactions generally were hampered by poor tenure security (only 18 percent of land is registered and titled); the lack of a credible system for valuing land; low incentives for landowners to rent their land; and high entry costs for land development ventures. To remedy the situation, especially in the metropolis of Kampala, Uganda urgently needs a credible system for documenting and valuing land. To be sure, local urban bodies also need financing support—to buy land and pay for infrastructure. But without sound planning, no amount of financing alone will solve Uganda's problems (World Bank 2012c).

Planning cities

Planning is fundamental to agglomeration economies in three ways. First, land use requires effective systems for land valuation. Second, land use must be allocated in a way that allows for infrastructure improvements. Third, the most basic infrastructure services—water, energy, sanitation, and solid waste management—need to be provided for all residents, urban, peri-urban, and rural alike.

Set up systematic and transparent systems for valuing land

The use and reuse of land is central to a city's expansion and development. For economic efficiency, land should be able to shift among various uses; in some cases, public intervention may be required to offset market failures (Henderson and Wang 2007). Urban land markets should efficiently allocate land between urban and rural uses (with

BOX 3.2   Urbanization, gender, jobs, and urban poverty

Women's labor, paid and unpaid, is crucial to the prosperity of cities. In turn, for women, urbanization opens up greater access to services and employment opportunities, offers advantages arising from lower fertility, and promotes increased independence. Indeed, women's growing participation in paid employment is a positive trend that is not only contributing to their empowerment but also improving individuals' and households' chances to move out of poverty. Increased movement of women between rural and urban areas is motivated by the greater availability of employment opportunities in urban centers and confirms the positive impact of urbanization on women's empowerment.

However, urbanization does not necessarily result in a more equitable distribution of wealth and well-being between men and women. Compared with men, women often remain at a disadvantage in equitable access to work and living conditions, income levels, health outcomes and education, assets, and representation in formal institutions and urban governance, as also discussed in *World Development Report 2012: Gender Equality and Development* (WDR 2012). This is especially so for the urban poor, especially slum dwellers, who face considerable environmental hazards, shelter deprivations arising from a lack of proper water and sanitation provisions, and difficulties in accessing health and education services. Unpaid care work for children, older people, and the sick or disabled at home is typically (though not always or only) performed by women in low-income settlements; this work can include food preparation, cleaning, and washing among other tasks. Limited access to water and sanitation puts an additional burden on women responsible for such activities, not only by making the chores more difficult, but also by requiring more time to perform them. This burden is further exacerbated by the type of employment that poor urban women engage in—typically low-paid

jobs with long working hours. Poverty generated by these factors therefore has a specific gender dimension. Women further face an unequal position in the labor market because of their lower income relative to their male counterparts, their limited ability to secure assets independently from male relatives, and their greater exposure to violence. In this sense, a gendered lens is not only essential for examining the nonincome dimensions of urban poverty but is also critical in understanding the broader issues of equality and social justice.

Social programs often do not sufficiently focus on efforts to improve the efficiency and productivity of household tasks. Often, this can be achieved through relatively simple infrastructure and provision of basic services and appliances, such as gas or electric stoves. In addition, policy makers can support initiatives that help reduce the time constraints caused by balancing paid work with unpaid care work. Some such initiatives already exist within the activities of grassroots and women's organizations, such as the Women's Network of Street Traders and Collective Kitchen initiatives in Lima (Peru), the Shack/Slum Dwellers International (SDI) savings groups in several developing countries, and Kenya's Home-Based Care Alliance. A lack of even basic data disaggregated by sex has prevented researchers from developing a more gender-nuanced picture of urban poverty. Data collection efforts on basic poverty indicators as well as more specific surveys of labor force participation and migration need to record respondents' sex at a minimum and make it available to researchers. Along with this, unpaid work needs to be incorporated within an understanding of how economies operate for the urban poor; without that, the impact of public policies directed at urban poverty reduction cannot be fully grasped.

Source: Based on Tacoli 2012.

incentives to conserve farmland and green space) and within urban areas (to prevent inappropriate land use and underserved neighborhoods).

What is the key to efficient land use? The answer is the price of land. Institutions

that improve the information foundations of the valuation process, including a cadre of appraisers trained in property valuation, help to ensure transparency and to make information about land values widely accessible. In Korea until the early 1970s, local government officials assessed the market value and replacement costs of assets for land acquisition purposes. In 1972, the government introduced the Basic Land Prices system to improve assessments. In this new system, land and buildings had to be assessed by certified private appraisers rather than government officials. Two appraisers had to provide estimated values for the property, and the final value was calculated as the average of the two values. If the two appraisals differed by more than 10 percent, a third appraiser was selected and the average recalculated. Since 2003, a third appraiser may be recommended by affected individuals as well (World Bank 2013a).

Developing countries often lack the systems to record and manage information on land transactions. The data may not reflect the true price of land because of black market transactions to save on duties, for example, or because of heavy public subsidies on housing and land use. Land registries are often archaic and lack the dynamic functions that allow them to be searched or updated quickly. These deficiencies translate into a dearth of data on real estate prices, preventing the critical analysis necessary for appraising land values. That, in turn, has heavy implications for local revenue generation, such as property tax collection and land sales or leases, that is based on real estate values.

Take India, where such information systems are in their infancy and the government often acquires land for industrial and infrastructure development. Farmers and other landowners are compensated with payments benchmarked to the stamp duties, a land transaction tax. But because the marginal rate for stamp duties has been as high as 12 percent historically, land and property values have long been underreported (World Bank 2013b).[1] Now, as India's policy makers amend the rules for changes in land use, the lack of independent and reliable land valuations is likely to result in public discontent and conflicts over land.

In Vietnam, too, official land prices fail to reflect demand. The country has two prices for land transactions—a market price, and

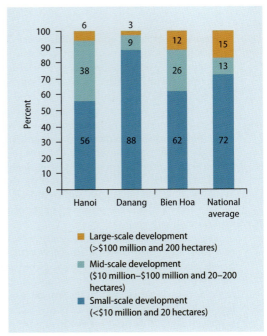

FIGURE 3.2 **Vietnam's dual land price system creates problems for the assembly of large plots of land needed for industry**

Large-scale development (>$100 million and 200 hectares)

Mid-scale development ($10 million–$100 million and 20–200 hectares)

Small-scale development (<$10 million and 20 hectares)

Source: World Bank 2011.

an imposed land price, a much lower value used by the government in acquiring land and allocating it to developers and investors (World Bank 2011). Such an inequitable system generates resentment over land acquisitions: over 1996–2005, there were more than 12,000 complaints. And conflicts over land, in turn, hinder the consolidation of plots for industrial development. More than 85 percent of available plots in Vietnam are smaller than 20 hectares, but industrial parks and districts typically need 150–200 hectares of contiguous land (figure 3.2). So the country's two-price system impedes efficiency and economic development.

In countries where land valuation is successful, standardized techniques enable appraisers to arrive at uniform and transparent valuations. In the United States, most states require appraisers and assessors to be certified. Appraisers generally work for private clients to determine the market value of property for real estate transactions, while assessors generally work for the government to determine property values for tax purposes. Both must follow the same regulations in valuing real estate. For practical purposes, however, and to avoid overestimation of prices, property prices for tax purposes are often set at about two-thirds of actual market value. In Bogotá, property values are usually set at 70–80 percent of estimated market value.

Public land valuation in developing countries is fraught with challenges, including the cost of hiring private appraisers (these countries lack standardized public valuation methods) and the need to update land price data. In addition, intergovernmental transfers of public land are often recorded as having zero value. These challenges can be overcome, however, as seen in at least two cases of innovation in public land valuation. Kuwait now requires two separate private appraisals for land involved in public-private partnerships (PPPs). And South Africa mandates that public land be taxed the same way as private land, which means that public land undergoes the same valuation processes (Peterson and Kaganova 2010). In other developing countries auctions are often used to reveal land values.

In contrast, federal regulation governs private land valuation in Germany. Germany has local land valuation boards that are charged with collecting and maintaining land price data as well as disseminating land price information (Lozano-Gracia et al. 2013). The United States allows each state to define its own method for private property valuation, and most states delegate this power to local governments, leading to a vast array of approaches. While the most common is the market value (or sales comparison) approach, there are at least two others: the cost approach, and the income approach. All three methods are often used in parallel to estimate property values. The state of New York, for example, uses these methods for different property categories. It follows the sales comparison approach to value small residential properties and vacant land, using

sales data of comparable properties for the previous three years. It adopts the income approach to value offices and businesses, taking an estimated income for the office rental, and dividing the net income by a capitalization rate. It uses the cost approach for new construction and renovations and for special properties such as stadiums, museums, and places of worship (Lafuente 2009).

Complementary policies that assign property rights and encourage trade of land are also needed to help settlements respond to the changing needs of the market. Fluid land markets help the transition out of agriculture, where rural land can be sold or rented for urban uses, and rural residents can seek more rewarding opportunities in nonfarm activities in urban areas. For instance in Vietnam, strengthening of land tenure security quadrupled participation in rural rental markets from 3.8 percent in 1993 to 15.8 percent in 1998 and resulted in an increase in rural-urban migration from 29 percent in 1993 to 64 percent in 1998. In addition, both rental and sales markets had positive impacts on productivity.

In conclusion, making land markets and land management work better requires improving and upgrading or reforming the underlying related legal system. Urbanization will increase the demand for land, and governments at the national and subnational levels will employ instruments such as land acquisition and land readjustment for accommodating urban expansion, or land monetization for financing infrastructure. Strong legal systems and credible institutions will be a precondition for success. In particular, these include carefully designed laws to assign and protect property rights; institutions that enable independent valuation and public dissemination of land values across uses; and a strong legal framework supported by a healthy judicial system to handle disputes and oversee the process.

For land acquisition, courts need to provide guidance on the legal scope of eminent domain. Given that the definition of public purpose constantly evolves, having a rigid and exclusive list of public purposes will pose stringent barriers to urban expansion. As an alternative, a flexible definition of public purpose can be combined with a strong judicial system to guide and evaluate acquisition decisions on a case-by-case basis. If a flexible definition is used, it becomes increasingly important to provide a clear definition of the process to adjudicate conflicts in cases where the "public purpose" of a particular acquisition is questioned, as well as to establish the institutions that guarantee that affected parties can voice their concerns.

Coordinate land management with infrastructure, housing, and transport

Manage densities

Just as valuing land and assigning property rights are challenges for accommodating urban expansion, so are managing densities within cities and finding ways to finance urban expansion and city renewal. One widely used tool for managing densities is the floor space index (FSI), or floor area ratio. This is the ratio of the gross floor area of a building on a lot divided by the area of that lot. If, for example, the FSI in an area of a city is 1:1, developers can only put up a building with a gross floor area less than or equal to the total lot area. While in some cases it may be possible to build a one-story building that covers the lot entirely, thus achieving an FSI of 1:1, developers typically construct buildings with a "footprint" or "plinth" that covers less than the whole lot, and so the structure has more than one story. For example, a developer could build a four-story building that covered 25 percent of the lot and still meet the FSI of 1:1.

Other planning regulations include setbacks (minimum distances to the front, rear, and sides of a plot) and maximum building heights. Both are designed to protect adjacent properties and preserve access to sun, air, and open space (parks and plazas). Finally, plot coverage ratio regulations limit the total area of a plot that can be developed (World Bank 2013a). There is no such thing as an optimal FSI. The "right" FSI for a specific area depends on the existing spatial structure

of the city, the street patterns and widths, the level of infrastructure (is there enough capacity to accommodate higher density, that is, higher FSIs?), and cultural and social factors (are skyscrapers acceptable?) (Bertaud 2004).

Although these regulations exist for good reasons, they often have unintended consequences. If an area's FSI is set far below the level at which investors might otherwise develop it, this repression of supply can push people into other areas, and the increased demand for those other areas can raise prices across the city (Annez and Linn 2010). Similarly, if the FSI is a uniform limit, it may increase housing prices by limiting the supply of land that would otherwise be built up. It may also encourage the allocation of land and buildings to less productive uses. Beyond slowing city growth in these ways, a uniform limit can also push poor households to distant suburbs, adding to their poverty by increasing their commuting costs and times. When households have no choice but to locate near jobs, they often join hazard-prone informal settlements.

Consider South Africa, where the government has focused on provision of subsidized housing, first introduced as part of the Reconstruction and Development Program. The benefits of the program have been questioned, however. The most common complaint is that households receiving the subsidized housing are not satisfied, because the housing is often far from employment centers; the new houses were often built in the "old" apartheid locations (which were deliberately sited far from urban centers and white neighborhoods). In addition, most households do not receive title deeds immediately but are allocated the housing administratively; whether they receive title right away or not, households are barred from selling or renting for a period of five years. Furthermore, even after the five-year period, the government has a preemptive right (the right of first refusal) on the sale of the property. In short, poor location and lack of fully tradable property rights are often cited as reasons for the limited impact of the subsidized housing.

Integrate land management with infrastructure

A central problem of urban planning is that of matching land use and infrastructure for the best possible outcome. Higher densities generate a greater need for infrastructure services (electricity, water, sewerage). But they also support environmental sustainability because they are better suited to public transport. To be sure, density must not overwhelm infrastructure. Yet it is equally important not to underuse infrastructure, imposing low-density caps where infrastructure can support higher ones.

To see what is at stake, compare Manhattan, New York City's archetypal borough, with Mumbai (map 3.2). Manhattan's density zones are typically small. Its restrictions on land use vary with street width and capacity, with infrastructure capacity, and with historical land use patterns (commercial office districts typically have higher FSIs than residential districts). This granularity helps to make Manhattan a good example of integration between land use and infrastructure.

In contrast, Mumbai's density zones are large and uniform across much of the city, and densities are generally low. India's urban planners justify such low formal densities as necessary to avoid overburdening existing infrastructure, which is severely limited. Rather than increase formal or planned densities, they have tried to preserve urban areas

MAP 3.2   **New York's density management is granular and integrated with infrastructure while Mumbai's is coarse and uncoordinated**

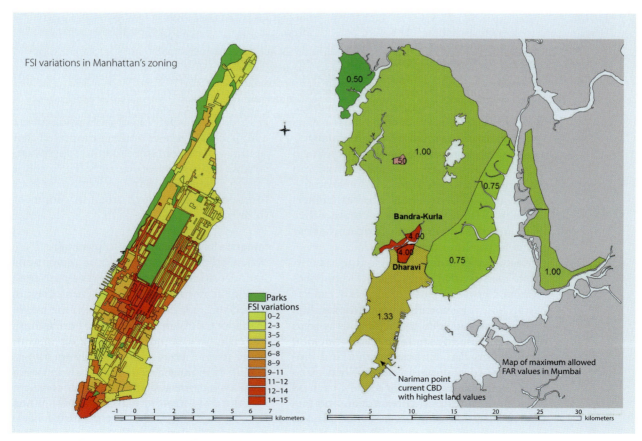

Sources: New York City Planning Department 2011 (left); Bertaud 2004 (right).
Note: In some zones, the floor space index (FSI) might be increased up to two additional units because of bonuses due to plaza, arcades, and the like. In some areas, the permitted FSI might not be reached because of setbacks and plot geometry.

BOX 3.3   **Do cities need master plans?**

Instead of drawing up a master plan and making a large effort to update it every 10 years, as is frequently the pattern, it may be better to produce a much simpler spatial strategy document that could be updated every year by staff of a city's urban planning department. The emphasis of such a document would be on the current spatial situation and spatial trends. Its main objectives would be to ensure housing and land affordability and adequate mobility. Such a process would focus on analyzing real estate prices and supply and demand constraints for all income groups, firms, and households. The plan would cover three topics: land use and spatially distributed demographics; road and transport networks; and land use and development regulations. Rather than attempting to cover all sectors, when the spatial strategy is approved by government, it could be distributed to line agencies that have the technical expertise to develop sectoral plans that are consistent with spatial distribution of people and jobs, as well as consistent with their budget constraints. It is important to provide the line agen-

cies with a constantly updated spatial distribution of populations so that they can adjust their investment programs to meet current and future demand.

This proposal is not revolutionary. Most master plans around the world are largely ignored (even in China). In Vietnam, master plans are often referred to as "hanging plans," suggesting that they often decorate the walls of planning departments but are rarely implemented. As in most countries, Vietnam line agencies typically make investment decisions based on their own population projections, which are rarely consistent with master plans and often differ between agencies. Changing the planning process to be more in line with market dynamics would lead to better and more consistent development outcomes. Singapore and Hong Kong are good examples of land use planning and internal consistency between spatial objectives and the provision of physical and social infrastructure.

Source: World Bank 2011.

by pushing development out to new towns and suburban industrial estates, disconnecting people from job opportunities (World Bank 2013b). But this strategy ignores an opportunity: India's cities could instead use rising land values to finance better, higher-capacity infrastructure, to increase office space, and to add affordable housing for low- and moderate-income groups.

Keeping densities low and failing to coordinate density with infrastructure suppresses economic growth, most importantly exacerbating housing shortages and affordability. Cities' plans and zoning designations need to reflect market realities. The consequence of master plans that artificially limit land supply can be soaring land prices. When plans underestimate required land uses, such as residential, industrial, commercial, and services, land prices for parcels zoned as such tend to sell at higher prices than would be set in the marketplace. In many cities in the developing world, urban planning consists of

designing the expansion of cities using norms and spatial choices that reflect the preferences of urban planners rather than to supply constraints and consumer demands. The result is often a master plan that is ineffective for both forecasting and guiding urban development (box 3.3).

Integrate land use and mobility planning

When urban land and building regulations limit densities in urban areas, they push people and firms to the outskirts. When cities are forced to grow out instead of up, the urban transport network becomes increasingly important as the only way to connect people to jobs. A good transport system allows people to make efficient trade-offs between the housing type and amenities they consume and the distance they travel to work. When the network is deficient, the problems stemming from stringent regulations in land markets are exacerbated. For example, people may be forced to live in slums close to job

BOX 3.4   **Publicly accessible information on urban hazard risk can improve household decision making**

With access to good information about hazard risk, households can make better decisions on where to live, depending on the location's proximity to job centers, the quality and cost of transport services, and the location's risk of exposure to natural hazards. Some examples of such information systems include:

- The Bogotá Disaster Vulnerability Reduction Project, launched in 2006, invested in information collection and vulnerability assessments for better targeting of risk reduction measures. One output was a database of earthquake vulnerability scores for all buildings in the city that helps prioritize upgrades and makes insurance markets more transparent (Prasad et al. 2009).
- Jakarta and Can Tho (Vietnam) recently carried out vulnerability assessments with World Bank support (World Bank 2012b). The studies demonstrate the use of geographically referenced data to pinpoint hazard risk and to support cost-benefit

analysis of various risk reduction strategies. Flood-prone Jakarta, for instance, is considering measures such as drainage improvement, river improvement, upgrading of retention ponds, and various options for a coastal defense infrastructure.

- Better risk information supported the introduction of the Turkish Catastrophe Insurance Pool, a risk transfer mechanism set up after the Marmara earthquake in 1999 that killed at least 17,000 people and damaged 120,000 houses in the Istanbul region. The program reduced households' financial damages by enabling them to have catastrophic insurance and encouraging physical risk mitigation.
- A joint study by the World Bank, the Asian Development Bank, and the Japan International Cooperation Agency assessed future climate risks for coastal megacities and found that by 2050, the frequency of major floods in Bangkok could increase from once every 50 years to once every 15 years. About 1 million inhabitants would be affected (ADB, JICA, and WB 2010).

centers, often assuming natural hazard risks, because they cannot afford to move into formal housing or cannot access cheaper land on the outskirts of cities for lack of an efficient urban transport system. In Santo Domingo, the capital of the Dominican Republic, 45 percent of the houses in the largest slum are located near a river and are flooded in heavy rains (Fay, Ghesquiere, and Solo 2003). The poorest live in the lowest-quality dwellings in the areas most at risk. Likewise, informal settlements in Rio de Janeiro and Caracas cling to steep slopes with large landslide risk during rainstorms. Publicly available information on hazard risk can enable households to make informed decisions (box 3.4), but lack of coordinated land use and mobility improvements will force them to make suboptimal choices.

Thus, plans to connect neighborhoods should be integrated with plans for urban land use, especially density plans. For any of

these policies to benefit the city as intended, they must be integrated throughout the planning process. Urban transport is often an "institutional orphan," however, with its responsibility often fragmented across agencies (World Bank 2013a). Land use planning is a core function of development authorities, with transport planning often limited to developing the road network. Such fragmentation of responsibilities results in inefficiencies. In Bangalore, a new airport several miles outside the city was close to being commissioned when city authorities realized that the road connecting the city to the airport was inadequate.

Land use planning is integral to transport planning because land use largely determines transport demand. Different cities need different mixes of transport types, and different neighborhoods need different modes. Mass transport generally suits compact areas; private vehicles, more sprawling ones.

Mixed-use plans can reduce the need for long trips by locating housing, shops, services, and jobs all within a short radius. Studies also suggest that higher densities are good for efficiency and for environmental sustainability, reducing energy consumption and emissions by reducing vehicle miles traveled (Newman and Kenworthy 1989; Mokhtarian, Bagley, and Salomon 1998; Schrank, Lomax, and Eisele 2011). Transport plans, in turn, shape land use by making specific sites more accessible. For example, a new road to undeveloped land can facilitate its development, or a new downtown metro connection can boost demand for redevelopment of the urban core.

However, increased prosperity leads in general to increased purchase of vehicles and even though the miles traveled in urban areas is smaller than in rural areas, this increase in vehicle ownership will have serious implications for carbon emissions. Controlling carbon emissions is a daunting challenge for policy makers in developing countries (Kahn forthcoming). As population and manufacturing firm densities in urban areas grow, so too do negative spillovers that affect the population's health, with significant effects on children's development, and that lead to environmental damage in the form of floods and droughts. The implications of both spillovers for the MDGs related to health and sustainable development are not trivial and have well-known policy implications for individual countries.

In the absence of urban planning, individual firms invariably locate in city centers to take advantage of industrial agglomeration, which contributes to high carbon emissions. Usually, labor-intensive industries choose countries with low wages, and electricity-intensive heavy industries pick locations where electricity is cheap. The challenge for developing-country policy makers of industrial cities is to foster sustainable urbanization policies to reduce carbon emissions without constraining industrial growth. The key to sustainable urbanization is designing city-specific and type of local pollution specific interventions.

A low-cost way for governments to break the link between industrial and pollution production is to encourage firms to locate in dedicated industrial parks such as China's special economic zones where government has encouraged the installation of industrial infrastructure to increase industrial productivity without compromising environmental damage. Another option to break the link is to invest in transport infrastructure to encourage suburbanization of manufacturing, which reduces industrial pollution exposure for people who live in the center city, while encouraging them to move closer to the suburban jobs. In China and the Republic of Korea, these policies also had the positive effect of attracting the industry's supply chain (intermediate goods suppliers) to the suburbs, causing population suburbanization.

"Smart" regulation includes allocating pollution permits to achieve the dual goals of pollution mitigation and continued industrial production. Under such a permit system, the government places a cap on total tons of pollution that may be released by industry in a given area surrounding the city and requires polluting firms to bid for permits to pollute in the area. This system discourages firms from polluting and gives them incentives to install production technologies that economize on pollution. Governments can disseminate information about industrial polluter activity by requiring firms to report their emissions levels. After the 1984 Union Carbide chemical disaster in Bhopal, India, the United States created the Toxic Release Inventory dataset, requiring U.S. manufacturing firms to publicize their emissions released to air, water, and land. Indonesia followed with success.

To economize on transportation costs, workers choose housing located close to firms. Government can invest in urban transportation to move goods and people within the metropolitan area, but richer people particularly continue to prefer private cars that add to carbon emissions. Some evidence suggests that a 10 percent growth in per capita income is associated with a 10 percent increase in per capita vehicle ownership. Policy options to minimize the environmental impact of private car ownership include a tax that influences a household choice to purchase a vehicle, the type of vehicle, and use of the vehicle. A gasoline tax that not only discourages driving but also increases fiscal revenues, pricing the use of public roads through tolls, and increasing public parking rates are other policy options to dampen the "heat-island effect" created by running vehicles. Government also can issue "pollution tickets," similar to speeding tickets to older cars and diesel trucks, and mandate the use of cleaner gasoline.

To encourage mass use of public transit, subways linked to city centers are popular. Investments in subways in Beijing and New Delhi are examples. But subways are costly and irreversible investments. The alternatives are investments in rapid buses, which offer competing speed and environmental benefits. Bogotá has done this with TransMilenio.

Urban households also use energy for air conditioning, heating, and appliances like refrigerators. These improve the quality of life but also add to carbon emissions. Governments can mitigate future climate change through flexible electricity pricing, which encourages consumers to keep energy use low. Smart cities use "smart meters" to monitor energy use but variable pricing penalizes the poor. Through block tariff rates with a low bottom rate for households that consume a low level of electricity, governments can make energy use affordable for the poor. In addition, poor urban households tend to choose the riskiest places where housing is cheapest. Policies to encourage energy efficient buildings can be helpful in these situations.

Leverage competitive forces to expand services

Governments have many choices in how to provide or expand basic services for their urban residents. In many instances, basic services are lacking altogether. Lack of electricity, for example, often forces households to trade off their health when they use alternate fuels for cooking and other uses. Indoor air pollution from solid fuels—wood, dung, coal, charcoal—continues to be widespread in areas where electricity is not available. This is a larger issue in rural areas but is still

significant in urban settings. In Sub-Saharan Africa, for instance, 83 percent of rural and 60 percent of urban households rely on solid fuels for cooking. Indoor combustion of solid fuels can cause severe health effects, especially among women and children who spend more time in the house (Bruce, Perez-Padilla, and Albalak 2000). These include lung cancer, pulmonary disease, low birth weight, cataracts, pneumonia, and tuberculosis. The World Health Organization estimates that exposure to solid fuel smoke causes 1.6 million deaths a year and the loss of 39 million disability-adjusted life years. With rising wealth in urban areas, households often switch to more convenient liquid fuels. Kerosene use is widespread in urban areas where electricity access is lacking, especially where kerosene is subsidized, such as in India and Nepal. Perhaps as many as 500 million households globally still use kerosene and similar fuels for lighting, as well as for cooking and heating. Apart from poisoning, fires, and explosions, kerosene poses risks from exposure to fine particulates, carbon monoxide, formaldehyde, and other potentially harmful emissions (Lam et al. 2012).

Basic services in many developing countries are distributed unevenly. Consider figure 3.3, which shows access to piped water for urban residents in Brazil, Colombia, India, Uganda, and Vietnam. In each of these five countries, water access varies with city size, but it does so differentially. In Vietnam, access is high but less equitable, with smaller cities showing lower access. In Brazil and Colombia, service coverage is high and fairly equitable. In India and Uganda, access is lower and less equitable.

Examine market structure

When policy makers consider how to expand infrastructure and improve the provision of basic services, they have a choice. Rather than give first priority to financing, as is often done, they can look at the structure of markets for basic services and determine what rules will work best. In particular, policy makers may consider rules for competitive pricing and cost recovery. Indeed, in many cases the expectation of cost recovery

FIGURE 3.3 **Share of population with access to piped water by country and across city size**

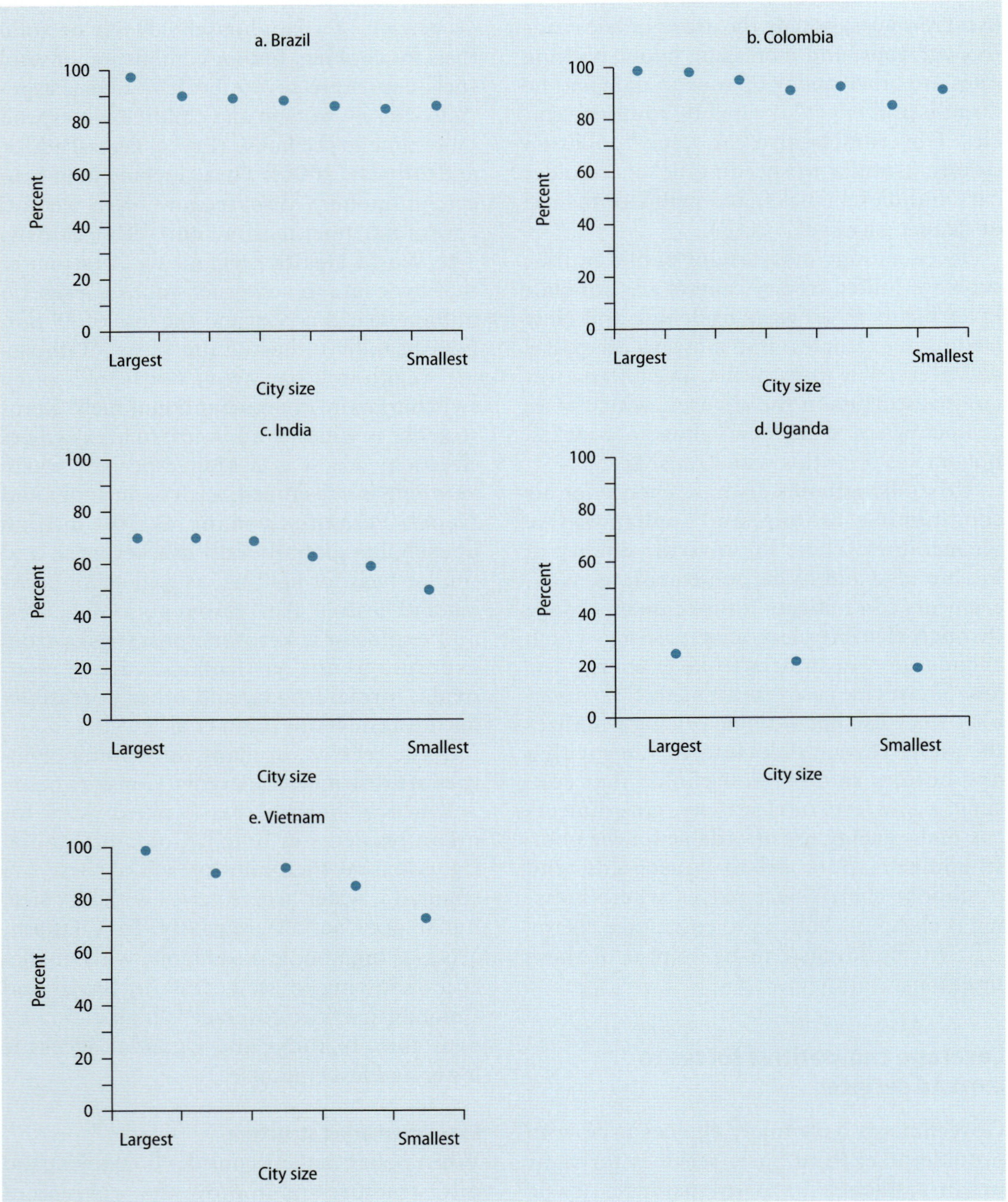

Sources: Brazil: Brazilian Institute of Geography and Statistics (IBGE), for 2000; Colombia: National Administrative Department of Statistics (DANE) for 2005; India: Ministry of Home Affairs for 2001; Uganda: Uganda Bureau of Statistics for 2010; Vietnam: General Statistics Office of Vietnam for 2009.

through fees will determine the availability of financing (box 3.5).

Recall Colombia's success in providing nearly universal access to water, electricity, and sanitation in cities nationwide. A big part of Colombia's success is that policy reforms allowed fees to nearly cover costs. For example, average residential water fees more

BOX 3.5   Expanding access to services: A tale of two sectors

For the most clear-cut demonstration of the role of prices and price formation processes, consider access to water versus access to phone services in Sub-Saharan Africa: just about everywhere in Sub-Saharan Africa, access to mobile phones is greater than access to modern water systems (figure B3.4.1). Official policy statements have been full of promises to enhance access to water for decades, yet similar statements have not been made regarding access to cell phones. Hence, official policy stance does not seem the key factor.

Maybe de facto administrative capability is more important. Both water and phones need some level of regulation. Yet the regulation of modern phone systems is conceptually more challenging than the regulation of water systems. In all systems, regulation needs to set prices that cover costs. Costs and an allowed rate of return need to be calculated. So it is for water systems that typically have monopoly providers in any given area. The mobile phone sector has both competitive and noncompetitive segments that require regulation. Multiple players pose challenges to regulating interconnection; as a result, telecommunications regulation should be more demanding than water regulation. However, many African countries have been able to provide a regulatory environment that enables penetration of mobile phone usage, even in challenging environments like the Democratic Republic of Congo, whereas they have not been able to achieve the same for water. Hence "capacity" to regulate does not seem to be the deciding factor either.

So what can explain the divergent patterns of access? A striking difference between the two sec-

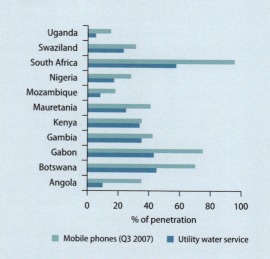

FIGURE B3.4.1   Water services versus mobile phones in Africa

Mobile phones (Q3 2007)   Utility water service

Source: Global Water Intelligence 2008.

tors is the level of prices relative to cost. In the water sector, prices typically barely cover operating costs and tend to be about 30 percent of total cost. In the mobile telephone sector, prices tend to exceed cost. Unsurprisingly, both public and private system operators, who can charge and collect prices that exceed costs, have an incentive to expand systems and can do so. Providers who receive less than full cost have neither the incentive nor the financial ability to expand access.

Source: Klein 2012.

than doubled over 1990–2001 (World Bank 2004). With almost 90 percent of households having a metered connection, household consumption was nearly halved. And that, in turn, reduced the need to develop major new infrastructure. Even with fee increases, water remains fairly affordable in Colombia. The fee structure allows the government to cross-subsidize: richer households and industrial users pay for the poorest consumers. As

a result, the average poor household spends less than 5 percent of its income on water.

Ugandan policy makers have started thinking about the rules that need to be in place to expand access to basic services. Water reform in 1998 focused on creating the right incentives for more efficient service provision, attributing responsibility to local service managers and increasing their accountability. Since 2000, the national government has been working with Uganda's National Water and Sewerage Corporation (NWSC), the autonomous public provider of water and sanitation to the country's large towns, to enforce performance contracts. Renewed every three years, the contracts include specific indicators that NWSC must meet at the end of the period (Banerjee and Morella 2011]). However, Uganda's reform has not yet attempted to promote cost recovery through user fees. The NWSC charges a uniform fee across all towns and customer categories served. In 2010, the fee covered production costs in only 6 of 23 areas served.

For some services such as urban transport, competition has to be regulated, because free market entry could undermine safety standards. The "penny wars" of Bogotá are an interesting example. Before a bus rapid transit system called TransMilenio was introduced in 2000, about 30,000–35,000 buses were operating in the city (Hook 2005). The government granted nonexclusive permits to the route operators, with whom bus owners were affiliated. The bus owners in turn charged their drivers fixed rents. The drivers' revenue thus depended directly on how many fares they collected. Cutthroat competition ensued, with unsafe results: drivers had a strong incentive to speed, cut people off, and carry too many passengers. The introduction of TransMilenio, together with a new regulatory framework, eliminated these "penny wars." The new framework included bidding for all parts of the service, from routes to infrastructure. TransMilenio allocates the market to operators according to their quality, among other factors, and it pays them by the kilometer, assuring them of a certain amount regardless of their passenger load (World Bank 2013a).

Direct competition may also not be feasible in sectors that naturally favor monopolies. Much of a city's networked infrastructure falls in this category: its duplication tends to be inefficient. A single network, fully built out, can often underbid any competitor (Klein 2012). Canada's cities are one example of a natural monopoly superseding market competition. Water utilities would at first compete to supply firms and households in a given market by laying separate pipelines. Then all the providers but one would fade away. In other cases, a monopoly provider started and was not challenged, either because competitors could not undercut it or because entry was forbidden by law. Natural monopolies can also appear in exclusive locations, such as airports and central metro stations.

Yet monopolies can abuse their market power, charging prices that are too high to be socially acceptable. Such prices can also make economies less productive and less competitive. So how can policy allow prices to cover costs while ensuring that prices stay close to costs, as opposed to fattening a monopoly with excessive profits?

Auctioning service franchises

Regulation can closely mimic the effects of competitive pricing even where monopolies exist. City leaders can auction the right to provide a service for a certain period, moving away from a monopolistic price and closer to the price that would arise from competition. Firms that lose at auction exit that particular market. If it is possible to put such a monopoly franchise up for auction fairly frequently based on the lowest price, the auction will act like a market to set prices.

Many cities, including Bogotá, London, and Santiago, auction bus routes, assigning operators to predefined itineraries. Santiago awards five-year contracts using criteria that include the fare offered by the bidder, along with quality variables. Before the auctions began, during a period of deregulation, bus fares had risen; with the auctions, the fares came back down. Where possible, franchise auctions repeated at intervals of one to three years can make price regulation essentially unnecessary. Such auctions have been used not only in bus transport but also in waste management. If a company loses a franchise, its assets—buses, garbage trucks—can be deployed elsewhere.

Public policy can set service prices below cost-recovery levels to meet social and environmental obligations. When prices are set to cover all the costs of an infrastructure project, including the cost of capital, systems will likely be built out to serve all customers who are ready to pay the service cost. But policy makers may also want access to infrastructure to be extended to other customers, both for equity and for environmental sustainability. Price discrimination and subsidies can boost coverage and access.

Establish subsidies for social equity

The poor often pay higher prices per unit of, say, water or energy than do wealthier people. Water vendors in poor urban areas may charge several times the unit cost of modern water service (Klein 2012). Price discrimination—charging rich people more and poor people less—is one way to restore equity. One method of price discrimination is to offer the poor a specially tailored price-quality mix. For example, poor people who can afford to buy water at times, but not regularly, can buy it by the bucket. Or the poor can be served by simpler pipelines. In other ways, too, the poor can be offered flexible service that is better than what they had before, yet not exactly what the rich receive. (Water that is not fully treated can still serve many common uses, such as flushing toilets. Poor people can make their water potable by boiling it.) Finally, the poor can be given more flexible payment terms, for example, through the use of electronic cards. In pursuing these possibilities, it can help to let unconventional providers, from for-profit vendors to community-based organizations, enter the market (Baker 2009). While these are clearly not the only solutions for improving access to water, they provide various second-best options to provide services of varying quality.

Governments can also provide subsidies to improve equity—but one must recognize that many subsidies do not increase access to services. For example, subsidizing an existing utility may help the better-off people who are already connected, but no one else (Komives et al. 2005; Estache and de Rus 2000). Accordingly, policy makers should focus discussions of subsidies on policies to expand access. They should target subsidies to poor people, either by conducting means testing (as in Chile's water subsidy system), by targeting areas where the poor tend to live, or by offering lifeline rates (for reduced service at a reduced price). Lifeline rates raise an objection, though, because they can benefit people at any income level. Such objections are a reminder that subsidies require careful design. Basing them on quantity or consumption does not necessarily promote equity. A study of 26 quantity-based subsidy cases in Africa, Asia, and Latin America suggested that 24 were regressive, and that where coverage is not universal, connection subsidies may be a solution for reaching the poor (Komives et al. 2005). A noteworthy innovation in enhancing access to services for the urban poor is through output-based aid, which links the payment of public funds or subsidies to the achievement of specified outputs and actual service performance (box 3.6).

Establish subsidies for environmental sustainability

Public transport can mitigate urban congestion: a bus carrying 40 or 50 people takes up no more road space than two or three private cars. And public transport pollutes less, generating fewer greenhouse emissions. Yet in many countries, public transport is unaffordable for the poor. For example, households in Kampala pay $13 a month for fares, about 8 percent of their budget (World Bank 2012c). Although that is consistent with global estimates of what people pay for transport, it is unaffordable for the poor. To use public transport, the poorest 20 percent of households would need to spend 41 percent of their income on fares. Similar patterns appear in other cities worldwide.

The predictable result is that in many developing countries, urban public transport ridership is low. In cities where transport fares do not cover the full cost of service provision, transport subsidies can boost ridership. But to succeed, such subsidies require strong contractual agreements and regulation. The problem is that even after fares are decoupled from full operating costs, transport providers still need assurance that their costs will be

BOX 3.6   Using output-based aid in urban projects

The people most affected by the lack of access to basic services in urban areas are the poor, who often obtain essential services such as drinking water or electricity from informal vendors at substandard quality and at a high premium. Given the growing demand for basic services, the need to improve service delivery in low-income urban settlements in increasing. One way to help the urban poor gain access to basic services is through output-based aid (OBA), which links the payment of public funds or subsidies to the achievement of specified outputs and actual service performance. Output definitions are designed to be as close to the desired development outcomes as is practicable and still within the scope of the service provider to deliver. Most urban OBA projects also require that a portion of the subsidy payment be withheld until sustainable service delivery has been demonstrated.

Targeting the urban poor: A core component of OBA is explicit targeting of low-income households. For the urban poor, a major hurdle to obtaining basic services is the high initial cost of access, such as a connection fee for water supply. OBA can help reduce this barrier by paying a subsidy to bridge the gap between the actual cost of access and what users are willing and able to pay. Geographic targeting can be effective in cities where poor households tend to be concentrated in slums and informal communities; alternative targeting strategies subsidize only those services that the nonpoor are less likely to use, or target beneficiaries based on their income or poverty level.

Risk transfer and access to finance: In OBA schemes, payment on delivery of specific outputs shifts performance risk to service providers, which can be public, private, or nongovernmental organizations. Since service providers are not paid the subsidy in full until they deliver outputs, they must have access to sufficient finance for the initial investments, a significant risk and one of the biggest constraints to developing output- or results-based projects. When service providers cannot afford to finance the whole project in advance, phased subsidy payments against intermediate outputs have been used. On rare occasions, small advance payments have been required for start-up costs and awareness campaigns. Most service providers meet prefinancing needs from internal cash flows or externally sourced funds, or both.

Designing OBA projects for the urban poor: A major obstacle to service provision in informal or slum settings is the often precarious tenure status of slum dwellers; many are ineligible by law for formal household connections. Residents also have no guarantee that their dwellings will be safe from demolition. Service providers may lack legal or regulatory authority to serve these informal areas and are also likely to lack incentives to do so for fear of low uptake or because they see it as a high-risk investment. For OBA schemes to succeed, they must have buy-in and commitment from local governments. Furthermore, the government agency should have the administrative capacity to manage OBA contracts and subsidies.

Lessons learned and prospects for scaling-up or replication: Although OBA is not the solution for all urban service problems, it is a tool to help increase the access of urban poor households to basic services, particularly where the cost of service access is unaffordable, and where service access needs to be built into urban project design. Land tenure issues must be addressed early on in the design stage. Active outreach and engagement with community-based organizations and political and community leaders is also key for successful project design and implementation. Incorporating OBA schemes into broader urban reform and slum upgrading programs can also be effective in bringing multiple stakeholders together, acting as a resource convener, and potentially playing an important role in shaping the urban development policy framework for service provision and service access for the urban poor.

Source: Adapted from Ahmed and Menzies 2012.

met by revenues. Cities such as Bogotá, Curitiba (Brazil), London, and Seoul have solved the problem with gross-cost contracts, which assure operators that their revenues will be based on performance, not on fare box collections (or not directly so). To cover costs fully, public agencies then seek other sources of revenue. Transport systems around the world vary widely in the share of operating costs recovered through fares. In a sample of

FIGURE 3.4   **Ratio of public transit fares to operating costs in a sample of large cities**

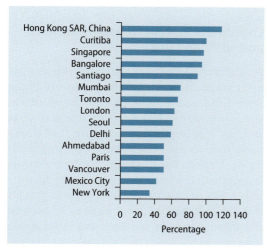

Source: World Bank 2013a.
Note: The numbers in this chart relate to bus and metro systems operated by public entities or large corporate entities. A weighted average was based on ridership across modes. Small private operators were not included because data were lacking.

20 public transit systems, only 5 fully covered their costs through fares. In New York City, 35 percent of costs were recovered through fares; in Mexico City, 40 percent (figure 3.4).

Connecting cities

Connections—between and within cities—benefit producers and consumers, both in urban and rural areas. They give producers access to input (including labor) and output markets. They give consumers options and, in many cases, better prices. And connections provide cities and rural areas with new economic opportunities. But policy makers who envision better transport connections for cities and neighborhoods face difficult choices. With limited resources, they cannot invest in everything. It is hard to know which new or improved connections will yield the highest returns over time.

Setting priorities for connective investment means picking winners and losers in the short run, but in the long run, thinking about priorities can make a vast difference for cities, surrounding rural areas, and even countries. To identify the most effective additions

and improvements to the networks connecting cities and neighborhoods, policy makers can take the steps described in the following three subsections.

Value the city's external and internal connections

For external connections to other cities and rural areas, policy makers can compare transport costs—and the density, quality, and capacity of roads, railways, waterways, and the like—with data from similar places. In this way, they can determine where improvement is most needed.

Systematically disaggregating transport costs can identify bottlenecks and reveal opportunities for infrastructure improvements that yield high dividends. A survey of truckers in India showed that transport costs were highest near large cities and their surrounding rural and peri-urban areas, a pattern similar to that found in Brazil and Vietnam. Freight rates for metropolitan transport in India, defined as trips shorter than 100 kilometers, averaged as high as Rs 5.2 per ton-kilometer ($0.12)—twice the national average of Rs 2.6, and more than five times the cost of such trips in the United States (figure 3.5).

Why are India's metropolitan freight transport costs so much higher than its long-haul

FIGURE 3.5   **Costs of moving freight in India**

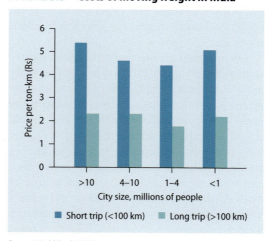

Source: World Bank 2013b.

costs? One reason is the use of smaller, older trucks on metropolitan routes. Another is the higher share of empty backhauls (truckers returning empty) on metropolitan routes. Finally, trucks on metropolitan routes clock about 25,000 kilometers annually, just a fourth of what they need to be economically viable. To improve coordination and reduce the cost of metropolitan freight movements, trucking firms could adopt logistics management systems; they could collaborate or consolidate with competitors; or they could form trucking associations. If India's high freight costs are not reined in, then they will affect national economic development, as happened in Vietnam, which, like India, has large concentrations of economic activity in and around metropolitan areas.

Alternatively, policy makers can identify possible transport cost reductions and connectivity gains that reflect the city's desired mix of economic activities and extent of specialization. In Colombia, lowering transport costs along the country's key trade corridors can enhance competitiveness for its cities and for the nation. For example, transporting freight by road from Bogotá to the Atlantic coast costs about $94 a ton while maritime transport from the Colombian coast to the United States costs about $75 a ton. High domestic transport costs undermine the competitiveness of goods produced in Colombia's largest cities, especially compared with other large cities around the world. Reducing domestic transport costs by 12 percent could lead to an increase in exports of about 9 percent.

For internal connections that link people with jobs, it is important to identify the problems: Are gridlock and lack of adequate public transport deterring residents from working outside their immediate neighborhoods (making labor markets inefficient)? Conversely, are long commuting times or high fares forcing residents to live in crowded slums so that they can walk to work? A city that faces one or both of these challenges needs a plan for a better transport system, including a desired mix of transportation modes. The plan must balance two main objectives: increasing the supply of affordable transport options

and ensuring that congestion and pollution remain within acceptable limits.

Coordinate among transport options and with land use

As discussed earlier, policy makers must systematically coordinate transport plans with land use policies and related infrastructure plans. Although each situation is unique, it is important to ensure that transport options are consistent with affordability. In Uganda for example, public transport is unaffordable to many at current income levels. Household survey data suggest that 64 percent of urban dwellers walk to work, and the share is as high as 70 percent in Kampala (figure 3.6). As cities in Uganda expand their spatial footprints, lack of viable commuting alternatives to walking severely limits labor market opportunities for people who live further away from economic centers and may even exacerbate slum formation, because many people will trade off housing quality to be close to jobs.

Typically, income determines transport choice. In Addis Ababa, 70 percent of trips are by walking, with an average distance walked of 5 kilometers; public transport is estimated to cost 3–37 percent of household income. In Nairobi, 48 percent of trips are by walking or other forms of nonmotorized transport, and the average trip is 4 kilometers; the poor pay 34 percent of their income on transport. And in Dar es Salaam, the average distance walked is 2.2 kilometers and the share of nonmotorized transport is 45 percent, with transport expenditures for the poor accounting for 53 percent of income (World Bank 2013a). These patterns are typical throughout Africa. Another challenge here is that although most (poor) people walk, hardly any facilities and safety standards are available to protect pedestrian road users. Improving sidewalks, streetlights, and other measures to protect pedestrian users should be important in an urban transport strategy.

Despite the challenges, policy makers can encourage the use of public transport and increase the geographic scope of the labor market. In Brazil, for example, the

FIGURE 3.6   **Modes for commuting to work in Uganda's urban areas**

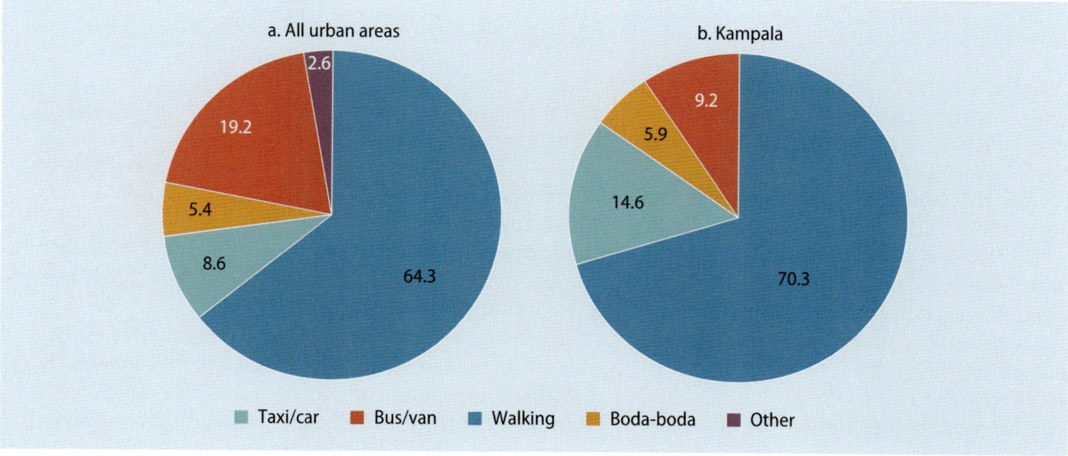

a. All urban areas

b. Kampala

■ Taxi/car   ■ Bus/van   ■ Walking   ■ Boda-boda   ■ Other

Sources: Uganda Bureau of Statistics 2010; World Bank 2013a.
Note: A boda-boda is a bicycle taxi.

government requires formal sector employers to provide transit tickets to their employees through a system called *vale transporte* (VT); firms then deduct the VT expenditures from taxable income. Although it applies only to the formal sector, the VT system effectively spreads the cost of transport subsidies between employers and the government.

In most rapidly growing cities, a useful mobility plan needs to make way for multiple options for shared travel. Metro rail systems and bus systems are the most common among them. There may also be multiple operators managing each of these systems. It is important that these are well coordinated and feed into each other rather than duplicate each other. Therefore, an important regulatory role will be to coordinate service planning.

Leverage investments that will yield the highest returns for cities collectively and individually

National leaders must identify the most efficient investments in connections among all the cities and rural areas in a country. Where is demand for the expansion of intercity and regional infrastructure and transport services highest? Which corridors are identified through spatial analysis and simulations as most central to the network, so that

improvements to them will yield the highest returns for efficiency and equity? Similarly, leaders must find ways to make transport within cities affordable while limiting congestion and pollution. This challenge is particularly important for infrastructure such as roads, where user charges alone cannot recover costs (box 3.7). Investments to increase capacity should be combined and aligned with other policies. Targeted subsidies, though not effective for all purposes or in all contexts, can sometimes be used to make transport more efficient as well as more equitable and safer for the environment. And other fiscal and regulatory tools can be used to manage demand for particular transport modes.

Financing cities

Having identified priorities for planning and connecting, policy makers confront the problem of financing those investments. The main difficulty is the need for money up front. Large capital outlays are needed to provide infrastructure and services, especially those that are not fully in demand now but will become so as urbanization picks up speed (Mohan 2009). The large capital investments that are needed in the construction phase, whether for transport, water provision, solid

---

BOX 3.7   Pricing and funding through ancillary services

A number of infrastructure services cannot be charged for easily. Roads are a prime example. Here it may be possible to use ancillary services to provide revenues for the venture. For example, a toll road franchise may be combined with the right to rent out service concessions for gas stations as well as restaurant or hotel services at rest stops along the highway. Going further, it is possible to provide a toll road company with rights to real estate development along parts, or all, of the highway. When granting a highway concession, the full package of rights and obligations can be auctioned to obtain the best price for the whole package. An example is airport franchises, where the rights to concession services (shops,

restaurants, and so forth) at the airport are a major source of revenue.

Such add-ons to the basic infrastructure service can make funding possible, while avoiding recourse to the regular government budget. Such add-ons can make an infrastructure service independent of fiscal processes and can help insulate the service provider from undue political influence.

At the same time, there is danger of excessive subsidization, particularly subsidization that makes it possible for economically unviable projects to go forward. Hence, cost-benefit analysis should routinely be used to ascertain that the infrastructure service is likely to be welfare enhancing.

---

waste management, or sewage removal and treatment, are likely to far exceed the budget of any city government. But financing can become more sustainable through taxes realized with increased economic growth, and with the ability of policy makers to leverage land markets and approach local currency debt markets.

How do policy makers bridge the gap between readily available resources and investment needs? What sources should they tap? To start with, the government can establish its creditworthiness by first securing cash flows from user fees and taxes and by leveraging the value of land in several ways, including through taxes. Only after that can the government begin to borrow money and attract private investment, making finance easier. Whether financing is public or private generally does not make the difference between successful and struggling cities. But there are at least two situations in which private financing may be the preferred course: when the government sees public-private partnerships as a way to improve efficiency in service provision, and when the government suffers from severe credit constraints that prevent it from obtaining credit for improvements to publicly run systems.

Value and develop creditworthiness

Without domestic credit markets, and often lacking the transparency needed in municipal bond markets, many city governments in developing countries cannot access long-term credit. Experience shows that subnational debt can work when clear regulations are in place to guide the issuance of debt, risks from borrowing are appropriately managed, and the conditions for subnational governments to issue debt (including the purpose, type, and amount of debt that can be issued) are clearly set forth.[2]

To make the issuance of debt to cities more transparent, Colombia has published "traffic light" ratings of the capacity of individual local governments to pay, with red, green, and yellow signals reflecting a combination of liquidity and solvency indicators. To rate municipalities' subnational debt, a red light identifies those whose ratio of interest to operational savings exceeds 40 percent and whose ratio of debt stock to current revenues exceeds 80 percent. Red-light municipalities cannot borrow. Green-light municipalities can. Yellow-light municipalities can borrow only after obtaining the approval of the central government.

Creditworthiness extends beyond local governments to their utility companies. In Kenya, the Water Services Regulatory Board calculated and published utility shadow credit ratings for 43 water service providers in 2011 and found only 13 providers to have investment grade ratings.

Smaller cities can seek short- and medium-term loans from higher levels of government and pool their credit. Thus, governments of smaller cities can use bond banks, loan pools, and guarantees to reduce lenders' risks. Two common types of municipal bonds are general obligation bonds, debt instruments secured by general purpose municipal revenue such as property taxes, and revenue bonds, debt instruments secured by the revenue generated from specific municipal assets (such as ports, toll roads, and water and wastewater utilities), with or without recourse to general revenues. Revenue bonds are particularly useful in cases where bond markets are not well developed. Colombia, India, Malaysia, Romania, the Russian Federation, the Slovak Republic, Slovenia, South Africa, and República Bolivariana de Venezuela provide examples of countries where cities have raised funds from municipal bonds.

In the absence of a well-developed bond market, financial intermediaries in diverse forms play important roles in mobilizing resources for urban infrastructure financing. In Colombia, a successful financial intermediary is FINDETER (Financiadora de Desarrollo Territorial S.A.), a government company created to finance regional urban infrastructure projects. More than 90 percent owned by the national government, with the remainder owned by the regions (departments), FINDETER provides resources for financial intermediaries who assign them to regional authorities. It has received funds from multilateral banks and has consistently received high credit ratings (Samad, Lozano-Gracia, and Panman 2012). Still, none of these methods can replace a creditworthy local government.

Coordinate public and private finance using clear and consistent rules

When city governments have constrained access to credit, private investors may step in to fill the gap. There are many types of partnership structures, with each one transferring different levels of risk to the private sector. They include service contracts, management contracts, leases, and privatization. Under any of these structures, property rights must first be clearly defined so that creditors need not depend on the government's promises. Then a PPP, with private sector selection mechanisms based on the market and on cost-benefit analyses, can improve project selection and ensure project sustainability while adding sources of infrastructure financing. Nevertheless, PPPs are no magic bullet: they require commitments to sustainable cost-covering tariffs or equivalent tax revenues. They cannot stand in for good financial management or good project evaluation. Clear rules must dictate the procedures, the requirements, the approvals, and the institutional responsibilities of the entities involved, and the allocation of risk.

Consider Ghana, where such rules were not in place. In 2002, the government of Ghana initiated a process to encourage several PPPs in the urban water sector, but the partnerships succumbed to lack of transparency and accusations of corruption in the selection process. In contrast, Chile put in place a clear and transparent procurement process, focusing on public awareness and a learning-by-doing approach that allowed for adjustments along the way. This process led to the award of 21 road projects on a competitive basis between 1993 and 2001 (Hodge 2006). The bidding started with smaller projects to test the market while also minimizing the risk for the private sector. More than 40 Chilean and international companies from 10 countries participated in the bidding through 27 consortia.

To successfully implement PPPs, city leaders will have to consider strengthening public sector capacity, laying out the appropriate legal and sector framework, promoting rigorous planning and risk assessment through feasibility studies, ensuring transparent and competitive procurement, building strong monitoring systems, and allowing flexibility for adapting to unpredictable events.

Leverage existing assets to develop new ones, linking both to land use planning

Land sales and leaseholds can provide initial capital for new infrastructure investments. Sales in Cairo, Istanbul, and Mumbai provide examples of the revenue potential of land auctions. For example:

- In Cairo in 2007, the auction of 3,100 hectares of desert land for a new town generated $3.12 billion, an amount 117 times greater than the country's total urban property tax collections, and about a tenth the size of national government revenue. The proceeds were to be used to reimburse the costs of internal infrastructure and to build a connecting highway to Cairo's ring road.
- In Istanbul in 2007, the auction of an old bus station and government building generated $1.5 billion, more than the city's total 2005 fiscal expenditures and infrastructure investments.
- In Mumbai in 2006–07, the auction of 13 hectares of land in the new financial center—the Bandra-Kurla Complex—generated $1.2 billion. That was more than 10 times the total 2005 fiscal spending of the Mumbai Metropolitan Regional Development Authority, and six times the total value of municipal bonds issued by all urban local bodies and local utilities in India in more than a decade. The proceeds were to be used primarily to finance projects identified by the Metropolitan Transportation Plan.

Yet policy makers should recognize that all successful land-based financing instruments require at least three kinds of rules to be in place. First are rules to assign and protect property rights. Second are institutions for the valuation and public dissemination of land values across various uses. Third is a strong legal framework, with a healthy judicial system to handle disputes and oversee the land-based financing process. Furthermore, a single planning strategy should integrate land-based financing with urban land use planning. With developing land management institutions, identifying infrastructure needs and integrating planning across sectors are the first steps in securing financing, because investors will be able to better assess risks and see the city as a good investment.

Managing decentralization

More generally, the financing of all local services is challenging: while services are best delivered locally, the local tax base is often narrow. That is true not only for cities but for all subnational governments (SNGs), including not only municipalities but also provincial and state or regional governments. All poverty is "local"—and given their proximity to citizens, SNGs are often better suited than higher levels of government to address these challenges. First, they have an informational advantage that makes them more efficient in discerning citizens' needs, which is particularly relevant for beneficiary identification in poverty programs. SNGs can direct resources toward these needs (*allocative efficiency*) and can also provide some services more efficiently than higher levels of government (*productive efficiency*). Political decentralization also lowers the "barriers to entry" for different groups of society, so they can more easily and directly participate in decision making (box 3.8).

Reductions in poverty can only be achieved if the net fiscal incidence remains pro poor (Boex et al. 2006). That is, regressivity of local revenue can be accepted as long as expenditures are progressive and lead to an overall positive incidence. That, however, also requires that the burden and benefit distribution of the tax system and public expenditures as a whole be considered, which in turn requires coordination across all levels of government. But achieving this coordination is becoming harder in the current urbanrural dynamics and now represents one of

---

BOX 3.8   Key design issues of decentralization

The three elements of decentralization are administrative, fiscal, and political. Administrative, or expenditure, decentralization relates to expenditures and services assigned to subnational governments; fiscal, or revenue, decentralization is related to the subnational government's own revenue, transfers, and debt; and political decentralization refers to elections and the delegation of authority, as well as citizen participation.

Countries are constantly adjusting and fine-tuning their intergovernmental relations. Given the several trade-offs that have to be faced, the three elements of decentralization constitute a never-ending balancing

act. In fact, decentralization is a "moving target"—there is no final model that countries can reach. What matters most is to fit the different design elements together coherently and avoid disjointed decision making.

The degree of fiscal, political, and administrative decentralization is not related to whether a country is federal or unitary. Relevant examples include unitary China, with about 76.5 percent of expenditure decentralization (accountability, in turn, is upward toward the central level). In contrast, in federal Mexico, the degree of expenditure decentralization is about 46 percent.

---

the challenges to achieving the MDG targets. As urbanization unfolds, the more populous areas acquire higher fiscal capacity (that is, their governments can generate more revenue). That implies they have more resources available to address poverty issues. Absent any convergence effect, SNGs in rural areas will face continued or even higher resource constraints. And because poverty is concentrated in these areas, the gap between needs and the means to address them will increase.

In any decentralized system, there are trade-offs to be faced. Decentralization of revenue-generating authority reduces the ability of central governments to redistribute. Decentralization of the spending authority implies that priority setting needs to be coordinated among the different levels. This failure to coordinate can affect the capacity to establish a "level playing field" in countries through fiscal equalization.

Decentralization also carries other risks: institutional capacity can be weak; special interests can capture government entities; and the poor and their priorities can be overlooked. Political party systems and electoral rules greatly influence the service delivery priorities of councilors, mayors, and governors, so services and resources may not always be directed to where the needs are greatest.

Urban areas are, in principle, more attractive for "vote seekers" than rural areas, and that can create an undesirable expenditure bias. Moreover, urban and rural service delivery gaps may not coincide with territorial boundaries, making coordination all the more necessary—and all the more difficult.

Weighing the risks and advantages of decentralization is prudent—but countries often have no choice: several levels of government need to find ways to cooperate if the MDG goals are to be reached. Many examples from across the world underscore not only that effective policies can be crafted, but that they can be crafted and coordinated by various levels of government working together.

Revenue challenges in rural areas
Because a large share of their population is poor, SNGs in rural areas have a relatively low fiscal capacity and are consequently more dependent on revenue transfers from higher levels of government. A large informal economy may further limit subnational taxation. Some rural governments can even be in a "transfer dependence trap," because there is no linear relation between increased tax effort and the level of expenditures that can realistically be achieved—a dilemma that

constitutes one of the "dangers" of decentralization (Prud'homme 1995). Assume, for example, a SNG whose total revenue is composed of 10 percent in taxes and 90 percent in transfers. All other things equal, financing a 10 percent increase in expenditures requires doubling the tax effort. That often exceeds the institutional capacity as well as the willingness to assume the political cost of raising taxes. Transfer dependence is particularly large for regional governments in many unitary government systems where policy decisions are channeled to subnational governing units for implementation (such as Bangladesh and Bolivia), because tax bases that are best suited to regional management (automobile taxes, for instance) have been given to municipalities. For SNGs in rural areas, therefore, the possibilities to engage in redistribution through local taxation are limited.

Redistribution therefore needs to come mainly from the expenditure side, which depends critically on the level of expenditure decentralization. More often than not, an SNG manages only parts of the service delivery: public investment and infrastructure. Human resource management, particularly in the social sectors (health and teaching personnel) has long been a politically sensitive area, and most management decisions remain centralized in many countries.

Given these uneven advances and levels of autonomy in expenditures, SNGs in rural areas are often constrained in their ability to provide packages of services to the poor and to target the incidence of spending so that services are directed where the needs are greatest.

In addition, the often low population density implies higher per capita costs in providing public services (Hon 2009; Kitchen 2006; McMillan 2007). Consider that the marginal cost in service provision for water and sewerage increases substantially in rural areas, and it is particularly high for tertiary education. Although education costs for primary and secondary education are often less affected by economies of scale than other services, factors such as very small class size can increase costs substantially even in rural areas. Roads can facilitate access between rural areas and economic centers, but, given the limited possibility to establish user fees and toll roads, financing by other entities or higher levels of government is required.

These challenges have important consequences. They require different levels of governments to contribute with grant financing to service delivery. These coordination requirements can be particularly significant at the regional or intermediate level of government, where there may be dual authorities. Investment funds can play a large role in rural areas because they cofinance or execute public works directly. Some of these entities have been trying to substitute for weak institutional capacity. But such efforts have also led to a bypassing of rural SNGs in service provision, creating an undesirable spiral of weak accountability and capacity.

The financing challenge of the MDGs in metropolitan areas

In contrast to rural areas, SNGs in urban areas have greater fiscal capacity and hence can influence outcomes much more through their own revenue decisions. Nevertheless the overall level of transfer dependence of metropolitan governments can be substantial. Some of the more financially autonomous metro areas include Addis Ababa, Melbourne, and Pretoria (Shah 2012). Cities like Berlin, Bucharest, and London, however, are dependent on central grants for about 80 percent of their revenue. Absent any convergence effects regarding how to structure revenues, fiscal capacity will increase as agglomeration unfolds. The tax incidence of revenue decisions naturally depends on the particular taxes and user fees applied. Common revenue sources are land-related revenue (property taxes, improvement levies, auctions, leases), which can affect the locational decisions and income of individuals; personal income taxes (applied at the local level in 13 of 27 Organisation for Economic Co-operation and Development [OECD] countries); and user fees, which are usually applied at uniform rates and therefore can have regressive effects.

Institutional changes often cannot keep up with rapid urbanization and therefore usually remain informal. It is no surprise then that many informal local institutions are merely

BOX 3.9   The complex structure of metropolitan governments

Metropolitan governance is complex in many cases, involving several single- or multiple-purpose jurisdictions covering a whole metro area or just parts of it. Metropolitan areas and their surrounding jurisdictions are either managed by subnational entities or have some central government involvement, given the complexity in finding purely local solutions. For example:

- New Delhi is affected by overlapping jurisdictions: power is divided among all three levels of government—the central government, the Union Territory of Delhi, and three municipal bodies (the Delhi Municipal Corporation, New Delhi Municipal Committee, and Delhi Cantonment).
- In Jakarta's metropolitan area, there are three urban municipalities and three rural municipali-

ties (districts) that are split among three provinces (Banten, Jakarta, and West Java).
- Mexico City's metropolitan area spans parts of two states and has a national capital district and more than 50 municipal-type local governments.
- The São Paulo metropolitan area (with 39 municipal governments) operates with relatively little coordination, because a suprametropolitan entity has yet to emerge.
- The Cairo region incorporates five contiguous governorates (the intermediate tier of Egyptian administration) and eight new cities. Governorates represent the central government. New cities were created to attract people from the Nile Delta to Cairo and have no formal relationship with local administration. They are overseen by the Ministry of Housing, Utilities, and Urban Development.

planning entities with no taxing powers, or that the central government influence is considerable. These institutional arrangements also affect if and how citizens are represented and can make their voice heard (box 3.9). The informality of these institutional arrangements has three consequences:

- It rules out more firmly establishing the authority to tax at these levels, which can be used to finance local expenditures.
- It limits possibilities for redistributing within metro areas or to other subnational units, which is critical for maintaining a level playing field for all entities. For example, redistributive efforts will be more difficult to be launched from subnational levels themselves—in contrast, in Argentina and Canada, for instance, the provinces are entitled to choose formulas for redistribution in some of the financial instruments. Although vertical equalization can achieve the same results from any level, such a subnational solution would need political consensus that would perhaps not exist on a nationwide scale.
- If revenues are further decentralized in urban areas, it can undermine the capacity

of the central government to redistribute to other areas, among them the rural SNGs.

Setting up a financing system that sets the right incentives for service delivery can be challenging for a metropolitan area (World Bank 2013a; Kim 2013; Shah 2012; Slack 2006; Sud and Yilmaz 2013). The high proportion of commuters leads to a breakdown of the tax-benefit principle: citizens may benefit from the public services provided by a metropolitan area but pay taxes at their residence in medium-size towns at the outskirts. Cross-territorial transactions can occur more frequently in areas with many entities and jurisdictions, affecting collection and distribution of sales taxes and corporate income taxes, for example, unless they are administered at a higher level of government.

Service delivery itself is challenging for several reasons—all of which limit accountability and efficiency:

- The multiple territorial boundaries of metropolitan areas can complicate the assignment of responsibilities for delivering the service, as well as accountability.

- In two-tier models, economies of scale may be limited at lower levels. As metropolitan areas encircle small municipalities, fragmentation may occur across jurisdictions, at the same time that further horizontal integration is limited for political reasons.
- Organizational arrangements can be complex: regional transport authorities, public enterprises, and special-purpose districts, among others, are common, and coordination among these and with entities of the SNG can be problematic.
- Metropolitan areas may not have the incentives to invest adequately in making complex services accessible in all sectors, including inpatient care, specialized medical treatment, and higher education, all of which have positive externalities and spillovers to other areas. Such underinvestment can be mitigated with grants from the central government, although that raises the question of alignment of the different compensation mechanisms. Bahl and Bird (2013) refer to India, where a large federal grant for urban infrastructure development and slum upgrading is allocated to cities on a matching basis. The program was introduced in 2005, and while it has succeeded in focusing increased attention on urban infrastructure issues, implementation progress has been slow. South Africa makes use of a more formal municipal infrastructure grant, designed primarily to improve services in poor neighborhoods. In Brazil, ad hoc grants are made to support specific projects.

As a consequence, coordination with other levels of government and within the metropolitan areas are significant and, if not done well, can limit accountability and efficiency.

Going forward: Three priorities for subnational governments

If rural and urban SNGs are to successfully address the challenges to delivering basic services necessary to achieve the MDGs, three areas of future action are critical: improving public investment; fiscal equalization; and governance arrangements for accountability.

Public investment

Public investment is directly related to attainment of the MDGs because of its importance in closing infrastructure gaps in urban and rural areas (Alm 2010; Bahl and Bird 2013; Frank and Martinez-Vazquez 2013; Pagano 2011; Romeo and Smoke 2013). But the level of efficiency in public investment varies substantially across both developed and developing countries. Surveys done for the World Economic Forum in a sample of 94 countries worldwide indicate that some advanced countries have seen decreases in the quality of infrastructure, while some countries in the developing world have taken respectable leaps forward.

Decentralized public investment is complex and might lead to inequity in spending. Project appraisal may not be sufficiently rigorous to weed out those with questionable impact, so cost and time overruns often do not become apparent until later stages—when sunk costs have to be accepted. Inequities in the distribution of assets across different jurisdictions can also be significant. Public investment often implies bulky infrastructure works offering localized benefits whose distribution is influenced by political economy factors. Together, these factors can undermine equity, one of the key aspects for achieving the MDGs.

Improved public investment will require three actions. First, coordination across levels of government should be strengthened. Experience in developed countries (France, Spain) has underscored that this coordination requires reasonably strong fiscal levers. Chile, for instance, is coordinating public investment through regional investment windows, including cofinancing with municipalities.

Second, institutional and process reform should allow "poor" projects to be weeded out before they gain traction and support—while projects with high returns should be selected. Korea, for instance, has successfully addressed the "optimism bias" by requiring reappraisal in projects with cost and time overruns.

Third, equalization of public investment spending should be strengthened. With infrastructure gaps shifting among urban and rural areas at a quickening pace, the need for "place-based" responses to the service delivery challenge is increasing. This adequacy in resources should be provided in terms of a country's entire expenditure needs, which include capital infrastructure, with the goal of creating a level playing field.

Fiscal equalization

The incidence of both revenues and expenditures is critical for MDG outcomes. These effects can be enhanced by establishing some level of equalization to address inequities in resource distribution (Blöchliger and Vammalle 2009; Boadway 2012; Dafflon 2012; OECD 2007). Changes in the patterns of urban-rural development imply three basic forces: *citizens' needs* change because of ongoing changes in their demographic composition, poverty profiles, and income levels; *costs of service provision* are affected; and *fiscal capacity* is affected. Fiscal equalization can help address these factors.

Equalization can be structured vertically (across different levels of government), horizontally (across and among jurisdictions), or as a combination of both. It requires defining the particular need, cost, and fiscal capacity issue to be addressed through a transfer; defining a group of representative taxes and representative expenditures to be equalized; and agreeing on the degree of equalization. All these decisions have both a technical and a political ingredient.

In short, equalization is a complex undertaking both politically and practically. As an outcome of political negotiation, transfers are often overburdened with objectives, which may weaken desirable compensatory effects. Some countries do organize spatially targeted programs aimed at stimulating regional development at large with a focus on the private sector. However, those programs that include incentives such as tax breaks or subsidies often challenge coordination among the different interventions, including service delivery and taxation, and specific poverty and social programs. For example, in Malawi, transfers are not establishing

sufficient levels of horizontal equity, as measured using a per capita standard as a reasonable comparator (World Bank 2012b). In Bolivia, distribution is driven by hydrocarbon revenues, which bear no relation to levels of poverty in the different provinces. If horizontal equity is recognized as a base for addressing the MDGs, then more effort needs to be put into fiscal equalization.

The type and degree of equalization is, in the end, a political decision. Given the prominence of infrastructure challenges in the urban-rural dynamics, however, it is unlikely that full equalization for all sectors can or should be achieved. The right balance is likely to depend on the type of infrastructure needed and may vary with specific circumstances, such as subnational capacity and credit availability. In the case of infrastructure for social services, such as health and education, recurrent equalization grants may be needed to cover continuing operation and maintenance costs. For utilities and other infrastructure whose costs can be largely recovered through fees, credit-facilitating policies may be the most appropriate means of equalizing expenditures. For network infrastructure where costs cannot be recovered through fees, such as no-toll roads, a conditional grant may be most appropriate.

Overall, it is clear that no country begins with a clean slate. More often than not, reforms of intergovernmental transfers are done at the margin and incrementally, as is demonstrated by Colombia's current royalty reform, which achieves more equality for royalty resources in a gradual fashion. Other noteworthy efforts are currently being undertaken by Ethiopia, Kenya, Morocco, and Tajikistan, although the results remain to be seen.

Governance for accountability

Accountability is critical to tackle the MDG challenge. Accountability depends on the way authority is constituted, but it also depends on human resources management, an often forgotten but critical element for accountability and efficiency.

All decisions on resource distribution require institutional arrangements and the authority to exercise those decisions. These determine, to some degree, if and how costs and revenue can be shared within and across jurisdictions. Institutional and governance arrangements reflect a country's political decisions, often based on its particular social, geographic, or political context. Subnational governments and their authorities can be elected or delegated; in some cases, parallel or dual authorities exist. Whatever the arrangement, as a guiding principle, a minimum level of accountability, vertically across levels and horizontally across the different territorial units, needs to be in place for MDG-relevant policies to be fully effective.

Human resources are a critical, yet often overlooked element of accountability. They establish institutional capacity, a necessary condition to addressing service delivery challenges. They define the "fine dividing line" in responsibilities among levels of government, which is key for accountability. And they are a significant cost driver that can impact fiscal responsibility. Three areas of institutional capacity are critical because they establish a basic level of transparency: financial management, procurement, and human resources. Efforts are under way to create integrated financial management systems in many countries, including Russia (as a centralized solution), and some Latin American countries (Guatemala, Peru).

Given deeply entrenched political economy factors, the risk of disjointed decision making is high. Hiring and firing decisions, along with salary policies, need to be made in a coordinated fashion. The example of Mexico underscores some of the challenges: because of political resistance, federal teachers were not decentralized to the states, resulting in a parallel hiring process at the state level that blurred the lines of accountability. In Colombia, the early decentralization process established central pay levels, while SNGs were supposed to cover the increased cost, which was shifted back to the center through higher transfers.

With growing interdependencies, human resources management needs to be strengthened in an intergovernmental fashion. Because these capacities are often "invisible" to citizens, which limits any demand-based

reform, they need particularly strong incentives to be sustainable. These examples underscore the fact that human resources reform constitutes a challenging area that can often progress only in limited, narrowly defined service delivery areas where sufficient demand for reform exists. In contrast, Kenya's ambitious territorial and devolution reform has forced it to engage in large-scale human resources reform, but the reform is still too new to evaluate the results.

Planning first, followed by financing

As urban centers continue their inexorable growth over the next decades, a strategy is needed to better manage the urbanization process through a coordinated, prioritized, and sequenced approach to the planning-connecting-financing formula of urbanization. Unplanned and uncoordinated urban development can pose risks, trading the hopes of those who migrate in search of a better life for unsanitary living conditions, joblessness, and high exposure to natural disasters. Public policy makers must act now to get this rapidly paced urbanization "right" by improving access to affordable and reliable basic services such as education, housing, transport, and health care for all, and by promoting effective land use management to influence the spatial structure of cities. Isolated efforts are unlikely to help. Experience in managing urban growth has varied considerably across countries (see box 3.10 for policies in the BRICS), but policy makers going forward will need to focus on getting land management "right" and integrating the intensity of land use with the placement of infrastructure, housing, mobility, and environmental amenities.

Of course, financing rapid urban growth is challenging, because large up-front capital investments are needed to build systems for transport and water, solid waste management, and sewage removal and treatment. Financing, however, needs to be closely tied to how urban areas are planned and connected. Often, getting the planning in place will allow cities to leverage land and credit

BOX 3.10   Learning from urbanization in the BRICS

The economic motors of development are shifting from the urbanized developed world toward the rapidly urbanizing developing world, and most famously those of Brazil, Russia, India, China, and South Africa (the BRICS). The BRICS provide some inspiring examples of how to seize the opportunities that urbanization can provide. Their governments all went through difficult periods when they tried to resist the predictable movement of people into cities, or steered people or enterprises to inappropriate urban locations. Several of the BRICS bear heavy burdens from past failures to accommodate urban population growth equitably and efficiently. To avoid such burdens, cities and nations need to plan proactively for urban growth, making use of both markets and planning tools, and engaging with all sectors of society, including the economically and politically weakest.

Rapid urbanization in the BRICS has generally accompanied economic growth and a shift out of agriculture. Nevertheless, governments have been ambivalent about urbanization, even causing some of the economic and social disruption that has attended this march toward urbanization; examples are China during the Cultural Revolution and South Africa during Apartheid. Each country illustrates different lessons about the opportunities and risks associated with urbanization.

Brazil's reluctant urbanization and the emergence of *favelas.* Brazil's world-famous slums or shanty towns also called *favelas* show how the failure to accommodate growing urban populations can lead to enduring social inequalities. Fearing that urban planning would encourage poor rural migrants, the Brazilian government did little to plan for rapid urban growth. Inaction did not slow the pace of urbanization, but poor planning did contribute to a very unequal urbanization, with large segments of the population inhabiting poorly located and ill-served informal settlements. Many inhabitants have done surprisingly well under the circumstances, but hazardous locations, enormous barriers to service delivery, bad relations with local authorities, and the like persisted.

In recent decades, pioneering approaches have emerged: participatory budgeting in Porto Alegre, sustainable travel in Curitiba, and condominial sewerage in various cities. These and other innovations have gained international renown. The national government has introduced some of the most inclusive urban legislation, as exemplified by its ambitious City Statute. Nevertheless, the problems of the divided city, stemming from past urban policies, remain a huge challenge. In retrospect, a more inclusive and proactive approach to rural-urban migration and urban growth from the start would have been more equitable at the time and very beneficial in the long run.

China's ardent urbanization and rapid economic growth. China's economic transformation, which began as a rural experiment, soon became urban, involving first a string of coastal cities, then larger urban regions, then inland cities. These innovative cities soon brought vast quantities of capital from around the world together with low-wage workers from China's agricultural regions. The central government progressively loosened controls on private investment within cities and on temporary rural migration into the cities. Economic powerhouses arose incrementally from locally driven but centrally sanctioned urban experimentation. City governments were given increasing powers and put under enormous pressure to raise economic production. A dominant model emerged of entrepreneurial city bureaucrats taking lead roles in land conversions. They oversaw the transformation of low-value urban or rural land into serviced plots whose long-term leases were sold at near-market prices to real estate developers, or at lower prices to investors promising industrial or commercial establishments.

China's stunning economic success highlights the importance of achieving moderately efficient urbanization for economic growth, but it is based on policies other countries would struggle to replicate and has brought unenviable environmental costs and social inequalities. China has recently tried to reduce these detractions while maintaining rapid economic growth, but it has been difficult to challenge the existing model, whose success is based on closely aligning local authorities' official and unofficial interests with market pressures, even when that causes environmental damage or amplifies inequalities. Urban experimentation could still hold the key to progress on social and environmental agendas, but local alliances of entrepreneurial bureaucrats and developers are unlikely to drive these agendas.

(box continues next page)

BOX 3.10   Learning from urbanization in the BRICS (continued)

Russia: Cities in the wrong places. Russia's urbanization history shows how long-term economic growth requires people and economic enterprises to move to productive urban locations—not just to anywhere in any city. This is a difficult process to direct unless markets are allowed to play a larger role than permitted by the Soviet authorities.

From an economic perspective, the Soviet system located many urban activities and populations in the wrong places. Central decision making that did not take markets into account left many cities exposed at the end of the Soviet era. The need for spatial restructuring brought heavy social and economic costs, adding to the traumas that accompanied the dismantling of the Soviet central planning system. Populations shifted toward newly vibrant cities and service centers in the south and west, and away from industrial cities with few amenities in the far north and east. That may have been the right response from an economic standpoint, but it involved considerable dislocation. Cities that produced goods for the military-industrial complex, or consumer goods protected from competition, have suffered enormously, even as those with natural resource bases or other strengths in the market economy have thrived.

South Africa's apartheid urban controls and its fragmented cities. South Africa's apartheid system was an extreme lesson in the dangers of exclusionary urban policies, particularly when combined with overt discrimination against particular social groups. Since apartheid ended, urbanization has rebounded, but the inherited social and economic divisions have proven to be intractable. The low density, fragmented form of South African cities has also had harmful social, economic, and environmental consequences, some of which are only beginning to be addressed. Low density has imposed additional barriers to employment for the poorest communities, added to the cost of bulk infrastructure provision and public transport, and fostered carbon-emitting private transport.

The creation of constitutional rights for the poor has helped to promote equity but has not always been backed by political will and sufficient government resources to meet people's basic needs for electricity, water, and sanitation. Equally needed are city-level leadership and investment plans that integrate fragmented cities more effectively, boost jobs and livelihoods, and work with poorer communities to improve essential services.

India: Ambivalence to urbanization offers an uncertain future. India is less urban than the other BRICS, and its ambivalence toward urbanization could impede economic progress, at least for the low-income groups who find it increasingly difficult to secure a place in India's cities. The size of India's still-growing population that has to find sustenance in rural settings is daunting. India's current challenges illustrate the importance of taking the rural implications into account when designing urban policies.

This is a particularly critical time for India's urban policies because they will help to determine whether economic growth is maintained, who will benefit, and what the environmental consequences will be. The Indian government has initiated several important programs intended to support equitable and efficient urban development, including the Jawaharlal Nehru National Urban Renewal Mission and Rajiv Awas Yojana. India has also pioneered civil society and grassroots efforts to improve conditions for deprived urban dwellers, including a partnership between the Society for the Promotion of Area Resource Centres, Mahila Milan, and the Indian National Slum Dwellers Association. To meet its urbanization challenge, India must not only address existing urban poverty but also create cities that can accommodate rapid urbanization and give even the poorest rural dwellers a fairer share of the benefits of economic growth.

Sources: Contributed by IIED and UNFPA.

markets to generate finances, as well as to encourage investments by the private sector.

Integrating planning, connecting, and financing can go a long way in ensuring that urban areas enhance job opportunities, productivity, and living standards by better managing densities, and by also reaching out and improving welfare in rural areas.

Annex 3A.1   International Financial Institutions and Urbanization

International financial institutions (IFIs) have long been engaged in supporting the urbanization process through different lending and nonlending mechanisms. These include a range of responses from financial support to improve housing conditions for slum dwellers to strengthening transport services to reduce congestion costs to integrating knowledge products that help countries plan better for anticipated migration from rural areas to its cities as well as address issues of congestion from natural growth of urban areas.

African Development Bank

The African Development Bank (AfDB) Group recognizes that the continent's cities and towns can be a major driving force for economic development. In 1992, its board approved an Urban Development Policy to provide guidance for AfDB Group operations in the urban sector, build a foundation for dialogue with counterparts, and promote cooperation with other development partners. The policy targeted regional member countries' capacity to plan and implement investment programs, promote private initiatives, support decentralization, and upgrade human resources. An important component was improving the living conditions of the urban poor. The AfDB has supported urban development over the years through projects in public utilities, industry, transport, education, health, and other social interventions. Between 1967 and 2007, roughly 15–20 percent of the cumulative financing provided by the AfDB Group benefited urban dwellers and enterprises either directly or indirectly.

In 2011, the AfDB developed its urban strategy , which was aimed at enhancing the effectiveness of its interventions in urban development in Africa (AfDB 2011). The main objective is to boost the viability and competitiveness of African cities to help them enhance their role as engines of growth and economic development. The strategy focuses on three main pillars in alignment with the AfDB's core areas of interventions: infrastructure development, urban governance, and private sector development. The urban strategy is based on the AfDB's medium-term plan for 2008–12 and the 2009 mid-term review of the African Development Fund (ADF), the concessional financing window of the AfDB. The urban strategy aims to help member countries progress toward the achievement of MDGs and to mainstream the key cross-cutting issues concerning all urban operations, namely, knowledge generation and management, regional integration, environment, climate change, gender, and empowerment of vulnerable populations.

Implementation of the AfDB's urban strategy will exploit the bank's existing financing instruments using the central governments' channels: loans and guarantees, mainly to middle-income countries, and private sector loans to middle- and low-income countries; loans or grants from the ADF to low-income countries and fragile states; and trust funds and other facilities. For financing in the case of creditworthy municipalities, the AfDB will invest in knowledge generation and lessons from other institutions concerned with this type of financing.

In recent years, the AfDB has supported some 70 urban-related projects and initiatives, such as: improving Zanzibar's water supply and sanitation services (special drawing rights [SDR] 28 million); the Dakar-Diamniadio Highway Project (SDR 45 million); the Nairobi-Thika Highway Improvement Project (SDR 121 million); and the Conakry Electrical Networks Rehabilitation and Extension Project (SDR 12 million). Since 2000, the AfDB's financial commitment

TABLE A3.1   AfDB's deliverables in energy, transport, and regional integration, 2010–12

Indicator	
Energy	
Length of transmission and distribution lines rehabilitated or installed (km)	13,129
Distribution substations and transformers constructed or rehabilitated (number)	Forthcoming
Power capacity installed (MW)	780
Staff trained/recruited in the maintenance of energy facilities (number)	1,963
People with a new electricity connection (number)	203,602
Population benefiting from new electricity connections (people)	6,498,853
Transport	
Roads constructed, rehabilitated, or maintained (km)	15,695
Feeder roads constructed or rehabilitated (km)	7,994
Staff trained/recruited for road maintenance (number)	13,950
People educated in road safety and HIV transmission (people)	810,000
People with improved access to transport (people)	40,326,880
Regional integration	
Cross-border roads constructed or rehabilitated (km)	471
Cross-border transmission lines constructed or rehabilitated (km)	597

Source: AfDB 2013.

for urban development interventions has amounted to SDR 2.26 billion (US$3.5 billion). The AfDB has also invested in various other interventions that have played a role in improving the socioeconomic levels of both urban and rural populations, through such means as increased access to energy and transport facilities and in regional integration. Table 3A.1 illustrates some of the key results delivered in these areas in 2010–12.

The AfDB has also undertaken economic sector work, such as a study on the expansion of Monrovia's water supply and sanitation system (SDR 1.5 million). Moreover, following its 2008 annual meetings in Maputo where the High-level Symposium addressed issues on urbanization, inequality, and poverty in Africa, in 2009 it embarked on a research program in partnership with the Swedish International Development Cooperation Authority aimed to yield knowledge products to assist AfDB staff and member countries in addressing urban development issues. A key product of this partnership is a book titled *Fostering Shared Growth: Urbanization, Inequality and Poverty in Africa*, due for publication in 2013.

An exemplary project illustrating the impact of AfDB's projects on the lives of the urban poor is the poverty reduction project in Ghana (Box 3A.1).

Asian Development Bank

The Asian Development Bank (ADB) has sought to facilitate the structural transformation for successful urbanization by providing various financial and knowledge-based instruments to its client countries. Of project financing identified for rural and urban development projects, approximately $3.3 billion was allocated for urban development and $2.3 billion for rural development in 2012. In rural areas, the transport and information and communications technology (ICT) sectors received the most, at 45 percent in 2012; agriculture was well behind, with 25 percent of the total allocation for rural development in 2012. In urban areas, transport and ICT is also the largest sector, receiving 35 percent of the total allocation for urban projects; energy received 24 percent, and water supply and other municipal services received 17 percent in 2012. Note that the ADB has slowly increased its allocation to support urban development from around 50 percent in 2008 to close to 60 percent of a growing amount of total resources available for both areas of development.

East Asia: China and Mongolia

Support for "urban-rural dynamics" in China and Mongolia is broadly in line with

BOX 3A.1   Tackling urban poverty in Ghana

As urbanization has proliferated in Ghana, particularly in the central and northern regions, the level of urban poverty has also been on the increase. An estimated 2 million urban dwellers in Ghana are classified as poor. In Accra alone, 45 percent of the population lives in the poorest neighborhoods and lack water, sanitation, and educational facilities. As a pilot country, Ghana benefited from the AfDB urban poverty reduction project worth about $40.25 million.

The objectives of this project were to develop urban settlements through participatory management, job creation, and strengthened public-private partnerships and local governance and management capacity; improve living conditions in urban and peri-urban zones by increasing access to basic quality services and socioeconomic infrastructure; and facilitate access to income-generating activities through capacity building and a strengthened urban small-scale enterprise sector.

The project covered 12 metropolitan, municipal, and secondary towns with a total population of 4.45 million. The expected benefits include improvement in the livelihoods of the urban poor through better access to good socioeconomic infrastructure, creation of 6,000 jobs for unemployed youth, and skills development training for at least 4,000 women. The project was expected to generate 350 urban and peri-urban socioeconomic subprojects and 50 environmental subprojects.

Source: AfDB 2011.

the ADB's support for inclusive growth. ADB operations help address regional and urban-rural disparities, improve rural livelihoods, and facilitate urbanization with job creation for migrant workers.

In China, more than 90 percent of the ADB's operations are focused on the lesser-developed central, western, and northeastern regions to promote regionally balanced and integrated urban-rural development. Transport operations have facilitated movement of people for better access to job opportunities and public services, particularly among migrant workers. Urban operations have supported integrated urban-rural infrastructure development and improvement of urban services, including provision of employment services and technical and vocational education and training. Natural resources and agriculture operations have supported biomass energy and water and natural resources protection, which help generate income and expand livelihood improvement opportunities.

The Chinese government is accelerating its support of the development of the country's small- and medium-size cities. The country's macroeconomic urban strategy aims to rationalize the unbalanced urban structure at all levels of the urban hierarchy, which currently provides a weak base for supporting sustainable and inclusive development. The approved loan amounts for urban development ranged from around $485 million in 2008 to $350 million in 2012. These projects aim to enhance the development potential of small- and medium-size cities, thereby directly and indirectly providing support to reduce regional imbalances and income disparities between urban and rural areas. The ADB has been a close partner to the Chongqing Municipality, the first provincial-level demonstration area for piloting urban-rural reforms in China. In 2010, the first $100 million in funding for the Chongqing Urban-Rural Infrastructure Development Demonstration Project was approved to finance key infrastructure of urban-rural roads and small-scale potable water supply plants in eight poor districts and counties of Chongqing. In 2013, the ADB and the national government are working on a proposed $150 million loan project for the second phase, which will further demonstrate more balanced and inclusive urban-rural development in Chongqing.

Mongolia's population was 2.8 million in 2011, including 1.3 million inhabitants of Ulaanbaatar City. Forty percent of Ulaanbaatar's population lives in the city core while 60 percent (approximately 800,000 people, or about 30 percent of the national population) live in peri-urban, or *ger*, areas. During the past five years, the population of the country increased by about 220,000; all but 10,000 of these were in Ulaanbaatar City. In addition, the countryside population decreased dramatically while the populations of the *aimag* (provincial) capitals and other small cities remained almost stable. The population growth of Ulaanbaatar City mainly happens in the *ger* areas, which, despite their size, are considered temporary settlements and have never been formally integrated into the city development process or infrastructure programming. Thus, the continuing *ger* area densification and sprawl is putting tremendous pressure on the urban environment. The huge gap between services in the formal and *ger* areas remains one of the most difficult challenges for the government, especially as projections indicate that they will add another 350,000 people over the next 10 years.

Approved loans for infrastructure in Mongolia during the past five years amounted to about $78.2 million. They included projects to improve water and other municipal infrastructure and services in small towns in the southeast area of the Gobi Desert ($15 million) and the improvement of urban transport in Ulaanbaatar City ($59.9 million). In 2011, a Public-Private Transportation Act was approved to prepare a multiannual financial framework for improving Ulaanbaatar City's urban services and *ger* areas development.

Central and West Asia: Multisector assessment for Kazakhstan and Uzbekistan

In addition to financial support, the ADB also provides analytical services to facilitate decision making by policy makers faced with urban and rural development challenges. For example, in Kazakhstan, the Country Partnership Strategy for 2012–16 includes a detailed sector assessment of urban transport and water and sanitation.[3] In Uzbekistan, the Country Partnership Strategy for 2012–2016 assessed issues surrounding water supply and sanitation, waste management, urban transport, and other municipal services.[4]

The urban regional technical assistance projects fostered the work of the Urban Community of Practice, one of the core knowledge management areas of the ADB, and, in particular, the Cities Development Initiative for Asia (CDIA), an international partnership program assisting medium-size Asian cities to bridge the gap between their development plans and implementation of their infrastructure investments. The CDIA uses a demand-driven approach to help identify and develop urban infrastructure investment projects in the framework of existing city development plans. These projects focus on urban environmental improvement, urban poverty reduction and gender, climate change mitigation or adaptation, and improved governance.

To facilitate these initiatives, the CDIA provides a range of international and domestic expertise and advice to help cities move from strategic master plans to concrete policies and infrastructure projects ready to present to financiers and project developers. Core city-level CDIA activities include:

- Advisory support for undertaking infrastructure investment programming and prioritization.
- Consultancy support for preparing prefeasibility studies on high priority infrastructure investment projects that demonstrate integration within a city's overall development process.
- Identifying financial sources for selected investments from domestic and international finance markets as well as opportunities for public-private partnerships (PPPs).
- Strengthening local institutional capacity through on-the-job training related to

infrastructure investment planning and programming and project management.

As of December 2012, the CDIA had approved applications from four cities in thirteen countries with a number of others under consideration. These interventions are estimated to lead to about $6.5 billion in strategic urban infrastructure investments. In the current portfolio, urban transport is the largest CDIA sector, followed by flood and drainage management, urban renewal, and wastewater management. While the ADB and the KfW (German government–owned development bank) are the primary downstream financiers, increasing emphasis is being placed on assisting cities to bring in additional financing through PPPs. Although the CDIA focuses on environmental improvement, poverty reduction, and governance aspects, its work has invariably contributed to a wider set of cross-cutting impacts. Especially through capacity strengthening, the CDIA has contributed to improved governance with city partner agencies (see also Linfield and Steinberg 2012).

European Bank for Reconstruction and Development

The activities of the European Bank for Reconstruction and Development (EBRD) that address issues related to urbanization differ from those implemented by other multilateral development banks. The EBRD has a specific mandate that identifies the main goal as support for its member countries in their transition to market economies. Through a variety of products (both investment and technical co-operation) offered to private and public sector clients representing a range of different sectors, the EBRD therefore has a specific role that indirectly addresses the urbanization issue. This role involves improving the business environment and removing infrastructure bottlenecks, both of which are crucial in facilitating the urbanization process in EBRD's 34 countries of

operation. Examples include specifically targeting micro, small, and medium enterprises in rural underserved areas for finance loans and supporting the involvement of farmers by extending backward linkages in agribusiness.

The EBRD also plays an active role in helping put adequate infrastructure in place to facilitate changing urban-rural dynamics and to minimize the negative impact of urbanization on cities. The EBRD's activities in the water and wastewater sector aim at achieving an enhanced and sustainable provision of services to urban populations. These operations are based on sustainable cost-recovery tariff structures; the development of robust regulatory approaches with a focus on the modernization of infrastructure; the promotion of appropriate environmental, social, health, and safety improvements that result in high-quality service delivery; and management efficiency. Since its inception, the EBRD has rapidly expanded its activities in the water and wastewater sectors throughout its countries of operation. To date, EBRD has financed over 130 water and wastewater projects, for a total of €2 billion.

Improvement in urban transport, in which the EBRD has been actively involved, is another essential component of facilitating urbanization processes. Urban transport has a unique ability to provide high-quality alternatives to use of private cars and is thus a viable antidote to urban congestion and pollution, two negative consequences of urbanization. Urban transport provides value added to the urban environment and increases the general quality of life for the urban population by improving air quality, reducing delays caused by congestion, and contributing to carbon reductions. The EBRD has financed more than 60 urban projects in different countries of operation, for a total of €1.4 billion. The EBRD addresses complex issues related to a variety of existing bottlenecks in the urban transport sector by implementing an integrated approach that consists of investments, technical assistance aimed at improving management capabilities, and policy dialogue with local and national authorities to

BOX 3A.2   The EBRD's integrated approach to transition challenges in Almaty's urban transport sector

Fueled by a number of factors, including economic, social, and structural changes in Kazakhstan over the past decade, the population of Almaty, the country's largest city, has been steadily growing. This growth is in large part a result of internal migration of the workforce from rural areas. The population of Almaty is expected to reach 1.6 million before 2015, up from 1.1 million in 2000. In the urban transport sector, population growth has been punctuated by a steady rise in private car usage, which subsequently led to a change in Almaty's transport pattern. The car fleet in circulation increased from 218,000 in 2003 to 560,000 in 2011. Greater reliance on cars has increased road congestion, and air quality in Almaty has been severely affected by pollution from traffic, and in particular, by emissions resulting from the use of low-quality fuel, a badly maintained and outdated private car fleet, and ever increasing congestion compounded by insufficient road management. In general, there has been an underinvestment in public transport solutions and traffic and parking management; institutional weaknesses and deficiencies in regulatory frameworks have also been identified as issues detrimental to the effective development of urban transport.

To address these complex challenges, the European Bank for Reconstruction and Development (EBRD) is pursuing an integrated approach to the urban transport sector in Almaty involving investments in target projects coupled with extensive technical cooperation and policy dialogue activities. Together, these activities aim at setting new standards for service quality in public transport, establishing a solid foundation for the introduction of a new regulatory framework in the sector, and integrating private operators into a single client-oriented system with significantly improved service standards. To address the

growing traffic problems and increasing dependence on private car usage, the EBRD's investments aim at increasing the capacity and standards of public transport services as an alternative to car usage and providing an overall balanced approach to urban mobility with viable travel choices for users. The investment projects include major investments in a modernized, clean urban bus and trolleybus fleet to provide a cost benchmark to the private sector. Finally, an integrated e-ticketing system operated under a build-operate-transfer concession will be implemented across all public transport services to allow for network benefits (that is, increased ridership spurred by free transport modal transfers) to accrue to the operators.

The EBRD's policy dialogue will focus on institutional development of the sector in Almaty and will include, among other activities, design and implementation of a robust regulatory approach through creation of a new urban transport authority; improvements in the contractual agreements to enable financing investments by private operators; and introduction of an integrated electronic fare collection system. In parallel, the EBRD's efforts will be complemented by assistance from the World Bank and the United Nations Development Programme to support the city in developing a computer-based traffic model, a new comprehensive route scheme, and carbon emission reduction assessment methodologies for the sector, all of which will help to improve the functioning of and benefits produced by the transport sector. It is expected that the EBRD's activities in urban transport in Almaty, in close collaboration with other international financial institutions, will contribute to creating efficient and effective market mechanisms in this sector and help mitigate negative consequences of urbanization in Almaty.

strengthen the regulatory and institutional framework (box 3A.2).

Inter-American Development Bank

The Inter-American Development Bank (IDB) established an Emerging and Sustainable Cities Initiative (ESCI) in 2011, since urbanization is taking place at a very fast

pace in Latin America and the Caribbean. Urbanization in the region rose from 62 percent in 1980 to 81 percent in 2011, making it the second most urbanized region in the world. If this trend continues, in 20 years 90 percent or more of the region's population will be living in cities. Although megacities are more prevalent in Latin America than in developing countries in other regions, it is now intermediate-size cities that are growing the fastest (Lora 2010). This pace of urbanization is creating daunting challenges for intermediate and emerging cities in the region.[5]

These emerging cities are still characterized by unacceptably high proportions of the population living in poverty, with limited governance and an enduring scarcity of resources. The challenges are multiplied when considering the efforts of cities to cope and adapt with the adverse effects of climate change. Events such as flooding and storm surge increasingly impact cities in the region, generating significant economic losses. Political decentralization has advanced substantially in the region over the last two decades. Local governments have assumed greater responsibilities for the provision of social services. However, fiscal decentralization has not kept pace, and most municipalities are not fiscally independent and do not manage their fiscal affairs well. They have very limited fiscal space to accommodate necessary investments in sustainability, and in most cases are not creditworthy partners to the private sector (PPPs transactions). Their capacities to improve the quality of life of their citizens are limited.

Emerging and Sustainable Cities Initiative

The first phase of the Emerging and Sustainable Cities Initiative (ESCI), launched in 2011, was a pilot test to develop ESCI's methodology and its application in five cities: Goiania in Brazil; Santa Ana in El Salvador; Trujillo in Peru; Port-of-Spain in Trinidad and Tobago; and Montevideo in Uruguay.

In February 2012, the Bank's Board of Directors approved the second phase of the ESCI, which includes scaling up of the program to a total of 26 cities in the region between 2012 and 2015. The purpose of the Initiative is to improve the sustainability and quality of life in emerging cities in Latin America and the Caribbean. The Initiative provides a set of tools that intermediate cities can use to identify key bottlenecks they may face in their path toward sustainability; weigh and prioritize the identified problems

to guide investment decisions in the sectors that may generate more positive impacts; find specific solutions according to their cost-benefit that would pave the way toward sustainability ("prioritized interventions"); and follow up on progress in closing gaps and reaching goals.

The Initiative works in three key dimensions:

- The *environmental and climate change dimension* is concerned with environmental management and local pollution control issues (including air and water contamination, solid waste management, and disaster prevention), climate change mitigation (through energy efficiency and other measures), and climate vulnerability reduction and adaptation measures.
- The *urban development dimension* refers to the effects of the city's design and footprint (or its ability to control its growth through effective planning and land use control), social inequality and uneven distribution of urban services, efficiency of its urban transportation network, economic competitiveness, and the level of public safety.
- The *fiscal sustainability dimension* is related to the ability of local governments to prioritize and finance needed investments, fund and maintain their urban and social services, control adequately their expenditures and debt, and make decisions in a transparent manner.

ESCI's methodology

Deployment of the Initiative in cities consists of two distinct stages. The first stage involves the development of an action plan, which begins with data collection, analysis and diagnosis, and prioritization through the application of different filters (environmental, economic, public opinion, expert opinion). The IDB ensures support for generation of expertise and diffusion of innovative experiences among the cities' governments.

The IDB, together with McKinsey & Company, has developed a rapid assessment diagnostic tool that analyzes 150 indicators and provides, in a period of six months, a comprehensive diagnostic of a city's situation with regard to the three dimensions of interest. The diagnostic is followed by a prioritization process that includes extensive consultation with civil society, academia, and local government as well as a public survey among citizens. This exercise leads to the development of an Action Plan, including key strategic interventions.

Once the action plan is developed and agreed among local stakeholders, the second stage—execution of the plan—begins. The Initiative assists in the design and development of the pre-investment components of at least one priority intervention as well as in the mobilization of financing from different sources (such as the public sector budget, private sector capital through PPPs, and commercial bank financing). The execution phase also includes the implementation of a monitoring system through the participation of local nongovernmental organizations (NGOs), the private sector, and academia.

The IDB has established a Special Fund ($25 million) to support provision of non-reimbursable technical assistance to cities adopting the ESCI methodology. The funding covers the development of all the phases in the ESCI methodology.

The World Bank

The World Bank has maintained a large presence in the area of rural and urban development. Recently, it has scaled up its knowledge-based services regarding urbanization, in particular through the Urbanization Knowledge Platform, which focuses on collaboratively building the evidence base for sustainable urban development.

Effectively managing the rapid change associated with urbanization is no easy task. And the risks are high, because many of the decisions that city leaders make today may lock cities onto a path of development that proves unsustainable. To help cities avoid this fate and harness urbanization for sustainable and inclusive growth, institutions like the World Bank must be more than producers of knowledge—they must also be customizers,

connecters, and catalysts for knowledge. That means translating global evidence and best practices into local solutions. It means connecting cities with one another to exchange best practices and learn from one another. And it means catalyzing new research by making data openly available to the public, so that others can validate conclusions, build from the findings, and contribute to development solutions.

To put this approach into action for cities, the World Bank launched a global knowledge partnership around the transformational topic of urbanization in 2011. The Urbanization Knowledge Platform (UKP) seeks to *convene and connect* city leaders, national policy makers, academia, the private and third-party sector, and development agencies from around the world to *co-create and customize* new insights on the most pressing challenges and opportunities faced by cities. Its mission is to put the world's best knowledge and data in the hands of policy makers so that they can better harness urban growth for sustainable and inclusive development.

The UKP began its activities by convening and cohosting more than 20 high-level policy consultations and knowledge exchanges in partnership with local think tanks, regional teams, and policy makers in 14 countries on 5 continents. Collectively, these events consulted more than 800 city leaders and 4,000 other stakeholders to facilitate extensive South-to-South knowledge exchange, convene regional stakeholders around common challenges, and lay the groundwork for future partnerships to jointly fill knowledge gaps. For instance, the platform facilitated regional knowledge exchanges among mayors for shared learning, including forming a community of city leaders from 8 countries in South Asia for unprecedented city-to-city learning that sidestepped inactive cooperation at national levels. And it nurtured global PPPs of more than 60 organizations to help harness the promise of "smart city" and "smart climate" innovations tailored to the needs of low-income countries.

Crucially, these global exchanges also led to the identification of the most pressing challenges and opportunities facing cities. The city leaders consulted through the Platform asked the World Bank: What must be done to create jobs? What must be done to improve living conditions in slums and hazard-prone areas and to bridge the social divide? What must be done to expand the coverage and quality of basic services?

So what has been learned to date? First, there are no straightforward answers to these questions, and the evidence base on many of these issues is filled with critical knowledge gaps. But the UKP's discussions with hundreds of city leaders from around the world also taught that, while all cities are unique, the challenges they face are remarkably similar, even across stages of development—with shared issues ranging from climate change to social inclusion. That means that "know how" and solutions are transferable—that the lessons learned from one city can, and should, inform the choices of cities on the other side of the planet. In other words, while there is no single blueprint for success, it is the case that some countries and cities have been more successful than others. There is a need, therefore, for new and expanding cities of today to learn what worked and what did not from those that have gone before and to collaborate on common solutions to shared problems informed by the evidence. Such shared learning and collaboration has been obstructed by a lack of facilitating global public goods (such as forums, knowledge platforms, and open data). The World Bank through the UKP aims to help fill this gap and to play the role of knowledge broker.

Second, most cities face not just a single bottleneck to sustainable development but a wide range of challenges that require integrated solutions and tight policy coordination across multiple agencies, jurisdictions, and disciplines that do not always have a natural incentive to collaborate. Most obviously, rapid urbanization has caused urban centers to spread beyond city boundaries and across disparate local governments that often fail to coordinate their actions, making it difficult to take a strategic approach to managing urban growth. A lack of sufficient policy coordination similarly hinders progress on several other aspects of urban development.

For instance, UKP-led discussions and follow-on research by Professors Paul Collier and Tony Venables on the persistence of informal settlements demonstrate that no single root cause explains the failure to deliver affordable housing. Rather, a number of inter-related impediments need to be addressed through integrated action across disparate policy domains—from financing to housing regulations to the cost of construction materials—because isolated progress on any one bottleneck will be of limited impact if the others continue to bind. For urban knowledge generators and development practitioners to help, they must lead by example by leveraging platforms like the UKP to collaborate across disciplines and sectors to build integrated solutions to urban challenges.

Third, the number one obstacle to providing city leaders with a fact-based understanding of their challenges and opportunities is the poor quality and tremendous fragmentation of city-level data. In fact, while many policy decisions are made and implemented at the local level, most statistical information is collected at the national level. As a result, more reliable data are available today on, say, the island-nation of Fiji—with a population of 860,000—than for the megacities of Delhi, Rio de Janeiro, or Shanghai, which each have populations in excess of 10 million. This imbalance creates an enormous mismatch between the scale at which information is available and the level at which urban development is conducted, and significantly constrains the growth of cumulative urban knowledge generation across countries, regions, and disciplines. To address this issue and respond to the overwhelming demand of its members and participants, the UKP has partnered with the Swiss government to, for the first time, systematically bring together and visualize data on cities for global benchmarking and evidence-based decision making. The goal is to work with cities and partners to harmonize, standardize, consolidate, and open-source city data to form a robust global evidence base on the challenges and opportunities faced by cities.

The World Bank through the UKP is committed to facilitating this shared learning across cities. But the Bank cannot do this alone. The key is for the urban community to come together to build a global pool of experience and evidence that all can draw and build from to better inform the tough and often irreversible decisions that city leaders need to make to harness urbanization for sustainable development.

Other organizations

Various bilateral agencies and United Nations (UN) agencies have also undertaken initiatives to assist urbanization. Such efforts include several led by the UN Population Fund (box A3.3) and a joint effort by various bilateral and multilateral institutions, known as the Cities Alliance (box A3.4).

BOX 3A.3   UNFPA's work on urbanization

Urbanization in the BRICS. The United Nations Population Fund (UNFPA) and the International Institute for Environment and Development (IIED) have collaborated for the past four years on a wide-ranging knowledge-building project focusing on urbanization in the BRICS (Brazil, Russia, India, China, and South Africa). These five countries provide some inspiring examples of how to seize the opportunities that urbanization can provide. All have gone through difficult periods when they tried to resist the predictable movement of people into their cities, or steered people or enterprises to inappropriate urban locations. Several of the BRICS bear heavy burdens from past failures to accommodate urban population growth equitably and efficiently. To avoid such burdens, cities and nations need to plan proactively for urban growth, making use of both markets and planning tools, and engaging with all sectors of society, including the economically and politically weakest.

Urbanization and gender dynamics. UNFPA also partnered with IIED to develop the conceptual and empirical foundations of the links between urbanization and gender dynamics. For example, a recent working paper highlights the tendency to plan against, rather than for, low-income urban residents and its implications from a gender perspective. This planning does not exclude the urban poor from income-generating activities but makes it difficult for them to secure decent living conditions. In so doing, inadequate urban policies place a disproportionate burden on reproduction rather than on production activities, and on women rather than men. A gendered understanding of urbanization and urban poverty highlights how urban disadvantage also includes limited access to shelter and basic services.

Urbanization, climate vulnerability, and adaptation planning. The UNFPA's work in this area points to the vital role that understanding population dynamics and extensively using demographic data has in developing preemptive and effective adaptation policies and practices. It also illuminates who is vulnerable and how to help build their resilience.

POPClimate web platform. Spatial analysis of population data is at the core of understanding and acting on climate vulnerability, particularly in high-concentration, high-exposure urban areas where vulnerability is dynamic and climate impacts threaten the lives and livelihoods of many. The POPClimate web platform was developed around UNFPA's manual on the analysis of census data for climate adaptation planning and was designed to bring together a community of data users, climate practitioners, and adaptation planners who can develop, share, and comment on new approaches for data-driven adaptation planning. The website is open to select users now and has been launched publicly (http://nijel.org/un_popclimate/).

Other UNFPA initiatives on urbanization. UNFPA contributed to the development of the World Bank's Urban Risk Assessment methodology, particularly focusing on the importance of a dynamic understanding of risk and vulnerability that integrates urban growth and change. It is also engaged in with IIED to come up with more innovative ways to manage densities in cities and is conducting joint research in the field of urban food security.

Source: UNFPA 2013.

BOX 3A.4   Cities Alliance: A new business model to promote systemic change and scale

The Cities Alliance is a global partnership whose members include multilateral and bilateral development agencies, donor and developing-country governments, international associations of local government, and two international nongovernmental organizations, one of which represents slum dwellers. Launched by the World Bank and UN-Habitat in 1999, the Cities Alliance was immediately successful in ensuring that the issue of slums was integrated into the international development agenda. Today, working through its members, the Cities Alliance seeks to strengthen and promote the role of cities in poverty reduction and sustainable development, improve synergies between and among members and partners, and improve the quality of urban development cooperation.

Good urban policies need to be based on solid data, the generation of which the Cities Alliance has supported: from the sophisticated and comprehensive HABISP model in São Paulo,[a] which provides comprehensive information on housing and other socioeconomic conditions of the urban poor, to the Know Your City campaign, which sees that slum dwellers collaborate with their local governments to find solutions to problems faced by slum dwellers.

To help its partners better respond to the challenges of urbanization, the Cities Alliance recently completely restructured its organization, adopted a new charter, and changed its business model. Moving decisively away from single, often ad hoc projects, the Cities Alliance used a $15 million grant from the Bill and Melinda Gates Foundation to move the fulcrum of its work program to longer-term, programmatic support in the form of multifaceted country programs.

The combination of multiple activities in support of a coherent national program holds very real promise for the systemic change and scale impacts that the Cities Alliance is seeking to support. In Uganda, for example, that support is focused on all 14 secondary cities, which is not only where the bulk of urbanization is taking place, but also where capacity constraints, infrastructure backlogs, and affordability challenges are most extreme.

With the support of Cities Alliance members, including both the World Bank and Slum Dwellers International, the government of Uganda is drafting a national urban policy. In small cities like Arua, Jinja, and Mbarara, slum dwellers are forming savings groups and carrying out slum enumerations. Slum dwellers and local governments are now talking to each other, land is being made available, and basic services are being provided. A $130 million World Bank loan will soon start to provide much needed critical infrastructure in these secondary cities.

a. www.habisp.inf.br.

Notes

1. In the United States, transaction taxes are around 1–2 percent of property values.
2. This includes national government clearing of subnational borrowing.
3. http://www.adb.org/sites/default/files/cps-kaz-2012-2016-ssa-03.pdf.
4. http://www.adb.org/sites.default.files/cps-uzb-2012-2016-ssa-04.pdf.
5. Emerging cities are defined as cities with populations of 100,000 to 2,500,000 that are growing—economically and demographically—faster than the national average. Currently, more than 140 cities, with a total population of about 70 million inhabitants, fit that definition.

References

AfDB (African Development Bank). 2011. *Transforming Africa's Cities and Towns into Engines of Economic Growth and Social Development.* AfDB, Tunis.

———. 2013. "Fostering Shared Growth, Urbanization, Inequality and Poverty in Africa." AfDB, Tunis.

Ahmed, W., and I. Menzies. 2012. "Using Output-Based Aid in Urban Projects." OBA Approaches Note 44. The Global Partnership on Output-Based Aid, Washington, DC.

Alm, James. 2011. "Municipal Finance of Urban Infrastructure: Knowns and Unknowns." Working Paper 1103, Tulane University Department of Economics, New Orleans.

Alpert, Pinhas, Olga Shvainshtein, and Pavel Kishcha. 2012. "AOD Trends over Megacities Based on Space Monitoring Using MODIS and MISR." *American Journal of Climate Change* 1: 117–31.

Annez, Patricia Clarke, and Johannes F. Linn. 2010. "An Agenda for Research on Urbanization in Developing Countries: A Summary of Findings from a Scoping Exercise." Policy Research Working Paper 5476, World Bank, Washington, DC.

Bahl, Roy, and Richard Bird. 2013. "Decentralization and Infrastructure: Principles and Practice." In *Decentralization and Infrastructure: From Gaps to Solutions*, edited by Jonas Frank, Martinez-Vazquez.

Baker, Judy L., ed. 2009. *Opportunities and Challenges for Small Scale Private Service Providers in Electricity and Water Supply. Evidence from Bangladesh, Cambodia, Kenya, and the Philippines*. Washington, DC: World Bank.

Banerjee, Sudeshna Ghosh, and Elvira Morella. 2011. *Africa's Water and Sanitation Infrastructure Access, Affordability, and Alternatives*. Washington, DC: World Bank.

Bertaud, Alain. 2004. "Mumbai FSI/FAR Conundrum: The Perfect Storm: The Four Factors Restricting the Construction of New Floor Space in Mumbai." http://alain-bertaud.com/AB_Files/AB_Mumbai_FSI_conundrum.pdf.

Blöechliger, Hansjorg, and Camila Vammalle. 2009. "Intergovernmental Grants in OECD countries: Trends and some Policy Issues." Paris: OECD.

Boadway, Robin. 2012. "International Lessons in Fiscal Federalism Design." *EJournal of Tax Research* 10 (1): 21-48.

Boex, Jameson, et.al. 2006. "Fighting Poverty Through Fiscal Decentralization." USAID, Washington DC.

Bruce, Nigel, Rogelio Perez-Padilla, and Rachel Albalak. 2000. "Indoor Air Pollution in Developing Countries: A Major Environmental and Public Health Challenge." *Bulletin of the World Health Organization* 78 (9): 1078–92.

Collier, P., and A. J. Venables. Forthcoming. "Housing and Urbanization in Africa." In *Cities in Development*, edited by E. Glaeser.

Creutzig, Felix, and Dongquan He. 2009. "Climate change mitigation and co-benefits of feasible transport demand policies in Beijing." *Transportation Research* Part D 14: 120-131.

Dafflon B. 2012. "Solidarity and the Design of Equalization: Setting out the Issues". *EJournal of Tax Research*. 10 (1): 138-164.

Estache, Antonio, and Ginés de Rus, eds. 2000. *Privatization and Regulation of Transport Infrastructure: Guidelines for Policymakers and Regulators*. WBI Development Studies. Washington, DC: World Bank.

Fay, Marianne, Francis Ghesquiere, and Tova Solo. 2003. "Natural Disasters and the Urban Poor." *En Breve* 32 (October), Latin America and Caribbean Region, World Bank, Washington, DC.

Frank, Jonas, Martinez-Vazquez. 2013. Decentralization and Infrastructure: From Gaps to Solutions.

Glaeser, Edward L. 2010. "Making Sense of Bangalore." London: Legatum Institute.

Gurjar, B. R., A. Jain, A. Sharma, A. Agarwal, P. Gupta, A. S. Nagpure, and J. Lelieveld. 2010. "Human Health Risks in Megacities due to Air Pollution." *Atmospheric Environment* 44 (36): 4606–13.

Hallegatte, Stéphane. 2009. "Strategies to Adapt to an Uncertain Climate Change." *Global Environmental Change* 19 (2): 240–47.

Henderson, J. Vernon, and Hyoung Gun Wang. 2007. "Urbanization and City Growth: The Role of Institutions." *Regional Science and Urban Economics* 37 (3): 283–313.

Hodge, Graeme A. 2006. "Public-Private Partnerships and Legitimacy." *University of New South Wales Law Journal* 29 (3): 318–27.

Hon, Vivian et. al. 2009. "A Framework for Bank Engagement in Lagging Areas, Spatial and Local Development Team," World Bank.

Hook, Walter. 2005. "Institutional and Regulatory Options for Bus Rapid Transit in Developing Countries: Lessons from International Experience." *Transportation Research Record* 1939: 184–91.

Kahn, Matthew E. Forthcoming. Sustainable and Smart Cities (Chapter 12). In *Rethinking Cities*, co-edited by A. Joshi-Ghani and E. Glaeser, Washington, DC: World Bank.

Kariuki, M., and J. Schwartz. 2005. "Small-Scale Private Service Providers of Water Supply and Electricity: A Review of Incidence, Structure,

Pricing and Operating Characteristics." Policy Research Working Paper 3727, World Bank, Washington, DC.

Kim, Ahyung. 2013. Megacities as Engines of Growth: Towards Inclusive and Sustainable Urban Development, World Bank forthcoming.

Kitchen, Harry, Enid Slack. 2006. "Providing Public Services in Remote Areas." In *Perspectives on Fiscal Federalism* edited by Richard Bird and Francois Vaillancourt. Washington, DC: World Bank Institute, pp 121-139.

Klein, Michael. 2012. "Infrastructure Policy: Basic Design Options." Policy Research Working Paper 6274, World Bank, Washington, DC.

Komives, Kristin, Vivien Foster, Jonathan Halpern, and Quentin Wodon, with support from Roohi Abdullah. 2005. *Water, Electricity, and the Poor—Who Benefits from Utility Subsidies?* Washington, DC: World Bank.

Lafuente, Mariano. 2009. "Public Management Reforms and Property Tax Revenue Improvements: Lessons from Buenos Aires." Working Paper Series on Public Sector Management. World Bank, LAC.

Lall, S. V., and H. G. Wang. 2011. "China Urbanization Review: Balancing Urban Transformation and Spatial Inclusion. An Eye on East Asia and the Pacific." East Asia and PacificRegion, World Bank, Washington, DC.

Lam, Nicholas L., Kirk R. Smith, Alison Gauthier, and Michael N. Bates. 2012. "Kerosene: A Review of Household Uses and Their Hazards in Low- and Middle-Income Countries." *Journal of Toxicology and Environmental Health* Part B: Critical Reviews 15 (6): 396–432.

Linnfield, Michael, and Florian Steinberg, eds. 2012. *Green Cities*. Manila: Asian Development Bank.

Lora, Eduardo. 2010. *The Quality of life in Latin American Cities: Markets and Perception.* Washington, DC: Inter-American Development Bank.

Lozano-Gracia, N., Cheryl Young, Somik V. Lall, and Tara Viswanath. 2013. "Leveraging Land to Enable Urban Transformation Lessons from Global Experience." Policy Research Working Paper 6312, World Bank, Washington, DC. http://wwwwds.worldbank.org/external /default/WDSContentServer/IW3P/IB/2013/0

1/14/000158349_20130114094647/Rendered /PDF/wps6312.pdf.

Markandya, A., and A. Golub. 2012. "Health Impacts of Fossil Fuel Use in ECA Countries." Metroeconomica Economics and Environmental Consultants, Bath, UK.

McKinsey Global Institute. 2011. "Urban World: Mapping the Economic Power of Cities." McKinsey & Company, New York.

McMillan, Melville. 2007. "Intergovernmental Transfers and Rural Local Governments." In *Intergovernmental fiscal transfers: principles and practice*, edited by Anwar Shah. Washington, DC: World Bank.

Mehta, Sumi, Hwashin Shin, Rick Burnett, Tiffany North, and Aaron J. Cohen. 2011. "Ambient Particulate Air Pollution and Acute Lower Respiratory Infections: A Systematic Review and Implications for Estimating the Global Burden of Disease." *Air Quality and Atmospheric Health*.

Mohan, Rakesh. 2009. "Global Financial Crisis: Causes, Impact, Policy Responses, and Lessons." Speech presented at the 7th Annual India Business Forum Conference, London Business School, London, April.

Mokhtarian, Patricia L., Michael N. Bagley, and Ilan Salomon. 1998. "The Impact of Gender, Occupation, and Presence of Children on Telecommuting Motivations and Constraints." *Journal of American Society for Information Science* 49 (12): 1115–34.

Newman, Peter, and Jeffrey R. Kenworthy. 1989. *Cities and Automobile Dependence: An International Sourcebook*. Aldershot, U.K.: Avebury.

OECD. 2007. "Fiscal Equalization in OECD Countries, OECD Network on Fiscal Relations Across Levels of Government." Working Paper no. 4, OECD, Paris.

Pagano, Michael A. 2011. "Funding and Investing in Infrastructure." Urban Institute, College of Urban Planning and Public Affairs, University of Illinois at Chicago. December 2011.

Peterson, George E., and Olga Kaganova. 2010. "Integrating Land Financing into Subnational Fiscal Management." Policy Research Working Paper 5409, World Bank, Washington, DC.

Prasad, N., F. Ranghieri, F. Shah, Z. Trohanis, E. Kessler, and R. Sinha. 2009. *Climate Resilient*

Cities: A Primer on Reducing Vulnerabilities to Disasters. Washington, DC: World Bank.

Prud'homme, R. 1995. "The Dangers of Decentralization." *World Bank Research Observer* 10 (2): 201–20.

Romeo, Leonardo, and Paul Smoke. 2013. "The Political Economy of Infrastructure Planning." In *Decentralization and Infrastructure: From Gaps to Solutions,* edited by Jonas Frank and Martinez-Vazquez.

Samad, Taimur, Nancy Lozano-Gracia, and Alexandra Panman, eds. 2012. *Colombia Urbanization Review: Amplifying the Gains from the Urban Transition.* Directions in Development Series, World Bank, Washington, DC.

Schrank, David, Tim Lomax, and Bill Eisele. 2011. "2011 Urban Mobility Report." Texas A&M University, Texas Transportation Institute, College Station, TX.

Shah, Anwar. 2012. "Grant Financing of Metropolitan Areas." Policy Research Working Paper 6002, World Bank, Washington DC.

Slack, Enid. 2006. "Fiscal Aspects of Alternative Methods of Governing Large Metropolitan Areas." In *Perspectives on Fiscal Federalism,* edited by Richard Bird, and Francois Vaillancourt. Washington, DC: World Bank Institute, 101-121.

Sud, Inder, and Serdar Yilmaz. 2013. "Institutions and Politics of Metropolitan Management." In *Metropolitan Government Finance in Developing Countries,* edited by Johannes Linn, Roy Bahl, and Debbie Wetzel. Massachusetts Lincoln Institute of Land Policy/The Brookings Institution. Washington, DC.

Tacoli, Cecilia. 2012. "Urbanization, Gender and Urban Poverty: Paid Work and Unpaid Carework in the City." Urbanization and emerging Population Issues Working Paper 7, United Nations Population Fund, New York, and International Institute for Environment and Development, London.

UNFPA. 2013. *The Demography of Adaptation to Climate Change.* New York: UNFPA.

World Bank. 2004. "Colombia: Recent Economic Developments in Infrastructure (REDI). Balancing Social and Productive Needs for Infrastructure." Private Sector and Infrastructure Unit, Latin America and the Caribbean, World Bank, Washington, DC.

———. 2008. *World Development Report: Reshaping Economic Geography.* Washington, DC: World Bank.

———. 2011. "Vietnam Urbanization Review." Technical Assistance Report. World Bank, Washington, DC.

WB 2011a on Findeter

———. 2012a. *Eurasian Cities: New Realities along the Silk Road.* Washington, DC: World Bank.

———. 2012b. *Inclusive Green Growth: The Pathway to Sustainable Development.* Washington, DC: World Bank.

———. 2012c. "Planning for Uganda's Urbanization. Inclusive Growth Policy Note 4." World Bank, Washington, DC.

———. 2013a. *Planning, Connecting, Financing Cities—Now.* Washington, DC: World Bank.

———. 2013b. *Urbanization beyond Municipal Boundaries: Nurturing Metropolitan Economies and Connecting Peri-urban Areas in India.* Directions in Development Series. Washington, DC: World Bank.

Appendix

Table A1.1 Classification of economies by region and income, fiscal 2013

East Asia and Pacific

American Samoa	UMC
Cambodia	LIC
China	UMC
Fiji	LMC
Indonesia	LMC
Kiribati	LMC
Korea, Dem. Rep.	LIC
Lao PDR	LMC
Malaysia	UMC
Marshall Islands	LMC
Micronesia, Fed. Sts.	LMC
Mongolia	LMC
Myanmar	LIC
Palau	UMC
Papua New Guinea	LMC
Philippines	LMC
Samoa	LMC
Solomon Islands	LMC
Thailand	UMC
Timor-Leste	LMC
Tonga	LMC
Tuvalu	UMC
Vanuatu	LMC
Vietnam	LMC

Europe and Central Asia

Albania	LMC
Armenia	LMC
Azerbaijan	UMC
Belarus	UMC
Bosnia and Herzegovina	UMC
Bulgaria	UMC
Georgia	LMC
Kazakhstan	UMC
Kosovo	LMC
Kyrgyz Republic	LIC
Latvia	UMC
Lithuania	UMC
Macedonia, FYR	UMC
Moldova	LMC
Montenegro	UMC
Romania	UMC
Russian Federation	UMC
Serbia	UMC
Tajikistan	LIC
Turkey	UMC
Turkmenistan	UMC
Ukraine	LMC
Uzbekistan	LMC

Latin America and the Caribbean

Antigua and Barbuda	UMC
Argentina	UMC
Belize	LMC
Bolivia	LMC
Brazil	UMC
Chile	UMC
Colombia	UMC
Costa Rica	UMC
Cuba	UMC
Dominica	UMC
Dominican Republic	UMC
Ecuador	UMC
El Salvador	LMC
Grenada	UMC
Guatemala	LMC
Guyana	LMC
Haiti	LIC
Honduras	LMC
Jamaica	UMC
Mexico	UMC
Nicaragua	LMC
Panama	UMC
Paraguay	LMC
Peru	UMC
St. Lucia	UMC
St. Vincent and the Grenadines	UMC
Suriname	UMC
Uruguay	UMC
Venezuela, RB	UMC

Middle East and North Africa

Algeria	UMC
Djibouti	LMC
Egypt, Arab Rep.	LMC
Iran, Islamic Rep.	UMC
Iraq	LMC
Jordan	UMC
Lebanon	UMC
Libya	UMC
Morocco	LMC
Syrian Arab Republic	LMC
Tunisia	UMC
West Bank and Gaza	LMC
Yemen, Rep.	LMC

South Asia

Afghanistan	LIC
Bangladesh	LIC
Bhutan	LMC
India	LMC
Maldives	UMC
Nepal	LIC
Pakistan	LMC
Sri Lanka	LMC

Sub-Saharan Africa

Angola	UMC
Benin	LIC
Botswana	UMC
Burkina Faso	LIC
Burundi	LIC
Cameroon	LMC
Cape Verde	LMC
Central African Republic	LIC
Chad	LIC
Comoros	LIC
Congo, Dem. Rep.	LIC
Congo, Rep.	LMC
Côte d'Ivoire	LMC
Eritrea	LIC
Ethiopia	LIC
Gabon	UMC
Gambia, The	LIC
Ghana	LMC
Guinea	LIC
Guinea-Bissau	LIC
Kenya	LIC
Lesotho	LMC
Liberia	LIC
Madagascar	LIC
Malawi	LIC
Mali	LIC
Mauritania	LMC
Mauritius	UMC
Mozambique	LIC
Namibia	UMC
Niger	LIC
Nigeria	LMC
Rwanda	LIC
São Tomé and Principe	LMC
Senegal	LMC
Seychelles	UMC
Sierra Leone	LIC
Somalia	LIC
South Africa	UMC
South Sudan	LMC
Sudan	LMC
Swaziland	LMC
Tanzania	LIC
Togo	LIC
Uganda	LIC
Zambia	LMC
Zimbabwe	LIC

High-income OECD economies

Australia
Austria
Belgium
Canada
Czech Republic
Denmark
Estonia
Finland
France
Germany
Greece
Hungary
Iceland
Ireland
Israel
Italy
Japan
Korea, Rep.
Luxembourg
Netherlands
New Zealand
Norway
Poland
Portugal
Slovak Republic
Slovenia
Spain
Sweden
Switzerland
United Kingdom
United States

Other high-income economies

Andorra
Aruba
Bahamas, The
Bahrain
Barbados
Bermuda
Brunei Darussalam
Cayman Islands
Channel Islands
Croatia
Curaçao
Cyprus
Equatorial Guinea
Faeroe Islands
French Polynesia
Greenland
Guam
Hong Kong SAR, China
Isle of Man
Kuwait
Liechtenstein
Macao SAR, China
Malta
Monaco
New Caledonia
Northern Mariana Islands
Oman
Puerto Rico
Qatar
San Marino
Saudi Arabia
Singapore
Sint Maarten (Dutch part)
St. Kitts and Nevis
St. Martin (French part)
Trinidad and Tobago
Turks and Caicos Islands
United Arab Emirates
Virgin Islands (U.S.)

Source: World Bank data.

Note: This table classifies all World Bank member economies, and all other economies with populations of more than 30,000. For operational and analytical purposes, economies are divided among income groups according to 2011 gross national income (GNI) per capita, calculated using the World Bank Atlas method. The groups are: low-income countries (LIC), $1,025 or less; lower-middle-income countries (LMC), $1,026–4,035; upper-middle-income countries (UMC), $4,036–12,475; and high-income countries, $12,476 or more. Other analytical groups based on geographic regions are also used. The names of countries and economies in this table comply with the World Bank's official listing.

Table A1.2 Country classifications in IMF's World Economic Outlook, 2013

Advanced Economies[a]

Australia	France	Korea, Republic of	Slovak Republic
Austria	Germany	Luxembourg	Slovenia
Belgium	Greece	Malta	Spain
Canada	Hong Kong SAR	Netherlands	Sweden
Cyprus	Iceland	New Zealand	Switzerland
Czech Republic	Ireland	Norway	Taiwan Province of China
Denmark	Israel	Portugal	United Kingdom
Estonia	Italy	San Marino	United States
Finland	Japan	Singapore	

Emerging Market and Developing Countries[a]

Central and Eastern Europe[b]

Albania	Lithuania
Bosnia and Herzegovina*	FYR Macedonia
Bulgaria	Montenegro
Croatia	Poland
Hungary	Romania
Kosovo*	Serbia
Latvia	Turkey

Developing Asia[b]

Bangladesh	**Myanmar***
Bhutan	**Nepal***
Brunei Darussalam	Palau
Cambodia	**Papua New Guinea**
China	Philippines
Fiji	**Samoa**
India	**Solomon Islands***
Indonesia	Sri Lanka
Kiribati*	Thailand
Lao People's Democratic Republic	**Timor-Leste***
Malaysia	**Tonga**
Maldives	**Tuvalu***
Marshall Islands*	**Vanuatu**
Micronesia, Federated States of*	**Vietnam**
Mongolia	

Sub-Saharan Africa[b]

Angola*	**Lesotho**
Benin	**Liberia***
Botswana	**Madagascar**
Burkina Faso	**Malawi**
Burundi*	**Mali**
Cameroon	Mauritius
Cape Verde	**Mozambique**
Central African Republic*	Namibia
Chad*	**Niger**
Comoros*	**Nigeria**
Congo, Dem. Rep. of*	**Rwanda**
Congo, Rep. of*	**São Tomé and Príncipe**
Côte d'Ivoire*	**Senegal**
Equatorial Guinea	Seychelles
Eritrea*	**Sierra Leone***
Ethiopia	South Africa
Gabon	**South Sudan***
Gambia, The	Swaziland
Ghana	**Tanzania**
Guinea*	**Togo***
Guinea-Bissau*	**Uganda**
Kenya	**Zambia**
	Zimbabwe*

Middle East and North Africa[b]

Afghanistan, Islamic Republic of*
Algeria
Bahrain
Djibouti
Egypt
Iran, Islamic Republic of
Iraq*
Jordan
Kuwait
Lebanon
Libya*
Mauritania
Morocco
Oman
Pakistan
Qatar
Saudi Arabia
Sudan*
Syrian Arab Republic*
Tunisia
United Arab Emirates
Yemen, Republic of *

Commonwealth of Independent States[b]

Armenia
Azerbaijan
Belarus
Georgia[c]
Kazakhstan
Kyrgyz Republic
Moldova
Russian Federation
Tajikistan
Turkmenistan
Ukraine
Uzbekistan

Latin America and the Caribbean[b]

Antigua and Barbuda	**Guyana**
Argentina	**Haiti***
Bahamas, The	**Honduras**
Barbados	Jamaica
Belize	Mexico
Bolivia	**Nicaragua**
Brazil	Panama
Chile	Paraguay
Colombia	Peru
Costa Rica	St. Kitts and Nevis
Dominica	**St. Lucia**
Dominican Republic	**St. Vincent and the Grenadines**
Ecuador	Suriname
El Salvador	Trinidad and Tobago
Grenada	Uruguay
Guatemala	Venezuela

Note: The names of countries and economies in this table comply with the IMF's official listing.

a. As used here, the terms "country" and "economy" do not always refer to a territorial entity that is a state as understood by international law and practice. Some territorial entities included here are not states, although their statistical data are maintained on a separate and independent basis.

b. Countries in bold typeface are low-income developing countries eligible for financial assistance under IMF's Poverty Reduction and Growth Trust. Countries with an asterisk are included in the World Bank's list of Fragile and Conflict-Affected States.

c. Georgia, which is not a member of the Commonwealth of Independent States, is included in this group for reasons of geography and similarities in economic structure.